Ius Gentium: Comparative Perspectives on Law and Justice

Volume 51

More information about this series at http://www.springer.com/series/7888

Rainer Arnold
Editor

Limitations of National Sovereignty through European Integration

Springer

Editor
Rainer Arnold
Juristische Fakultät
Universität Regensburg
Regensburg, Germany

ISSN 1534-6781 ISSN 2214-9902 (electronic)
Ius Gentium: Comparative Perspectives on Law and Justice
ISBN 978-94-017-7469-7 ISBN 978-94-017-7471-0 (eBook)
DOI 10.1007/978-94-017-7471-0

Library of Congress Control Number: 2016930106

Springer Dordrecht Heidelberg New York London

Printed on acid-free paper

Springer Science+Business Media B.V. Dordrecht is part of Springer Science+Business Media (www.springer.com)

Foreword

Limitation of sovereignty by European integration is a key issue of contemporary law in Europe. This book collects the perspectives of researchers from various European countries on the topic. The constitutional orders of the Member States of the European Union are the basis for the integration process. The traditional sovereignty concept is in conflict with the supranational power of the EU created according to the provisions of the national constitutions. This conflict is reflected by the debate on constitutional identity which seems to be the new version of a "supranationalised sovereignty". Identity in this sense draws the borderline between national autonomy and supra-nationality. Integration must be based on an equilibrium of both.

The introductory contribution (*Rainer Arnold*) explains, with the use of Germany as an example, how the Constitution enables the legislator to put into effect "open Statehood" and how the Constitutional Courts in Germany and other countries are trying to find the above mentioned equilibrium. The concept of constitutional identity and the question of the competence to decide what it entails are of major importance. The jurisprudence of the French *Conseil constitutionnel* developing the criterion of the *conditions essentielles d'exercise de la souveraineté* as well as the rigid and questionable English doctrine of *parliamentary sovereignty* are taken into consideration.

How European integration, which is characterized by the existence of various constitutional levels, affects the traditional doctrinal basics of Constitution-making and reforming power is dealt with in the reflection of *Francisco Balaguer*.

National and constitutional identity as an emerging key concept of integration is double-sided: a national and a supranational perspective has to be applied and adequately harmonized. *Luca Mezzetti* and *Sinisa Rodin* give an insight into the two approaches.

Significant developments in limiting the impact of supranational power on national constitutional law appear in the jurisprudence of the Italian Constitutional Court on the "*controlimiti*".

Approval or criticism is given to the EU-related jurisprudence of the new Member States, Poland (*Boguslaw Banaszak*), Hungary (*Peter Kovacs*), Czech Republic (*Jirí Zemánek*) and Romania (*Manuel Gutan*).

European integration affects not only the EU Member States but also third states linked to the EU by international agreements. The question how to characterize Association Agreements in this context is dealt with by *Viktor Mouraviov* while *Arta Vorpsi* explains the Europeanization of Albanian Constitutional law, a manifest expression of the reception of European concepts as a form of "open statehood".

For their important help to prepare this book I would like to thank my collaborators Jessica Pham, Stephanie Lodola, Bethany McGhee and Stefan Nigam from Cambridge University, Lisa Poth and Samuel Cross from Oxford University, Nevila Saja from Albania, Timothy Wojewodka from Poland, and Sebastian Seefried from Germany.

I also want to thank the Springer Publishing House, in particular Diana Nijenhuijzen, for their continuous support of this project.

Regensburg, Germany Rainer Arnold
May 2015

Contents

Contributors

Rainer Arnold Juristische Fakultät, University of Regensburg, Regensburg, Germany

Bogusław Banaszak Faculty of Law and Administration, University of Zielona Góra, Zielona Góra, Poland

Francisco Balaguer Callejón Department of Constitutional Law, University of Granada, Granada, Spain

Diana-Urania Galetta Dipartimento di Diritto pubblico italiano e sovranazionale, Università degli Studi di Milano, Milan, Italy

Manuel Guţan Faculty of Law, Lucian Blaga University of Sibiu, Sibiu, Romania

Péter Kovács Péter Pázmány Catholic University, Budapest, Hungary

Luca Mezzetti School of Law, Advanced School for Legal Studies, University of Bologna, Bologna, Italy

Viktor Muraviov Institute of International Relations, Kyiv Taras Shevchenko National University, Kiev, Ukraine

Sinisa Rodin University of Zagreb, Zagreb, Croatia

Arta Vorpsi Law of Faculty, University of Tirana, Tirana, Albania

Jiří Zemánek Faculty of Law, Charles University, Praha 1, Czech Republic

Chapter 1
Limitation of Sovereignty by European Integration: The German Experience in a Comparative View

Rainer Arnold

Abstract The contribution reflects on the limitation of national sovereignty which has been effectuated by a transfer of national competences to the supranational institutions. The EU member states have opened their formerly closed legal orders through such transfers and accepted that EU law has direct normative effect. Primacy of EU law is generally accepted, but not regarded as being absolute. In tendency, the core elements of a Constitution are safeguarded by the constitutional courts which have elaborated the concept of constitutional identity.

1. Limitation of sovereignty by European integration has its normative basis in the constitutional law of the member states. For Germany Article 23 of the Basic Law (BL) authorizes the state to participate in the European Union and to transfer "sovereign powers", that is internal competences, to this organisation. The predecessor of this constitutional provision created in 1993, in the moment when the first European Union was established by the Maastricht Treaty, has been Article 24 BL, dating from 1949, the year of the creation of the BL, with the finality to limit German sovereignty by the internationalization of national state powers to be attributed by a federal law to "interstate bodies". This should enable Germany to associate with the international community, a new approach of anti-nationalism after the end of the dark phase of her history. The new perspective is now "open statehood" as a basis of Germany's integration into the European, and worldwide, family of nations. The preamble of the BL as well as various key

R. Arnold (✉)
Juristische Fakultät, University of Regensburg, Regensburg, Germany
e-mail: jean.monnet@gmx.de

R. Arnold (ed.), *Limitations of National Sovereignty through European Integration*, Ius Gentium: Comparative Perspectives on Law and Justice 51,
DOI 10.1007/978-94-017-7471-0_1

provisions of the Constitution, the most far-reaching being article 24 BL, provided for a highly important relativization of national sovereignty.

Both articles, 24.1 BL, which served as a constitutional instrument for co-foundation of the European Communities in the 50s, and 23.1 BL, destined to participate in the European integration from the decisive year of 1993 on, have as their constitutional nuclei the authorization to "transfer sovereign powers" what means, as it has been explained by the German Federal Constitutional Court (FCC) in its famous *Solange* I decision of 1974 (FCC 1974, 280), that Germany "opens" her formerly closed legal order, limiting her sovereignty by renouncing the normative exclusivity of national law within its territory.

Article 23.1 BL has been enlarged in its scope in comparison with article 24.1 BL, now featuring *four finalities*:

(a) To Europeanize national policy fields by the transfer of competences to the EU, the traditional core aspect of open statehood;
(b) To guarantee that the powers Europeanized in this way will be exercised in a context which corresponds in its basic features to the basic values of Germany, to "democratic, social and federal principles" as well as to the principles of the rule of law and subsidiarity, and which guarantees the protection of the individual by the fundamental rights in a way comparable to the own constitutional system;
(c) To safeguard the nucleus of the constitutional order, in later jurisprudence called "constitutional identity", as it is protected by the "eternity clause" of article 79.3 BL which excludes some fundamentals of the German constitutional system from even a formal constitutional reform: Article 1 with human dignity as the supreme value of the legal order and the ideological and normative basis of the comprehensive fundamental rights catalogue, as well as the principles of Article 20 BL defining the basic constitutional structures of Germany; democracy, the social State principle, rule of law (explicitly referred to by paragraph 3 of the eternity clause only with respect to primacy of the constitution over the legislator and of the legislation over executed and judiciary, in fact, the basis of the modern rule of law concept), and federalism (this in a threefold way: federalism in general, the territorial subdivision of the country into Member States (*Länder*), and the institutional involvement of the latter in the federal legislative process).
(d) To apply a qualified procedure which underlines the importance of the transfer process and ensures a broad democratic and federal consensus: a two thirds majority of the members of Federal Parliament as well as two thirds of the votes of the Federal Council (*Bundesrat*) for the foun-

dation of the EU and the alteration of the EU Treaty foundations or for comparative regulations which alter or supplement the BL or make this possible. For a transfer of competences it is indispensable that the Federal Council gives its explicit consent.

Article 24.1 BL did not contain such qualified requirements and made a transfer of powers possible with a simple majority vote in Parliament and the ordinary participation of the Federal Council (giving it the competence to make objections against Parliament's vote which could be regularly set aside by a new vote in Parliament with absolute majority). The aggravation of the transfer requirements by the wording of article 23.1 BL seems to be a consequence of the constitutional jurisprudence that existed until 1993, in particular of the two *Solange* decisions of 1974 and 1986 (FCC 1986), as well as of the political debate which increasingly focused on the defense of their own constitutional achievements against a too incisive exercise of supranational power.

It shall be noted in comparison to other member states of the EU that the constitutional basis for a transfer of competences to international or supranational organizations are different in their wordings, ranging from the limitation of sovereignty (Italy, France until the constitutional reform of 1992) to the transfer of competences for a common exercise by the European institutions (e.g. France after the reform of 1992, text adapted various times to the ongoing integration, Spain) to the transfer of sovereign powers (Germany, 1949 and 1993). Many of the constitutions refer quite generally to the transfer of competences to international organizations and only some of them explicitly to the European Union as such. All the member States have ratified the same treaties establishing or reforming the supranational institutions. This means that the normative result of such transfers which have led to the creation of the supranational power as defined in a classic way by the ECJ in Costa v. ENEL (ECJ 1964) has been the same. In other words: despite the differences in the constitutional formulations, the functional content of the transfer or limitation norms in all the member states constitutions must be regarded as being the same. Teleological interpretation of these constitutional provisions is necessarily determined by the result of these transfers, which means the characteristics of supranationality as defined by the ECJ jurisprudence have an essential impact on the substance of the integration provisions of the national constitutions. Constitutional interpretation must conform to this fact. Therefore the functional content of these provisions is harmonized within all the member States. It can also be said that these provisions are to some extent "supranationalized", determined from outside the State, from the EU. This seems to be a sort of constitutional interpretation or even constitutional reform effectuated from outside.

The transfer of national competences must be limited: sovereignty and even statehood would be threatened by the global shift of functions from the State to the multistate organization. It is of common opinion that such a global transfer is not authorized by the existing Constitution. Therefore numerous Constitutions, in particular in the new democracies of Central and Eastern Europe, explicitly permit only a transfer of "certain", "determined competences". They express this limit in the wording of the constitutional texts while in other countries often jurisprudence has underlined it in a general perspective.

The reason for the prohibition of an undetermined power transfer is that such a loss of national competences could endanger the functional existence of the State. A Constitution keeps the State alive, safeguards statehood. As it was pointed out, "open statehood" is favored by a modern Constitution which implies the limitation of sovereignty but not its abandon.

Of course, the constituent power, the people, could integrate, by a new Constitution the existing State into another State or into a union of States with the effect that the integrating State loses its statehood. This can be effectuated by a formal step, e.g. a solemn act of proclaiming a European (Federal) State, or by a functional integration, a sort of implicit creation of a new constitutional order by an unlimited, maybe gradually ongoing transfer of national competences eroding statehood.

For this reason a Constitution only allows a well-determined power transfer which does not shift core competences of a State, at least not fully, to another State or a multistate, supranational organization. The FCC worked out, in its Lisbon Treaty decision (FCC 2009, para. 252–260), a list of "democracy-related" and therefore "statehood-related" matters which must remain, to an essential extent, in the hands of the State. This position listing the singular matters exempt from (total) transfer is under criticism from doctrinal critics for too much restriction of the dynamic integration process and by denying a common or shared exercise of these competences by the EU and the Member States. Neither the Czech (ÚS 2008) nor the Polish Constitutional Court (TK 2010) dressed up such a list.

Statehood can be endangered by the State itself by giving away too many powers or by the supranational power which has been constituted by the will of the Member States if it extends the transferred competences by interpretation beyond the limit of "ultra vires" or affects by its normative regulations the core elements of the national constitutional order, called "constitutional identity", a term newly used by the German FCC (FCC 2009), the French Conseil Constitutionnel (CC 2006, para. 28) and the Polish Constitutional Court (TK 2010).

The national constitutional courts defend the fundamental national orders but have also to respect the acceptance of a limited sovereignty, of "open statehood", in accordance to the wish of the Constitution itself. They can draw the borderline between transfer of national powers and limitation of sovereignty on the one hand, and abandon statehood on the other hand. They express the national perspective when doing so, and claim their exclusive competence for this. The power to have the "final word" on what is compatible with statehood and with constitutional identity is essential to a State, inherent to statehood as such and not transferable to a body outside the State such as the EU. This includes the competence to define what statehood and constitutional identity are and to hinder a supranational act incompatible with this to be applied on the national territory. The German FCC has distinctly elaborated this vision both in the Maastricht (FCC 1993) and the Lisbon Treaty decision, a vision which has been relativized, but not abandoned, by the Mangold decision in 2010 (FCC 2010).

The problem is that the national constitutional court competes with the CJEU insofar as supranational law is involved. The problem does not arise if only national law is in question. If national legislation is contrary to constitutional identity or to national sovereignty, it is considered to be void for unconstitutionality and can be annulled by the constitutional court, no matter whether it is incompatible with the core elements or other of the constitutional order. The problem arises when two autonomous legal orders, the national and the supranational order, enter into conflict. They can conflict because both have normative force within the Member State, a specific consequence of the fact that the State has "opened" its legal order by the transfer of competences to the supranational organizations.

In case of such a conflict the CJEU claims the exclusive power to limit or to stop the normative validity or the application of a EU legal act. This is deep-rooted in the jurisprudence of the supranational Court and, indeed, contrasts with the German FCC's position to claim the final word and the power to suspend the application of EU legislation on the German territory, in accordance with its own appreciation.

The mentioned Mangold decision had the merit to liberalize the "ultra vires" concept of the FCC as developed in the Maastricht decision by restricting an "ultra vires" act of the EU to a "manifest and serious" trespassing of the competence scheme as laid down in the Treaties which would clearly affect the competence distribution system between EU and Member States.

As to the relation between the two courts, the Mangold decision declares it obligatory for the FCC to ask a preliminary question to the EU Court of

Justice. This does not mean that that FCC accepts the final decision of the supranational Court in ultra vires matters, but it is to ensure that the EU primary or secondary law in question is interpreted in the way that the EU Court understands it. This gives the national constitutional court the clarity about the meaning of this law and allows the EU Court to practice an interpretation "in conformity to national constitutional law". The possibility of such an interpretation goes alongside with the EU obligation to respect as far as possible the basic legal orders of some member states, in particular their constitutional identities as it is expressed by article 4.2 EU Treaty. A case of this type occurred a short time ago in Germany when the FCC (FCC 2014) made, in January 2014, its first preliminary question to the EU Court of Justice on how to interpret the primary law provisions on the European Central Bank concerning the acquisition of government bonds on the secondary capital market. The FCC has in mind, with this preliminary question, to give the EU Court of Justice the "chance" to interpret the relevant EU primary law in a sense which would be conform to the opinions of the constitutional judges and therefore avoid the FCC declaring such an activity of the bank unconstitutional for being ultra vires.

2. The FCC has been revealed to be a protector of the basic achievements of legal culture, which finds its particular expression in the fundamental legal order, the Constitution. As the constitutional provisions and values form a coherent order, the elements of the internal and external dimension of the Constitution have to be equilibrated. This means that the State-related elements of the Constitution, its internal dimension, have to be weighed out with the elements referring to the international and European community, the external dimension of the Constitution. "Closed" statehood (embracing the purely national matters) and "open" statehood must be brought into the right equilibrium. The internal and external elements of the Constitution can conflict and need to be reconciled.

In its jurisprudence, the FCC has safeguarded the core elements of the constitutional order: an efficient standard of fundamental rights protection without exclusively attributing it to the national level (FCC 1974) and quite generally the preservation of the constitutional identity (FCC 2009). As it has been pointed out, the concept of identity, as the FCC has developed it, is linked to the matters which fall within the scope of the eternity clause. The identity argument is now in the focus of the Court's deliberations and has been a crucial issue in the financial crisis jurisprudence where the budget power of Parliament was considered to be at the heart of democracy and therefore an aspect of constitutional identity (FCC 2011).

The ultra vires debate is an expression of the mentioned equilibrium between the internal and external dimensions of the Constitution because it stresses the rule of law basis of the integration process. The act of approval of the integration treaties voted by the national Parliament is the concrete connection between the two legal orders which are integrated one into the other, the national and supranational order. This act is the national side of the integration "coin" while the integration treaties can be considered as the supranational side of it. This act is seen as a legitimation for the control function of a national constitutional court over the activities of the supranational institutions. It contains the "integration program" (FCC 1993) and implies the "integration responsibility" of the member State (FCC 2009). Furthermore, it is considered to be the legal reason for supranationality, in particular of its major aspects, the direct effect and the primacy of supranational law. *Ultra vires* therefore means to trespass the limits of what has been attributed to the supranational institutions by the Member States through the act of approval of the integration treaties. It is an important aspect of the principle of external rule of law to act within the competences transferred from the State to the supranational organization.

To respect the scope and limits of transferred competences, that is to act *intra vires*, is therefore the observance of the right equilibrium between statehood and integration. The only controversy is the question *who* interprets what *intra* and *ultra* vires is: national or the supranational Court?

The answers of the FCC and the EU Court are different.

The EC/EU Court of Justice focuses its argumentation on the preliminary question system which intends to ensure a Europewide uniform interpretation of EU law and makes it obligatory for the last instance courts (as well as for the constitutional courts) of the Member States to request for the centralized interpretation by the supranational Court. This implies the final word competence of this Court and not of the national courts. While the supranational answer is based on primacy and uniform interpretation of EU law, the answer of the FCC is based on statehood and preservation of national constitutional identity.

It can be stated in a comparative view that limitation of sovereignty by European integration has led, in the constitutional orders of most of the Member States, to an equilibrium which is characterized by the respect of supranationality by the Member States on the one hand and respect of the constitutional core elements, i.e. the constitutional identity, by the EU. Only in some countries the impact of supranational law on national constitutional law is totally refused, such as in Poland (TK 2005) and Lithuania (Constitutional Court 2006). It is obvious that a European perspective has entered into the national legal orders, not only into the legislative infrastructure, but also into the very center of the national order, the Constitution. This means the progressing Europeanization of legal culture, the reception of common European concepts which, themselves, are based on the diversity of national constitutional identities. What is often called "cross-border fertilization" takes place significantly in this context. This equilibrated, balanced State – EU relation is fundamental for the integration process and accepted by most of the Member States' constitutional courts as well as by the EU itself, as article 4.2 EU Treaty clearly shows. The major point of divergence is the question; which institution is judicially responsible for safeguarding this equilibrium. Of course, it is in part a matter of cooperation between the national and supranational courts which is essentially based on the preliminary question system. However, the final word competence is highly controversial and a sort of battlefield between both sides. To mitigate potential conflicts the judges on both sides have developed "peacekeeping" instruments such as the obligation to interpret the national law, including the national constitutional law, in conformity with supranational law as far as it is possible in methodology (e.g. ÚS 2006). This corresponds to the obligation of the supranational judges to interpret supranational law in conformity with common principles of the Member States, a consequence of the reciprocal loyalty obligation within the Union.

It seems that the procedural reflection of this diversity of standpoints is, among others, the hesitation of some constitutional courts to practice the preliminary question mechanism outside the ordinary justice system. Regarding this question, the new tendency is to align with the EU perspective Italy (Corte Costituzionale 2008a, b), France (CC 2013) and recently Germany (FCC 2014) while other constitutional courts in Austria (Österreichischer Verfassungsgerichtshof 2012), Belgium (Cour constitutionnelle 2013) have no problems in this respect.

3. We can state as a result the national concepts of sovereignty have essentially been relativized by European integration. Even in significantly traditional systems, such as the English constitutional order based on the principle of sovereignty of Parliament, or the French order focusing on the "souveraineté indivisible", European law has been the starting point for fundamental changes. The Factortame case in the UK (House of Lords 1990) has weakened the old dogma, and the new chapter on the EU introduced into the French Constitution has fundamentally modified the concept of sovereignty which is considered now, insofar as the EU is concerned, as divisible, meaning not only a "limitation" but also a (partial) "transfer" (see CC 1976).

In France, the relation between national sovereignty and supranational power is basic. Most of the issues related to European integration which have been dealt with before the *Conseil constitutionnel* have focused on the question whether the impact on sovereignty is conform or not to the Constitution. Several approaches to sovereignty have been examined by the

Conseil: is a limitation of sovereignty ("limitation de souverainté") or a "transfer of sovereignty" ("transfert de souverainté") concerned? Are the essential conditions of the exercise of national sovereignty ("les conditions essentielles d'exercise de souverainté nationale") affected? Is the constitutional identity ("identité constitutionnelle") disregarded?

These questions show the variety of possible modes and intensities of impact on French constitutional law by supranational law. The main criterion in the jurisprudence of the *Conseil constitutionnel* has been the "essential conditions" formula (CC 1970, 1985, 1991a, b, 1992, 1997, 2004, 2007). However, additional criteria such as "contrary to an express clause of the Constitution" or incompatibility with the constitutional guarantee of fundamental rights have been used (Haguenau-Moizard 2008, para. 29–31). The criteria for indicating unconstitutionality have not been clearly distinguishable. In particular the "essential conditions" formula had to be filled up in detail by jurisprudence (Favoreu,Philip 2011, 358–359). A similar ambiguity has been inherent to the term "constitutional identity" used as a yardstick for unconstitutionality of national laws implementing EU directives (Isaac, Blanquet 2012, 422–423). The CC deriving from article 88-1 of the French Constitution the obligation to implement EU directives claims the right to examine the due fulfillment of this obligation but abstains from reviewing the conformity of the national legislation with the other parts of the Constitution if the contents are strictly predetermined by them. However, the limit of this abstention is an encroachment on identity not consented to by the Constitution (CC 2006; Mayer, Lenski, Wendel 2008, 69–72).

The basis for the foundation of European Communities in the fifties was the preamble s. 15 of the IVth Republic Constitution which expressly permitted "limitations" of sovereignty (*"limitations de souveraineté nécessaires à l'organisation et à la défense de la paix")*. In contrast to this, a "transfer" of parts of sovereignty was originally seen as unconstitutional what could be legitimated by constitutional reform. A series of constitutional reforms (Rideau 2010, 1231, 1234, 1236, 1240–1241, 1242; Ardant, Mathieu, 2010, 436–437) have taken place for *constitutionalizing* important steps of the integration process which had not been conform to the Constitution initially.

Sovereignty of Parliament is, in theory, the keystone of the constitutional architecture in United Kingdom, with particular adhesion force in England. Developed in the nineteenth century it continues to be defended by the courts though it has suffered considerable losses: devolution, the impact of the ECHR through the Human Rights Act, the Factortame decision, the upcoming use of the referendum etc. Parliamentary sovereignty might formally be upheld, functionally it is in decline.

As in 1972 also in 2015 the very basic legal idea of the UK relationship with supranational organizations is that the European Communities Act 1972 which enabled accession for 1 January 1973 incorporates, by section 2, all law of the EEC, EC and EU *ex ante* and *ex post* into the internal British legal order. It remains, is a normative source, supranational law but is introduced in an equal position as the own legislation, submitted, as a consequence of parliamentary sovereignty, to be potentially repealed by later legislation. As the deep-rooted dogma confirms, Parliament, and also the EC Act of 1972, cannot bind a successor. However, interpretation of English legislation has to be effectuated in favor of supranational law so that open conflicts can often be avoided. Interpretation cannot go beyond a clear intention of the legislator. This would be contrary to separation of powers as well as to the doctrine of parliamentary sovereignty.

It has to be taken into account that sovereignty of Parliament is not (not yet) abandoned and finds its formal expression in the mechanism of the EC Act 1972 (which has been confirmed by the later EU Acts 2008 and 2011). United Kingdom Parliament (Sovereignty) Bill 2013–14 which has not completed its passage through Parliament before the May elections 2015 would, if enacted, repeal essential elements of the 1972 Act in detriment to the rooted EU concepts on supranationality developed and also widely accepted by UK. However, the intention to safeguard and sharpen sovereignty of Parliament would be limited by the concept of parliamentary sovereignty itself. A new law more favorable to European integration would easily repeal the blockade established by such an Act.

Sovereignty of Parliament as a historical meaning and underlies the ongoing political and social changes. The more the need for power differentiation in particular in the framework of uprising Scottish autonomy becomes urgent the more the formal constitutionalization of the legal and political system is preceded as an indispensable step forward. Constitutionalization if intended to be efficient implies the adoption of a supreme law charter. Sovereignty of Parliament will then transform into sovereignty of the Constitution. It seems that this fundamental change is not far away.

Limitation of national sovereignty by integration means Europeanization of the legal order and, at the same time, upholding the national identity whose main aspect is constitutional identity. Integration also requires the adaptation of traditional sovereignty concepts which do not permit, in their original meaning, "open statehood" but close up the State. It can be seen that tradition cannot exclude progress in integration.

Europeanization also means transformation of the State's national legal concepts into European concepts. Also this transformation process is a limitation of sovereignty. The conceptual influence which is exercised by the

European Convention of Human Rights on the national orders means a gradual transition into a common multistate rights system. Integration is not only a political–institutional operation but also a conceptual adaptation process.

National sovereignty in the European Union is a new form of supranationalized State power. The formula for this new phenomenon is national and constitutional identity but no longer sovereignty in the traditional sense.

References

Ardant, Philippe, and Bertand Mathieu. 2010. *Institutions Politiques et Droit Constitutionnel*, 22nd ed. Paris: LGDJ.

Conseil Constitutionnel (CC). 1970. DC No. 70-39 du 19 juin 1970. Rec., p.15. ECLI:FR:CC:1970:70.39.DC. http://www.conseil-constitutionnel.fr/conseil-con..-dc/decision-n-70-39-dc-du-19-juin-1970.7185.html.

Conseil Constitutionnel (CC). 1976. Déc. No. 76-71 DC du 30 Déc. 1976 http://www.conseil-constitutionnel.fr/conseil-constitutionnel/francais/les-decisions/acces-par-date/decisions-depuis-1959/1976/76-71-dc/decision-n-76-71-dc-du-30-decembre-1976.7453.html.

Conseil Constitutionnel (CC). 1985. Déc. No. 85-188 du 22 mai 1985. Rec., p.15. ECLI:FR:CC:1985:85.188.DC. http://www.conseil-constitutionnel.fr/conseil-con..-dc/decision-n-85-188-dc-du-22-mai-1985.8148.html.

Conseil Constitutionnel (CC). 1991a. Déc. No. 91-223 du 23 juillet 1991. Rec., p.77. ECLI:FR:CC:1991:91.293.DC. http://www.conseil-constitutionnel.fr/conseil-con.. decision-n-91-293-dc-du-23-juillet-1991.8762.html.

Conseil Constitutionnel (CC). 1991b. Déc. No. 91-294 du 25 juillet 1991. Rec., p.91. ECLI:FR:CC:1991:91.294.DC. http://www.conseil-constitutionnel.fr/conseil-con.. decision-n-91-294-dc-du-25-juillet-1991.8764.html.

Conseil Constitutionnel (CC). 1992. Déc. No. 92-308 du 9 avril 1992. Rec., p.55. ECLI:FR:CC:1992:92.308.DC. http://www.conseil-constitutionnel.fr/conseil-con..c/decision-n-92-308-dc-du-09-avril-1992.8798.html.

Conseil Constitutionnel (CC). 1997. Déc. No. 97-394 du 31 décembre 1997. Rec., p.344. ECLI:FR:CC:1997:97.394.DC. http://www.conseil-constitutionnel.fr/conseil-constitutionnel/francais/les-decisions/acces-par-date/decisions-depuis-1959/1997/97-394-dc/decision-n-97-394-dc-du-31-decembre-1997.11129.html.

Conseil Constitutionnel (CC). 2004. Déc. No. 2004-505 du 19 novembre 2004. Rec., p.173. ECLI:FR:CC:2004:2004.505.DC. http://www.conseil-constitutionnel.fr/conseil-constitutionnel/francais/les-decisions/acces-par-date/decisions-depuis-1959/2004/2004-505-dc/decision-n-2004-505-dc-du-19-novembre-2004.888.html.

Conseil Constitutionnel (CC). 2006. Déc. 2006-540 DC du 27 juillet 2006. Rec., 88. ECLI:FR:CC:2006:2006.540.DC. http://www.conseil-constitutionnel.fr/conseil-constitutionnel/francais/les-decisions/acces-par-date/decisions-depuis-1959/2006/2006-540-dc/decision-n-2006-540-dc-du-27-juillet-2006.1011.html.

Conseil Constitutionnel (CC). 2007. Déc. No.2007-560 du 13 décembre 2007. Rec., p.459. ECLI:FR:CC:2007:2007.560.DC. http://www.conseil-constitutionnel.fr/conseil-constitutionnel/francais/les-decisions/acces-par-date/decisions-depuis-1959/2007/2007-560-dc/decision-n-2007-560-dc-du-20-decembre-2007.1166.html.

Conseil constitutionnel (CC). 2013. Décision n° 2013-314P QPC du 04 avril 2013. http://www.conseil-constitutionnel.fr/conseil-constitutionnel/francais/les-decisions/acces-par-date/decisions-depuis-1959/2013/2013-314p.qpc/decision-n-2013-314p-qpc-du-04-avril-2013.136588.html.
Corte Costituzionale. 2008a. Sentenza No. 102/2008. http://www.cortecostituzionale.it/actionSchedaPronuncia.do?anno=2008&numero=102.
Corte Costituzionale. 2008b. Ordinanza No. 103/2008 giurcost.org/decisioni/index.html. http://www.giurcost.org/decisioni/index.html.
Cour constitutionnelle belge. 2013. Referring judgment of the Constitutional Court: 172/2013 of 19-12-2013. http://www.const-court.be/ Preliminary rulings from the Court of Justice.
European Court of Justice (ECJ). 1964. Costa/ENEL, 6/64, EC Rep. 1964, 585 (English Special Edition).
Favoreu, Luis, and Loïc Philip. 2011. *Les grandes décisions du Conseil constitutionnel*, 16th ed, 348–361. Paris: Dalloz.
Federal Constitutional Court (FCC). 1974. Solange I, vol. 37, 271.
Federal Constitutional Court (FCC). 1986. Solange II, vol. 73, 339.
Federal Constitutional Court (FCC). 1993. Maastricht, vol. 89, 155.
Federal Constitutional Court (FCC). 2009. Lissabon, vol. 123, 267 BVerfG, 2 BvE 2/08 of 30 June 2009. English version http://www.bverfg.de/entscheidungen/es20090630_2bve000208en.htm.
Federal Constitutional Court (FCC). 2010. Mangold, vol. 126, 286 BVerfG, 2 BvR 2661/06 of 06 July 2010. English version http://www.bverfg.de/entscheidungen/rs20100706_2bvr266106en.html.
Federal Constitutional Court (FCC). 2011. vol. 125, 385; BVerfG, 2 BvR 987/10 of 07 September 2011. English version http://www.bverfg.de/entscheidungen/rs20110907_2bvr098710.htm.
Federal Constitutional Court (FCC). 2014. BVerfG, 2 BvR 2728/13 of 14 January 2014. English version http://www.bverfg.de/entscheidungen/rs20140114_2bvr272813.html.
Haguenau-Moizard, Catherine. 2008. Frankreich. In *Handbuch Ius Publicum Europaeum, Offene Staatlichkeit - Wissenschaft vom Verfassungsrecht*, vol. II, ed. Armin von Bogdandy, Pedro Cruz Villalón, and Peter M. Huber, 37–69. Heidelberg: C.F.Müller.
House of Lords UK. 1990. R v Secretary of State for Transport. Ex p. Factortame Ltd. and others July 26, 1990. http://www.bailii.org/uk/cases/UKHL/1990/7.html.
Isaac, Guy, and Marc Blanquet. 2012. *Droit général de l'Union européenne*, 10th ed. Paris: Dalloz.
Mayer, Franz C., Lenski, Edgar, and Wendel, Mattias. 2008. Conseil d'Etat – Arcelor -Entscheidung vom 8. Februar 2007 (Übersetzung). Der Vorrang des Europarechts in Frankreich(Anmerkung) *WHI – Paper (Walter-Hallstein-Institut der Humboldt-Universität Berlin) 11/08*. www.whi-berlin.eu/documents/whi-paper1108.pdf. Printed also in *Europarecht (EuR)* 2008, Heft.1. 57–87.
Österreichischer Verfassungsgerichtshof. 2012. G 47/12-11; G 59/12-10; G 62,70,71/12-11 28.11.2012. http://www.vfgh.gv.at/cms/vfgh-site/attachments/5/9/4/CH0007/CMS1363700023224/vorratdatenspeicherung_vorlage_eugh_g47-12.pdf.
Rideau, Joël. 2010. *Droit institutionnel de l'Union européenne*, 6th ed. Paris: LGDJ.
Trybunal Konstytucyiny (TK). 2005. EU membership K 18/04.

Trybunal Konstytucyjny (TK). 2010. Lissabon K32/09.
Ústavní Soud (ÚS). 2006. Europ. Haftbefehl PL ÙS 66/04.
Ústavní Soud (ÚS). 2008. Lissabon I PL ÚS 19/08.

Rainer Arnold Dr. Dres.h.c. Professor at the University of Regensburg, in 1979 appointed holder of the Chair of Public Law, in 1999 nominated holder of the Jean Monnet Chair of EU Law and in 2008 holder of the Jean Monnet Chair ad personam "Legal Relations of the EU with Central, Eastern and Southeastern Europe". Nominated in 2000 hostujíci professor at the Charles University Prague. Corresponding Member of the Academy of Sciences of Bologna, Membre titulaire de l'Académie international de droit comparé, Fellow of the European Law Institute, in 2008 Fernand Braudel Fellow at the European University Institute, Fiesole/Florence, former Visiting Professor at the University Paris I (Panthéon-Sorbonne), Paris II (Panthéon-Assas), Strasbourg, Toulouse, Rome La Sapienza, Bologna and other.

Chapter 2
European Integration and Limitation of the Power of Constitutional Reform

Francisco Balaguer Callejón

Abstract This paper reflects on the changes that occur in the sovereignty of Member States of the European Union as a result of the process of European integration, through the analysis of constituent power limitations. Constituent power is the primary expression of sovereignty in constitutional States and the European integration process is changing some of the traditional profiles of this power. In the context of the European integration process, a fragmentation of constitutional matters occurs and therefore, these matters are not only in national constitutions. This means that constitutional reform cannot be analyzed solely from a national viewpoint. The fragmentation of constitutional matters is also the fragmentation of constituent power, what means fragmentation of Member States sovereignty and implies specific limits on reform. On the other hand, it must be considered along with the limits on reform derived from EU membership, an exercise of an external power of reform in relation with the constitutions of Member States. In summary, we have to take into account the dialectical relationship that is developing among constitutional spaces, which also leads us to consider that the facilitation of reform of fundamental norms is necessary for the effective interaction among constitutional systems.

2.1 Constitutional Reform and Constitutional Pluralism

The dialectical interaction among diverse constitutional spaces in Europe is altering classical concepts of national constitutional law, such as those of constituent power and the power of constitutional amendment. In the

F. Balaguer Callejón (✉)
Department of Constitutional Law, University of Granada,
Plaza de la Universidad, 1, 18001 Granada, Spain
e-mail: balaguer@ugr.es

R. Arnold (ed.), *Limitations of National Sovereignty through European Integration*, Ius Gentium: Comparative Perspectives on Law and Justice 51,
DOI 10.1007/978-94-017-7471-0_2

context of European integration we can no longer see the constitutional systems of the Member States exclusively from a "national perspective", nor can we see the legal system of the European Union purely from a "European perspective", as if they belonged to separate spheres (Häberle 1991, 1995, 2004a, b). This interaction is creating a dualist understanding of a European constitutional law: in a strict sense as the constitutional law of the European Union, and in a broad sense as the constitutional law of several constitutional levels of Europe (i.e. European, national, and regional); (Balaguer 2013a).

In the context of this plurality of constitutional spaces, the amendment process should be considered from a different perspective than has traditionally been done. This perspective must start with a methodological premise, which arises from one basic fact: since "constitutional issues" today are not only regulated by national constitutions, "constitutional reform" cannot be discussed only with reference to the text of these constitutions. This is a consequence of a pluralism of legal systems, to which the constitutions of Member States of the European Union are open.

At the same time the fragmentation of constitutional matter results in the division of constituent power, which means there are specific limits on reform (Balaguer 2002, 99–130). These limits are displayed and expressed at all constitutional levels. At a European level they are evident in the clause which safeguards the constitutional identity of Member States; Article 4.2 TEU, amended by the Lisbon Treaty, which provides that: "The Union shall respect the equality of Member States before the Treaties as well as their national identities, inherent in their fundamental structures, political and constitutional, inclusive of regional and local self-government. It shall respect their essential State functions, including ensuring the territorial integrity of the State, maintaining law and order and safeguarding national security. In particular, national security remains the sole responsibility of each Member State."

At a national level, although these limits are not explicitly established, they are present as a result of the process of European integration; so that today they operate in relation to the possibility of national constitutional reform as long as States remain a part of the European Union. National constitutions cannot be reformed, in practice, against the law of the European Union although there is no legal impediment to such reform.

Starting from the diversity of constitutional spaces, we can better understand the amending capabilities in relation to the constitutional needs of the different levels. For that purpose, we must take into account the dialectical relationship created among the different legal orders and the need for reform that it causes. In a system of legal pluralism there is a need to facilitate the reform of fundamental norms in order to achieve an effective interaction among the different legal systems.

In a context of constitutional plurality-such as that which exists amongst the Member States of the European Union-some of the functions of constitutional rigidity must be diminished. For example, the excessive rigidity of fundamental principles as a mechanism to guarantee protection of minorities and the democratic system itself largely makes no sense, if we consider the transformation that is involved in the process of European integration. Accession to the European Union is currently the principle safeguard against the regression of democracy that European States had previously tried to combat by means of intangible regulations (eternity clauses) established by their constitutions or by very rigid reform procedures intended to prevent presiding majorities from changing the foundation of the constitution, thereby violating the rights of minorities.

Excessive constitutional rigidity, which does not, in and of itself, contribute substantially to the democratic stability of Member States of the European Union, hinders the implementation of genuinely necessary constitutional reform. The indefinite postponement of reform does not help to streamline the system and has the cumulative effect of amplifying issues that are essentially of minor, technical nature, and turning them into major political issues. Given this situation, it is necessary to promote a more open constitutional culture that isn't based on the idealization of fundamental texts but on the consideration of their dynamics. These are norms and regulations that must positively serve society and they should be adapted to deal with new societal needs.

2.2 The Constitutional Status of Reform in the Context of the Diversity of Constitutional Spaces

The important functions of reform in the constitutional system are well known. One of these functions is the guarantee of the supremacy of the constitution over the power of the legislature and establishing the line between constituent power and constituted power. Enshrined therein is a legal (or external) division of power as transcendent as the political (or internal) division that makes the judicial review of actions of the legislature possible on the basis of constitutional regulations (Balaguer 1991).

Reform is reaching a nuclear position in the constitutions thanks to the theory of constituent power (Sieyès 1789). Although this theory is slightly ambiguous, it has played an important role in demonstrating the difference between the source of power that leads to the establishment of a new constitution, and the powers that may be exercised pursuant to that constitution. From this point of view, it can be stated that constituent power is political power, which has no strict legal limits. This lack of limits does not imply a lack of social and political constraints. Some of which can even be formulated legally, although only political or social grounds can ensure the linking of constituent powers to themselves.

A second characteristic of constituent power is its extinction at the point when the constitution is enacted. Whatever can be expressed in a constitution afterwards is nothing else but constituted powers to which the constitution itself grants diverse regulatory potency, including the modifying of its fundamental system, the reform of the constitution. Whatever powers are granted in this last order to the constituted powers, the foundation of the constitutional system, maintained within the framework of the constitution, would never be able to be legally altered. Unlike the sources of law that produce rules within the constitutional system, which are governed by a principle of inexhaustibility (Pugliatti 1958, 142), the constitution is a source that is depleted in its own production, as the power that gave it life disappears.

These two characteristics of constituent power correspond to those of sovereignty itself (Zweig 1909). On one hand, the politically and legally unlimited character of sovereign power; and on the other hand the inevitable contradiction between the constitutional principle of sovereignty and constitutional democracy itself which demands that all powers be subject to the law (Kriele 1975; Friedrich 1961; 1968, 60). People's sovereignty can only be exercised at the time of approval of a constitution, because only then there is the subject (the people as a homogeneous group) and the object of that principle (sovereign power); (Balaguer 1992, 28; 2000, 194).

In any case, the fact that the constitution is not subject to the principle of inexhaustibility of sources of law, allows for a distinction to be drawn between the constitution and constitutional reform. This distinction allows us to respond to some of the doctrinal questions about the possibility of establishing limits on the power of reform (Balaguer 1992, 37). It is true that a source of law is unable to bind itself in a way that would affect its future legislative power. This theory is correct, but it is not applicable to the constitution as a source of law. Hence the idea that the constitution cannot determine its own reform procedure (and therefore impose limits on it) is not acceptable, nor the idea that an amendment to the constitution is held to be at a higher level than the constitution itself (Ross 1929, 359). Precisely the opposite is true: an amendment of the constitution is located on a lower level to the constitution and is completely subject (whilst acting as legal power) to the constitution.

The apparent logical paradox can be explained easily: the postulate that a proposition cannot refer to itself is not applicable to the amendment of the constitution. In effect, reform is not a proposition that refers to it, because reform and the constitution are two different sources of law, both are expressions of legislative will of a different nature, of unequal legal potency and subject to different rules. Reform is subject to legal rules; the constitution only to political ones. Reform is an expression of constituted power the constitution is an expression of a constituent power. Only if we detract from reform its legal nature, thereby turning it into constituent power, can we say that this is a source of law, which, as the constitution, can legally enforce a limit to amending itself only if it is regarded as a higher source of law. Yet within the theory of constituent power, the apparent contradiction, which the prevision of procedures for constitutional reform poses, can be easily resolved. Indeed, constituent power is exhausted by the coming into force of the constitution, so there is not, from a legal point of view, any self-limitation of the power of political nature which is extinguished at the precise moment that the legal power (the constitution) begins to operate.

Constitutional limits on amendment are not, strictly speaking, limits on the constituent power, but the expression of a different power, of a legal nature (the power of reform), which intervenes solely within the constitutional framework. Moreover, power of reform cannot be regarded as superior to constituent power or to the constitution itself, because it is a general principle of law that no source of law can create another of a higher value (Zagrebelsky 1988, 5). What the constituent power actually creates in the constitution is constitutional reform and it is subordinated to the constitution, because it must be governed by the constitutionally established rules.

It is undoubtful that the distinction between constituent power and power of reform is something of a fiction. Like all legal formulation it indicates a qualification of a particular type that only makes sense from a legal perspective. It is from this perspective that it can be said that the power of reform is a limited power, since nothing prevents, from a political standpoint, the fundamental alteration of the constitutional system, through ways that are considered appropriate and by those who have the means to do so. If that happens, constituent power will have intervened once more leading to a new constitution. However, with that same act it will also be extinct until sometime in the future a new constitutional system is found by a new constituent power. Nonetheless, there is no more 'self-limitation' in the dialectal relationship between constituent power and power of reform than is present in the dialectal relationship between constituent power and the constitution. If one refuses to accept the metamorphosis of constituent power with the same token one is denying the supremacy of the constitution. The possibility of the existence of sovereign acts within the constitutional system is what is being admitted in that case. There is no self-restraint, but instead a transformation from an unlimited power to one which is legally controlled – not as a consequence of the will of the sovereign, but as a logical demand of the democratic conformation of the constitutional order. Otherwise, if the theory of the alleged (and rejected) restraint of constituent power is accepted, the constitutional system would collapse at the outset.

The problem which now arises from the process of European integration is whether from a legal perspective constituent power can really be distinguished from the power of reform, not because the power of reform acts (effectively) without legal limits, as does constituent power; but because the latter cannot actually act without legal limits as has traditionally been thought. Therefore, the problem is not whether the power of reform could turn into constituent power on a factual level; but if the power of reform can, legally, turn into constituent power: in other words, if it is still possible to speak about constituent power in the manner in which constituent power and power of reform have traditionally been discussed and differentiated, namely the absence of legal limits on the former power.

Above all, what must be dealt with is analyzing the impact that the gradual fragmentation of constituent power is having on the traditional relationship between constituent power and power of reform and whether, in the context of legal pluralism, it may still be possible to draw a coherent distinction between constituent power and power of reform. In short, if it is possible to maintain the doctrinal categories that we have inherited and, if so, to what extent.

If the process of European integration has diminished the sovereign power of States, leading to a real transfer of sovereignty to the European Union, it raises the question of whether the concept of 'constituent power' itself continues to be applicable, as primary source of power without legal limits to constituent power which can currently be exercised by the Member States of the European Union. At the same time, since a part of constitutional matters are external from the State, we have to accept that it is not possible to talk of 'constitutional reform' only by reference to the State and national constitutions. From that perspective, we will have to evaluate to what extent the EU is exercising a power of reform that can affect not only its own constitutional system, but also its relationship with the State and with national constitutions.

2.3 The Fragmentation of Constituent Power and the Limits on Reform

The process of European integration has reached such an intensity that it is difficult to speak of a primary constituent power in Member States. Indeed, there is no doubt about the existence of material limits to reform, derived from integration into the European Union. To the extent that this process is slowly becoming irreversible, we can speak of the impossibility of primary constituent power intervening in national constitutional systems. This leads to the effective transformation of constituent power into a mere power of reform. This is the main result of the fragmentation of constituent power. Moreover, with the advancement of the process of European integration, the material limits will be stricter and therefore the power of reform will have less room for maneuver.

Certainly the previsions on the voluntary withdrawal of Member States that have been incorporated to the Treaty of Lisbon (amended to Art. 50 of the Treaty on the European Union) could be opposed to this. The legal possibility of withdrawal from the Union is therefore accepted by the European Union itself. A different question is whether withdrawal is still possible for States integrated into the Eurozone, whose economies are heavily dependent on their membership of the European Union. Beyond the factual difficulties (or, rather, impossibilities) of withdrawal from the Union, a legal question may also arise for all Member States. Since even if we accept that voluntary withdrawal is legally possible, that does not mean that the States retain primary constituent power. Through their voluntary withdrawal, they can recover the constituent power that has been lost through their integration into the European Union but they do not possess it while they are inside the EU.

Whilst Member States remain being part of the European Union, they can only wield limited constitutional power, as they have to respect the obligations arising from their membership of the European Union. They cannot, for example, recover through constitutional reform (or through exercise of constituent power) the powers that they have transferred to the European Union. Nor can they establish a catalogue of fundamental rights that limits those established by the Charter on Fundamental Rights of the EU.

The limitation of the constitutional power of States does not mean that the constituent power exercised by the European Union in relation to its own fundamental rules, is a primary power. On the contrary, the European Union's ability to structure its fundamental norms is clearly determined by the Member States. On that point States have established specific constraints to European law through a clause safeguarding the constitutional identity of the Member States (Article 4.2 TEU, amended by the Lisbon Treaty). The clauses are an acceptance, or 'Europeanisation', of the so-called 'contro-limiti' that had been advocated by national constitutional doctrine and constitutional jurisprudence of the Member States, and incorporated into some constitutional systems.

What we have seen here is a clear example of the interaction between the European and national constitutional systems. This interaction also shows that neither the European constituent power nor that of the State can confer upon itself an originative condition that it is lacking. For this reason, we must assume that constituent power is a fragmented power under the condition of constitutional pluralism.

The gradual fragmentation of constituent power raises some issues for national constitutional law. If this fragmentation resulted in a full equivalence of the power of reform and constituent power (the disappearance of the legally unlimited nature of the latter), the functions of constituent power and the very distinction between constituent power and power of reform would be brought into question. However, it must be said that such equation does only occur in the partial aspect concerning the limits that the fragmentation of constituent power introduces in practice. Apart therefrom, the substantial distinction between power of reform and constituent power remains.

One must bear in mind that the unity of the constitution and the legal system is a reflection of constituent power. This unity may be compromised if there is no exercise of united constitutional power, in any area of the system. Moreover, constituent power allows for a legal order that aims to be systematic, because it is not merely partially acting but setting up an entire constitutional system. This does not occur with the power of reform. The power of reform can lead to essential changes in the constitutional system. However, it always would be partial modifications (otherwise, there would be a genuine exercise of constituent power and a new constitution).

All this should not prevent us from taking into account that constituent power and the power of reform are of the same nature. The result of the exercise of both powers is a constitutional regulation. From this perspective the line between originative constituent power and derivative constituent power will always be ambiguous. From the point of view of the final result, both provide constitutional rules to the legal system (de Cabo Martín 2003, 64).

Although the same result is reached by different methodology, constituent power and constitutional reform correspond to different *raisons d'être* and therefore cannot be regarded as identical. The establishment of a constitution can never be fully equated to an amendment, even if the constituent power is subject to prior legal limitations. Not only because the establishment of a new constitutional system always has a note of plenitude which reform lacks, but also because to the legal limits that may condition the constituent power, this can add additional limits to the power of reform. It is clear, therefore, that the gradual fragmentation of constituent power does not diminish the usefulness of the theoretical distinction between constituent power and power of reform. Fragmentation implies only that the distinctive feature of original constituent power can no longer be the one of a strictly political power and devoid of material limits. However, beyond its new limits, constituent power intervenes with full capacity for political decision making in setting up a new constitutional system.

2.4 The "Reform Power" of the European Union in Relation with the Constitutions of Member States

We have seen so far which the impact legal pluralism can have on the fragmentation of constituent power when it comes to the passive aspect of this process: the limits of reform and the relative similarity between constituent power and power of reform. Now we should dwell on the active side: the impact of legal pluralism on the constitutional transformations of the systems with which they interact.

The procedures of constitutional reform do not include formal mechanisms with which the EU can decide on a constitutional reform by itself. In any case, it is natural that supra-national integration impinges at a constitutional level as it does at an infra-constitutional level. Recent examples of this issue referred to national constitutional reforms, which have been informally promoted by certain European institutions.

Constitutional interaction in these areas is therefore inevitable and the effects of this interaction have been repeatedly discussed. We could say that the EU is already exercising constituent power belonging to the Member States, even though it is not an originative, but derived constituent power. This exercise of power of reform is consistent with the transitional phase, which the process of integration is currently in. At this point, we can say that Member States have already lost much of the status of originative systems, whilst the European Union has not yet acquired that status. The interaction between the emerging constitutional system of the European Union and the established constitutional systems of the Member States is an increasingly tangible reality and must be assessed in a methodological manner. The European 'level' can no longer be ignored in the study of national constitutional law. The European integration process requires assessing national constitutional institutions considering such variables with a new methodological approach. The interaction between the European 'level' and the national one is set to become increasingly intense and therefore must increasingly be taken into account when pursuing the singular analysis of these levels.

References

Balaguer, F. 1991. Notas sobre la estructura constitucional del Estado español. RDP: n. 32.

Balaguer, F. 1992. *Fuentes del Derecho*. Madrid: Tecnos.

Balaguer, F. 2000. Constitución y ordenamiento jurídico. In *Teoría de la Constitución. Ensayos escogidos*, ed. M. Carbonell. México: Editorial Porrúa/UNAM.

Balaguer, F. 2002. *El status constitucional de la reforma y la fragmentación del Poder Constituyente, AAVV, La democracia constitucional. Estudios en homenaje al Profesor Rubio Llorente*, vol. I. Madrid: Congreso de los Diputados/Tribunal Constitucional.

Balaguer, F. 2013a. (Coordinador) Cámara Villar, G., López Aguilar, J., Balaguer Callejón, M., Montilla Martos, J. Manual de Derecho Constitucional, vol. I. Madrid: Tecnos.

Balaguer, F. 2013b. Crise économique et crise constitutionnelle en Europe, Constitutions avril-juin.

De Cabo Martín, C. 2003. *La reforma constitucional en la perspectiva de las fuentes del Derecho*. Madrid: Trotta.

Friedrich, C.J. 1961. *Demokratie als Herrschafts- und Lebensform*. Madrid: Tecnos.

Friedrich, C.J. 1968. *Man and his Government: An empirical theory of politics*. Madrid: Tecnos.

Häberle, Peter. 1991. Gemeineuropäisches Verfassungsrecht. EuGRZ: 261.

Häberle, Peter. 1995. Die europäische Verfassungsstaatlichkeit. Kritische Vierteljahresschrift für Gesetzgebung und Rechtswissenschaft: 3/1995.

Häberle, Peter. 2004a. Europa como comunidad constitucional en desarrollo. Revista de Derecho Constitucional Europeo, n° 1, Enero-Junio.

Häberle, Peter. 2004b. *Tienen España y Europa una Constitución?* Sevilla: Fundación El Monte.

Kriele, M. 1975. *Einführung in die Staatslehre. Die geschichtlichen Legitimitätsgrundlagen des demokratischen Verfassungsstaates*. Opladen: Westdeutscher Verlag, 1990.

Pugliatti, S. 1958. Abrogazione. EdD: V. I.

Ross, A. 1929. *Theorie der Rechtsquellen. Ein Beitrag zur Theorie des positiven Rechts auf Grundlage dogmenhistorischer Untersuchungen*. Leipzig: Franz Deuticke.

Sieyès, S. 1789. *Qu'est-ce que le Tiers État?* Madrid: CEC, 1988.

Zagrebelsky, G. 1988. *Manuale di Diritto costituzionale. I. Il sistema delle fonti del diritto*. Torino: UTET.

Zweig, E. 1909. *Die Lehre vom Pouvoir Constituant. Ein Beitrag zum Staatsrecht der französischen Revolution.* Tübingen: J.C.B. Mohr.

Francisco Balaguer Callejón Professor of Constitutional Law at the University of Granada and *ad personam* Jean-Monnet-Professor of European Constitutional Law and Globalization.

Chapter 3
National and Constitutional Identity as a Legal and Political Instrument

Luca Mezzetti

Abstract This work delves into the issue of the theory of constitutional justice that assumes the shape of a ring of essential conjunction between the theory of the Constitution on one hand and the theory of constitutional interpretation on the other hand. The continuum theory of the constitutional justice-theory of constitutional interpretation denotes the tight interdependence of the segments that compose it and the mutual osmosis of the factors that characterize it, and it necessarily implies a systematic approach to arrange the second element of the trinomial in light of the first one (the theory of the constitutional justice in the optics of the theory of the Constitution) and the third element of the trinomial in the light of the second one (the theory of the constitutional interpretation in light of the theory of constitutional justice). Such an approach has been variously conceived by the different doctrinal positions that have faced the above-mentioned problem and in this work it will be offered an overview of the most important of them, as developed in a comparative perspective. Moreover, this work analyses the role and the functions of constitutional justice organs in contemporary democracies showing as the reasons of their legitimation, can be evaluated in a partial and sectorial perspective (coinciding with the judgment of constitutionality of the laws) or in a systemic perspective, to embrace the functions of the organs themselves in their complexity.

L. Mezzetti (✉)
School of Law, Advanced School for Legal Studies, University of Bologna,
via Belmeloro 12, 40126 Bologna, Italy
e-mail: luca.mezzetti@unibo.it

R. Arnold (ed.), *Limitations of National Sovereignty through European Integration*, Ius Gentium: Comparative Perspectives on Law and Justice 51,
DOI 10.1007/978-94-017-7471-0_3

3.1 Theories of the Constitutional Justice and Constitutional Identity

The problem related to the democratic legitimisation of the constitutional jurisdiction is of fundamental importance in a democratic State. A reference to the people of the constitutional jurisdiction as a demonstration and exercise of State sovereignty is essential, particularly if the jurisdiction is conferred the attribute of annulling laws as unconstitutional if approved by the popular representation elected by the people. The theoretical structure finalized to embody the constitutional justice within the democratic legitimation which is founded upon the sovereignty, has the objective of preventing the constitutional jurisdiction, founded to safeguard the constitution, become an uncontrolled excess of power in comparison to the others and as such threaten the democratic constitutional structure, instead of protecting it.

In this way, the theory of constitutional justice assumes the shape of a ring of essential conjunction between the theory of the Constitution on one hand and the theory of constitutional interpretation on the other hand. The continuum theory of the constitutional justice-theory of constitutional interpretation denotes the tight interdependence of the segments that compose it and the mutual osmosis of the factors that characterize it, and it necessarily implies a systematic approach to arrange the second element of the trinomial in light of the first one (the theory of the constitutional justice in the optics of the theory of the Constitution) and the third element of the trinomial in the light of the second one (the theory of the constitutional interpretation in light of the theory of constitutional justice). Such an approach has been variously conceived by the different doctrinal positions that have faced the above-mentioned problem.

3.1.1 The Italian Doctrine

According to the *realist* theory elaborated by V. Crisafulli, no model of constitutional justice can boast full democratic legitimacy, and this is also true for the system of the Italian constitutional jurisdiction.

Nevertheless, the apparent antinomy is overcome, according to the author, only when considering the contradiction as inevitable and immanent to the liberal-democratic Constitution, representing the constitutional justice not as an antinomy, but rather an *alteration* of the democratic-parliamentary scheme, an alteration intentionally set by the constituent authorities, functional to a precise political plan, in which is expressed, at the highest level, the liberal and therefore guaranteed component, that qualifies the constitutional democratic regime.

The constitutional Court is a factor that converges to characterize and define a form of government.

The problem of the democratic legitimation of the constitutional courts, "*longae manus* of the constituent power", has also been faced by A. Ruggeri and A. Spadaro; that upsetting the traditional formulation and questioning the very legitimisation of the democratic regime, observed as the "natural lack of democratic legitimisation" of the constitutional courts rises from their function as custodians of the meta-democratic framework of values that limit the strength of the same democratic regime: "guaranteeing the equilibrium of the two poles of the popular sovereignty, on one hand, and of the supremacy of a system of constitutional values on the other hand, the courts – even though not practicing the activity of political direction in the narrow sense – take the shape of judicial organs endowed with political strength, with juridical-arbitration functions of custody-guarantee also, if not above all, towards the same laws in which popular sovereignty expresses itself". Such functions bring the constitutional courts, even though not elective, to work in the name and in the interest of all members of the society.

Besides as arbiter, the organ of constitutional justice is a component of a balanced system of weights and counterweights characterized by the presence of remarkable functions of guarantee conferred to other organs (as the President of the Republic, the independent administrative authorities etc.) and in which results the difficult to imagine, according to Ruggeri and Spadaro, the hypothesis of a court that misuses its powers, trying to impose its hermeneutic tools against the "learned" interpretation of the jurists and the "diffused" interpretation of the profanes.

The factor that induces the authors to see with a sense of proportion, and to circumstantiate the lack of democratic legitimation of the constitutional organs coincides with the power belonging to the power of constitutional revision, to restore any normative declared unconstitutional by constitutional courts.

Indefectible, under the logical-juridical profile, "closing organs" in the constitutional system and the necessity to recognize, "by convention", a unique system of constitutional controls, the hypothesis of an organ that can verify the correctness of the interpretative path on one hand not being possible; the non-self-applicable nature of the decisions of the organs of constitutional justice and the ordinary unavailability of the same organs of instruments of realization-execution of their decisions, on the other hand, constitute more factors as insuperable limits to the "sovereignty" of the Constitution's custody organs.

The power of such organs is in a tight relationship, and in direct proportionality with, the social consent of the Constitution and with the attitude of the members of society to observe the precepts and the jurisprudentially elaborated reading keys.

3.1.2 The German Doctrine

The approach to the problem of the democratic legitimacy of the constitutional jurisdiction has taken place in the German doctrine along three essential coordinates: (a) interpretative methods of the organs of constitutional justice; (b) delimitation of the spheres of attributions of the organs of constitutional justice in comparison to the representative organs; (c) systemic approach.

3.1.2.1 Interpretative Methods of the Organs of Constitutional Justice

An object of analysis has been, by many doctrinal positions and under a plurality of visual angles, the contribution of the Federal Constitutional Court to the purpose of the enunciation of new rights and values in the constitutional context of the Basic Law, as well as formulating warnings and concrete directions to the legislator and the executive in various material sectors: such instruments bring a "colonization of the political sphere" (Haltern 1998, 207), that consequently is "juridified". Such "juridification" is assimilated to an ossification as the borders of correction-overcoming of the decisions of the organ of constitutional justice by the legislator are considered extremely narrow: this explains the quantitative prevalence of the studies that have tried to identify the borderline of the attribution spheres of the representative assemblies and of the *Bundesverfassungsgericht*, as well as an acceptable justificatory criterion of the power of the Constitutional Court – an organ deprived of a direct democratic legitimacy – to annul acts of the Assemblies, organs for excellence expression of direct democratic legitimacy (Chryssogonos 1987; Landfried 1988; Jekewitz 1980; Stern 1997).

3.1.2.2 Delimitation of the Spheres of Attributions of the Organs of Constitutional Justice in Comparison to the Representative Organs

The theoretical location of the constitutional jurisdiction had given place to a vivacious doctrinal debate and raised controversies already at the epoch of the Weimar Constitution: the alleged reasoning cannot be referred restrictively to the polemic between Kelsen and Schmitt. In the context characterized by the tension established among the configuration of the pole of the parliamentary legality and the pole of a legitimacy superior to the same positive Constitution, you can distinguish the doctrinal positivistic and the anti-positivistic currents, articulated themselves in two sub-currents (Hinkel 1984; Wendenburg 1984).

The conservative anti-positivism of H. Triepel, R. Smend and of E. Kaufmann was sceptic as regards the attitude of the *Staatsgerichtsbarkeit* to resolve political conflicts at the central level; such scepticism turned, as it is known, in a radical negation in the position elaborated by Schmitt (1981). The quoted authors maintained on the other hand a positivist attitude towards the constitutionality control, in an incidental way, practiced by the *Reichsgericht* starting from 1921 with the famous decisions of 28.4.1921, of 21.10.1924 and of 4.11.1925. The jurisdictional control of the norms met a definite rejection by the socialist orientation current of the anti-positivism that qualified it as a "degeneration of the rule of law principle" (Heller, Neumann).

A conciliatory position was assumed by the positivistic school that in its liberal variation (whose eminent representatives were R. Thoma e G. Anschütz) and in its socialist variation (coincident particularly with the position of G. Radbruch) was favorable to the attribution of the control function to a centralized constitutional court.

More recently, the intent to individualize the borderline between the parliamentary decision and that of the constitutional justice organ, as well as the search of the legitimation source of the pronunciations of the latter, has implicated the elaboration by the German doctrine of theories on the base, respectively, of the principle of separation of powers, of the political questions doctrine, of the judicial self-restraint principle, of the juxtaposition between right and politics principle, and of the juridical-functional principle.

With reference to the first of the mentioned profiles, the separation of powers principle is shaped – as the base of the state's system of competences – as a central criterion to determine the position of the constitutional jurisdiction in the democratic system (Adamovich 1987), identifying the constitutional justice as a "fourth power" to be referred with a certain difficulty to the classic separation of powers scheme (Roellecke 1980).

On the second profile, the automatic and mechanical applicability to the German system of constitutional justice of the political questions doctrine of North American origin has been treated by the German doctrine with extreme caution and scepticism (Stern 1980; Friesenhahn 1976; Schneider 1980; Rau 1996), some doctrinal positions (Chryssogonos 1987; Bryde 1982) remarking that in principle it is extraneous to the Basic Law the concept of constitutional dispositions that cannot act as a parameter for the exercise of the constitutionality control.

Likewise, the judicial self-restraint principle has been considered of scarce reliability for the identification of the legitimation source of the constitutional jurisdiction (Chryssogonos 1987; Böckenförde 1991; Schneider 1980).

The juridical-functional approach seems to denote a better attitude for the identification of the spheres proper of the legislator and of the constitutional justice organ and of the legitimation requisites of the latter. It is an analytical method followed, among others, by E.W. Böckenförde that identifies the primary function of the constitutional jurisdiction in the protection of the Constitution.

The peculiarities of the constitutional jurisdiction inside the State powers structure, particularly in comparison with the ordinary jurisdiction, are individualized by the author in the constitutional jurisdiction, in the parties of the constitutional trial, in other words, of the subjects that take part to the constitutional controversies, in the unusual interpretative strength proper of the constitutional jurisdiction.

How can the dilemma of the democratic legitimation of an actor with such a meaningful role and so penetrating in the dynamics of the contemporary State be resolved? The guarantees offered by the formalities of election, nomination and duration of the constitutional judges mandate, remaining in any case to the constitutional jurisdiction the "last word" on the interpretation of the constitution, appear insufficient to Böckenförde.

A possible answer to the above mentioned question is identified by the author in the institute of deferment to the representatives of the people of a law declared unconstitutional by the constitutional justice organ, and in the possibility that the representative assembly re-approves it with the (qualified) majority requested for the constitutional revision, contemplated by the Polish Constitution up to July 1999. In such case the "last word" would remain with the organ of popular representation: it is a solution not exempt from critical relief, pertaining particularly the possibility that would proceed from it, the modification of the constitution for the single case without proceeding to a formal constitutional revision, implicitly admitting no limitation to constitutional changes.

3.1.2.3 Systemic Approach

Paradigmatic and preliminary to the reconstruction of the systemic approach it is the classical doctrine of Bachof (1963). For Bachof, a characteristic feature of the Basic Law, that not only differentiates it from the anterior

German Constitutions, but also from a lot of contemporary Constitutions, is given by the function assigned to the judicial power in the constitutional system: the expansion of the judicial power attributions, and particularly of the Federal Constitutional Court, that in the German legal order is incorporated in the sphere of the same power, is testified according to the author by the introduction of the constitutional control of the law, by the direct claim of constitutionality to protect the fundamental rights (*Verfassungsbeschwerde*), and by the resolution of the inter-organic and inter-subjective conflicts. Such competences are not nevertheless able *per se* to justify the practical effectiveness of the control practiced by the judicial power: the same effectiveness derives from the energetic ambition of validity of the material norms of the Constitution; of an order of values that directly binds the three state powers and expressly reveals itself in the discipline of the fundamental rights; of a value order that has been considered by the Constitution as anterior to the same one; of a value order that has not been created by the Constitution, but that recognizes and guarantees, and whose last base of validity is recovered in the basic values of the western culture, in a conception of the man based on such values (Bachof 1963, 39–40).

The direct and immediate applicability of fundamental rights and the immediate validity of the ethical order of values subtended by the Basic Law, is applicable, according to the German lawyer, to the political system in the narrow sense: for the decision adopted by the Constitution for the democracy and the form of parliamentary government, for the separation of powers as a principle of the rule of law to prevent abuses in the exercise of the power, and for the principles of the social State and the federal State as the articulation of the competences among the different state organs is concerned (Bachof 1963, 31).

The material substance of the Constitution, the order of values altogether that characterizes it, operationally rest on the position of the courts: the judges have been attributed the responsibility of the last protection of the Constitution. The fundamental reason for the subjection of the legislator to the control of the judges has to be found, according to Bachof, in the total change that has interested the relationship between the men and the law: a feeling of depth discomfort and of radical mistrust towards the law has risen, founded upon the dominant impression that the law, once the shield of liberty and of law, turned instead into a threat for such good (Bachof 1963, 48). The law has become, therefore, actions of political direction as well as an expression of will of a political nature conditioned by the contingent cases and occasional circumstances.

To the objections of the control function attributed to the constitutional justice organ – violation of the separation of powers principle, inherent antidemocratic nature of the decision on the value constitutional system submitted to an organ with a restricted composition rather than to the Parliament, the danger of the politicization of justice – the author answers through a triplex order of considerations.

As for the first objection, Bachof considers that the meaning of the separation of powers consists of preventing the concentration of power and of a possible abuse of the same. Currently, in the modern social State, the necessary character that has for the men, their total dependence from the government apparatus, implicates correlatively a total control of such apparatus: the limitation of power that Parliament and Government experiment implies a necessary correction for the reestablishment of the equilibrium (Bachof 1963, 58).

As the supposed antidemocratic character of the judicial power is concerned, the author says, on one hand, that other organs or subjects are not in a relationship of direct derivation by the people (the Government, the President of the Republic, the civil servants), on the other hand that criterion of reference must not be the type of mandate but rather the function: to administer the justice in the name of the people means for the German lawyer to maintain by the judge a constant and continuous dialogue with the trial parties, with the colleagues, with the technical-juridical and scientific world and with the public opinion (Bachof 1963, 60).

Regarding the risks of politicization of the judges, finally, the author observes that the experienced judge knows the consequential dangers proceeding from the introduction of emotional and irrational elements in his/her judgments: his professional formation, the necessity of a nonstop dialogue and the same independence of the judge guarantee, according to such a vision, an elevated level of objectivity.

The concrete danger that the constitutional justice organ slides toward a judicial paternalism that could implicate the transition from the parliamentary legislative State, to a State characterized by the prominence of the jurisdictional power of the Constitutional Court, is a risk that can be avoided, according to Alexy (1986 526 et sqq.), through the successful incorporation of the constitutional jurisdiction in the democratic process. This implies that the Constitutional Court is conceived as a centre of reflection of the political process and is approved as such. To this purpose, the constitutional justice organ must demand the result of the political process doesn't contradict the parameters of the fundamental rights and must found its own pretensions so that the citizens can rationally approve the reasoning of the Court. The fundamental rights must be interpreted, according to the German lawyer, in conformity to a "public moral conception" that makes apparent a common representation of the correct conditions of social cooperation in a world characterized by the pluralism: the constitutional justice organ must not oppose its own thought, in a preconceived way, to that of the legislator, but to aspire to shape it through proceeding by topics which represent the citizens.

The Constitution prescribes and prohibits certain actions through fundamental norms and the formal principles establishing a legal framework as a fundamental order; it leaves open, on the other hand, borders of manoeuvre, structural and epistemic, attributing a certain trust to the legislator to the realization of fundamental rights. Likewise, the intervention of the constitutional justice organ, when consisted of a violation of the competence by the legislator, doesn't produce an institutional move of the competence of the Court within the legislation. Such intervention, Alexy signals, not only is permitted, but it is prescribed by the Constitution in the measure in which the latter determines the sphere of action of it. The essential nucleus of such a sphere of attribution consists in the protection of a legal framework that simultaneously establishes a fundamental order (Alexy 1986, 529).

The consideration of the functions of the constitutional justice organ in the most general social dynamics, is criterion followed by the authors that they have reserved to the problem of the legitimation of the constitutional jurisdiction a *systemic approach*, centred on the reference to juridical-constitutional criteria, but also founded upon the appeal to social, political, economic, historical and cultural criteria.

An example is given by E. Stein (1972) that identifies seven functions of the Federal Constitutional Court in the German political system. According to such doctrinal position, the constitutional justice organ develops a *function of stabilization of the Constitution*, it contextually facilitates a controlled social change (*evolutionary function*) also acting as a valve able to prevent (or to obviate to) phenomena of stagnation of the political and social forces (*valve- function*). As control organ competent to verify that the formation process of the political will develops inside the channels and the limits assigned to it, the Federal Constitutional Court rectifies, in a binding way, behaviours conflicting with the Constitution (*control function*). The composition of the conflicts realized by the constitutional justice organ contributes to the formation of social peace and resolves political and social conflicts through a jurisdictional procedure (*pacification function*). The realization of fundamental rights promotes the liberty (*educational function*) and the maintenance of the open character of the political process, particularly through the protection of minorities, it may overcome the crisis of legitimation of the political system, bringing about the realization of democracy (*integration function*).

Apart from doctrinal positions conferring a plurality of tasks and functions to constitutional justice, others have identified more specific aims. Criticizing the capitalistic model, Massing (2005) understands the constitutional jurisdiction as a central component of the political-administrative government system of the late-capitalistic Interventionist State, endowed with the function of developing and preserving equilibrium and stability in the same system. The Federal Constitutional Court, as an instrument of the creation of consent in a binding way and of the influence on the collective imperatives of action, is conceived by the author as a factor of management of the political crisis of the late-capitalistic State and of support to a system of forces structured according to an oligopolistic model.

Analogous is the reasoning advocated by Schlothauer (1979).

The integrationist conception of the constitutional jurisdiction has always had a primary importance, at least starting from the theory of R. Smend on the integrative force of the Constitution (Smend 1966). More recently, the pluralist theories of the constitutional justice have become an object of reconsideration, particularly, by the doctrinal positions of Häberle and of Ebsen.

The organization of the constitutional justice takes place in the works of Häberle, both of general character (Häberle 2005) and specifically devoted to the subject (Häberle 1980, 2006), to the light of the idea of the Constitution: "Constitution" is the fundamental legal order of state and society; it is not only a limit of governmental power, but also authorization of governmental power; it contains State and society. Constitutional justice as a political force acts from the beginning outside of the dogma of the division of State/society (Häberle 2005, 158). The configuration of the Federal Constitutional Court as a "constitutional court" of the *res publica* as a whole implies that the constitutional justice organ doesn't adhere to a theory or doctrine, but pursues the pragmatic integration of elements of different theories.

The pluralism in the constitutional procedures and the conception of the Federal Constitutional Court more as a "court of the society in general" than as a "state" court implies a peculiar general responsibility attributed to the constitutional justice organ in the guarantee and in the development of the constitution as a social contract, engraving on its continuous process of realization and it is forced toward the pluralism in this. The function of constitutional justice is the limitation, the rationalization and the control of the state and social power, it cooperates, from the point of view of the content, to the general consent and is based on the guardianship of the minority and the weak, in the flexible and timely reaction to the new dangers for human dignity, in its apolitical character of guide and answer (Häberle 2005, 159–160).

Likewise, according to the theory of the constitutional justice elaborated by Ebsen, in the democratic constitutional State three fundamental tasks are attributed to the organs of constitutional justice: maintenance of a broad political process, that implies the legitimacy of the majority principle; guarantee of the measure socially allowed for the protection of the individual towards the governmental force; integration of the particular interests as far to make possible the majority decisional system (Ebsen 1985, 229). The three tasks imply, according to the author, a determined degree of consent: the function of maintenance of the open character of the political process is founded upon the consent at the meta-level of the social relationships; the normative function of guardianship of the liberty is preferable to the elements of the general concept of liberty, brought in principle by the material constitutional consent; the consent, that implies the function of integration on one hand, but on the other hand is finalized to guarantee it, pertains to a further meta-level featured by the objective to guarantee and to implement the social compromise formed in the constituent assembly (Ebsen 1985, 322).

3.1.3 The French Doctrine

With reference to the factors able to accredit or to strengthen the legitimacy of the jurisdictional control of the laws, L. Favoreu points out six functional elements: the history, the form of government, the jurisdictional technique, the Constitution (*rectius*, the constitutional text), the control's organ, and the structure of the State (Favoreu 1986).

To bring back the legitimacy of constitutional justice to the history means to evoke the experiences and the historical heritage of Countries that have experienced periods of dictatorship in which it has absolutely appeared necessary to found a jurisdictional control of laws with the purpose to subtract the exclusive dominion to the majorities as fundamental rights are concerned: the examples alleged by the French lawyer are those of Greece, Portugal and Spain, that have experienced their constitutional transitions at the mid of the seventies of the twentieth century, then taking a sure walk of democratic consolidation. You can add the cases of the countries of Eastern and Central Europe and of the ex-Soviet area that have opted in mass, after 1989, for the creation of systems of centralized constitutional justice.

The legitimacy of the jurisdictional control of the laws subsequently acts as a function of the modalities of operation of the form of government. The author ascertains that the Countries of Western Europe endowed with a system of constitutional control of the law are characterized by a form of parliamentary (Italy, Germany, Spain, Belgium) government or semi-presidential (Austria, Portugal, France). In the mentioned experiences (apart from Italy) there is a stable parliamentary and government majority, strong and cohesive, faced by the opposition. The latter needs a counterweight – the constitutional justice – that cooperates with it to face up to, and to withstand, the majority: it is the institutional logic that erects or develops an institution as a reaction against the excessive power of another institution (Favoreu 1986, 47). In Italy, it is the weakness and brittleness of the Parliament that implicates an intervention of the Constitutional Court, which is able to replace the absence of decisive choices by the legislator. Furthermore, the legitimacy of the constitutional jurisdiction depends on the jurisdictional technique used, whereas the American technique of the diffused control of constitutionality appears to the author, without doubt, less fit to assure the same legitimacy in comparison to the European technique of the centralized control (already Cappelletti had pointed out various reasons in such a direction). The legitimacy of the constitutional justice finds its own source, furthermore, in the same nature of the constitutional text, whose vanished, inaccurate or evanescent character and whose historical origin eventually exalts, at least doesn't devalue, the adapting function of the constitutional judge.

Organization and workings of the constitutional justice organ are shaped as further factors of conditioning the legitimacy of the same organ. In contrast to the criticism related to the non-democratic and not representative nature of the constitutional courts, Favoreu sets in evidence the common feature of the majority of the courts, composed by members designated in prevailing measures by elective organs endowed with full democracy and representation: the politicization of the designation and composition of the constitutional jurisdictions is a necessary element of such systems.

The legitimacy of the constitutional justice in the structural function of the State-legal order, is made finally evident by the necessity of the control of constitutionality of the law in federal and regional States, or in the experiences founded upon a delicate equilibrium between ethnic and linguistic communities (Belgium).

The control of constitutionality can contribute, in a different measure, to improve the working of democratic regimes thanks to the beneficial effects that it is able to produce in the juridical and political sphere: in such a direction, Favoreu identifies six fundamental functions that the constitutional justice develops and that, in their complexity, denote the attitude to increase the legitimacy of the same: the function of pacification of the political life, the function of regulation and authentication of the political changes and the alternation, the function of strengthening of the cohesion of the political society, the function of diffusion and rootedness of fundamental rights, the function of protection of fundamental rights, the function of adjustment and updating of the Constitution (Favoreu 1986, 62–66).

A configuration of the constitutional jurisdiction of *dynamic* nature as an adaptable model to the mutable reality of the democracy in its actual phase, introducing shaped as *continuous democracy*, has been elaborated on in the French doctrine, particularly, by Rousseau and it implies the affirmation of three new forms of representation of the opinions in the political competition, the form of the inquiries, the media form, that realizes itself through the means of communication, the *constitutional form*, that is realized through the constitutional courts or, in the case of France, the Constitutional Council (Rousseau 1995, 1998, 2006).

Differently from the positivist school and from the natural law school, that found the legitimacy of the constitutional justice upon a definition *a priori* of the democracy, the author proposes another hypothesis, that is formulated in the followings terms: the control of constitutionality of the laws is legitimate because it produces a definition of the democracy that legitimates it (Rousseau 2006, 2). The objective of identification by D. Rousseau is not the relationship among democratic truth and mechanism of constitutionality control, but the democratic truth that makes possible such mechanism, legitimising it.

Today the constitutional justice produces a new language, "a new representation of the democracy that founds the legitimacy of the re-composition of the institutional framework upon the principle of the prominence of the Constitution and consequently of the constitutional judge" (Rousseau 2006, 3). Such a new configuration of the democracy, denominated elsewhere by the author "continuous democracy" (Rousseau 1995, 9 et sqq.), "legitimates a constitutional judge that, through his/her jurisdictional activity, behaves as the builder of the autonomy of the public space and the builder of the making norm of the word of the sovereign" (Rousseau 2006, 4).

The first delineated perspective is dominated by an epochal overturn of scenery, characterized by the passage from the Constitutional separation of powers to the Constitutional guarantee of rights and by the connected development of the constitutional jurisprudence.

The space built between the civil society and the political society is therefore occupied by the constitutional jurisdiction; the main effect produced by the distinction rulers-ruled in the sense now described consists in the representation of the representation.

If the affirmation of the superiority of the people in comparison to its representatives is fulfilled through the mediation of the constitutional justice organ, the mirror that reflects its image of sovereign people is, according to D. Rousseau, the jurisprudential charter of rights and liberties that the constitutional judge introduces to the people to make them aware of their own sovereignty and to the representatives to make them aware of their subordination to the sovereign.

In the second of the delineated perspectives, the continuous democracy is characterized by an (apparent) contradiction, consisting in the mean – the organ of constitutional justice (of non-elective nature) – that realizes the mediate (and not direct) superiority of the people in front of its representatives. Such antinomy is overcome, according to D. Rousseau, considering that, through its own interpretative work, the constitutional justice organ confers normativeness to the Constitution entering a game of relationships of force with other institutions, of different nature, contributing within the continuous democracy, as a privileged entrepreneur among legislative entrepreneurs (*entrepreneurs législatifs*) that participate in the enunciation of the norms in their complexity, to the delineation of a regime of competitive affirmation of the norms: on one hand, in fact, the formation of the law appears the fruit of the work of three competing institutions (Parliament, Government, the organ of constitutional justice), on the other hand the interpretation of the Constitutional Council could sometimes be derived from free and arbitrary choices, but it is the consequence of a series of ties, "of a game that puts different actors in competition ": the members of the Parliament, law professors, the category organizations, press, and the same constitutional jurisprudence.

The necessity and legitimacy of constitutional justice in our times are given by the fundamental role that it develops in the last type of democracy: it enriches it with the protection of rights of the individuals and of the minorities, it opens individual and sectorial new spaces of participation, it strengthens the pluralism and the competition in public processes, it represents in a new way the public opinion, it improves the formation of the general will, that is no more as a will of a simple parliamentary majority, and it widens the field of the deliberation in the production of the norms, going beyond the limits imposed by the pure representative democracy.

3.1.4 The Latin American Doctrine

Close to reasons of traditional nature, four fundamental reasons are alleged by N. P. Sagüés to the identification of the factors of legitimisation of constitutional justice (Sagüés 2002, 51 et sqq.): the concrete procedure of selection and designation of the constitutional judges (for instance through the representative assemblies) that, as programmed by a democratic Constitution, enjoys a meaningful quota of democratic legitimisation; the formation and the cultural heritage of constitutional judges; the legitimacy of exercise of the constitutional jurisdiction, particularly the formalities of behavior of its members; the compatibility among democracy and effectiveness of the institutional system, the democratic regime not having necessarily to be revealed in pure or absolute forms when the same ones are able to jeopardize the functionality of the political system (it is for instance the case of the military, diplomatic or judicial career).

The attempt to individualize the reasons of the legitimacy of the constitutional justice outside, at least partially, of the democrat-representative circuit, also through the reference to meta-democratic values and principles, can also be found in the work of A. R. Brewer-Carias (1996).

It is democratic and legitimate, according to the Venezuelan author, the power recognized for the judges or for determined constitutional organs in order that they watch over the violations of fundamental rights, as the same power is immanent and connatural to every representative and democratic regime and finalized to the strengthening of the liberties of the citizen.

The democratic legitimacy of the jurisdictional control of the constitutionality of the laws derives therefore from the relationship of identification among the protection of fundamental rights and is based on the formalities of distribution of powers adopted by the Constitution, both to vertical level and to horizontal level, both as articulation of the State legal order and structure of the State-apparatus (second reason of the legitimation). The separation of powers has ensured the institution of an independent mechanism to guarantee the organic content of the Constitution: the indefectible nature of the constitutional jurisdiction as a working tool in the constitutional system of weights and counterweights, which derives from the necessity to preserve the equilibrium on which the same Constitution holds up. The constitutional control (and the organ that manages it) doesn't appear, according to Brewer-Carias, a spurious element in comparison to the separation of powers: the apparent collision among the necessity to establish a jurisdictional control of the Constitution and the principle of the separation of powers is an antinomy that is resolved updating the conception of the same principle, considering it inclusive of an organ and a procedure more in comparison to the traditional connotation.

The legitimacy of the jurisdictional control of constitutionality proceeding from the legitimacy of the constitutional State that determines the normative force of the Constitution and the necessity of its protection against the action of the constituted powers that want to violate it is a central syllogism in the work of H. Nogueira (2004). The supposed invasion by the constitutional jurisdiction into the sphere of legislative power is a critique that neglects the existence, according to the Chilean lawyer, of a deeper division among the constituent power and the constituted powers, in which the constitutional jurisdiction develops to protect the Constitution against the "breakers" (*embates*) aroused by the "constituted" constitutional organs.

To the critique that underlines the lack of legitimacy of the constitutional jurisdiction in comparison to the popular representation and the irresponsibility of the first one towards the electorate, the author proposes five fundamental objections. The democratic legitimacy of the constitutional jurisdiction proceeds, in first place, from the same decision and legitimacy of the constituent power that establishes the Constitution, a power that confers legitimacy to the constituted organs and determines the form of integration. In the largest part of the cases the members of the organs of constitutional justice are chosen or designated by political organs (Parliament and Government), a factor according to which the constitutional jurisdiction is endowed with suitable representativeness (Nogueira 2004, 14).

Second, the constitutional jurisdiction is shaped as an institution to protect fundamental rights against possible abuses of political organs, to preserve the distribution of the powers and competences determined by the Constitution, rationalizing and legally framing the action of political actors, resolving the conflicts, strengthening the working of the constitutional democratic State, protecting the rights of the individual and the groups, and increasing the quality of the democracy and a suitable governability (Nogueira 2004, 15).

The third reason of the legitimacy of constitutional jurisdiction is given according to Nogueira by two factors: on one hand, by the general rule according to which organs of constitutional justice are usually banned from proceeding *ex officio*, on the other hand, as the decisions of such organs must find a juridical and rational justification, have to be endowed with a base, congruent and founded upon the sources of constitutional law, which makes a control of the scientific (particularly, legal) community and the society as a whole on the work of constitutional courts possible (Nogueira 2004, 15–16).

An additional test of the legitimacy of constitutional jurisdiction is given, according to the author, by the increasing generalized acceptance of the same by the democratic constitutional framers of States that, at the beginning of twenty-first century, in the different continents realize processes of constitutional transition and attempts of democratic consolidation: in such contexts constitutional justice is conceived as a pillar and a fundamental axle around which the constitutional democracy develops and consolidates, as not merely representative, but also deliberative and continuous, in which constitutional judges contribute to express the actual will through the construction of the constitutional jurisprudence (Nogueira 2004, 16).

Finally, it is seen with a sense of proportion the power of constitutional jurisdiction, "whose word is not the last word", considering that the political body of the society and the power of constitutional revision, if they believe that the constitutional judges have gone beyond by the idea of law valid and in force in the society, they can always modify the constitutional text, inducing the constitutional jurisdiction to act in the direction pointed out by it (Nogueira 2004, 16).

The reconstruction of the functions and of the reasons of the legitimation of the constitutional justice featured by great systematic nature can be found in the Spanish doctrine in the work of J. Acosta Sánchez (1998).

The author identifies three fundamental goals that the constitutional jurisdiction has to pursue: the purification of the legal order from unconstitutional norms and the purification of law, the guarantee of the rights and the fundamental liberties, and the resolution of conflicts of competence, particularly as the territorial organization of the power is concerned (Acosta Sánchez 1998, 349). To these three goals, others of unwritten nature are added: the participation to the legislative process or creation of norms on the legislative plan, the creation of constitutional norms, and the constitutionalisation of all law branches (Acosta Sánchez 1998, 354).

The explications offered by the doctrine of such functions as a whole are classified by the author in two categories, that of the *exorbitant explications,* and that of the *reasonable explications* (Acosta Sánchez 1998, 362). The first category is joined by the configuration of the constitutional justice organ as the third Chamber, the conception of the constitutional jurisdiction as "continuous constituent power", " secondary constituent " and "performer or commissar of the constituent power" and the consideration of the constitutional justice as "paradox" and fundamentally antidemocratic.

Other "exorbitant" explications present the constitutional jurisdiction as continuous constituent power, secondary constituent and commissar of the constituent power. The first configuration has its origin in the North American experience and has been coined by W. Wilson qualifying the Supreme Court as continuous constitutional Convention (Wilson 1895).

The expression that presents the constitutional judge as a secondary constituent is used in France by the realist theory of the constitutional interpretation, that has in M. Troper its most representative figure (Troper 1998). According to this theory, every interpretation assumes a creative function, taking the shape of an action of will in virtue of which the interpreter recreates the text, that misses the objective sense before the interpretative work. The organs of constitutional justice are, particularly as supreme interpreters of the Constitution, able to make an interpretation "authentic" as invested by the same Constitution of the power to interpret it, give an interpretation that enters into the legal order leaving out of consideration the meaning it assumes, and not being their decisions object of annulment, you must consider that they participate in the exercise of the constituent power as a secondary constituent.

The third explication of the constitutional jurisdiction considers the competent organ as performer or commissioner of the constituent power, defining it as entity commissioned by the Constitution (Marcic 1963, 204), as performer of the will of the constituent power (Weber 1986, 70) or conceiving the juridical position of it as commissioner of the constituent power. The third exorbitant explication conceives the constitutional jurisdiction as "paradoxical" and antidemocratic.

The paradox of the constitutional judge has been shaped as an application of the general paradox of the judge in a democratic society: the paradox would consist of the necessity of the jurisdictional control of the laws produced by assemblies formed by subjects that represent the will of the people, or at least by its majority. A parallel exists among the situation of the ordinary judge, that is never not totally faithful to the democracy as his/her interpretation of the law always takes the risk to deviate from the will of the legislator and that of the constitutional judge, that is forced to adopt, or at least to establish, anti-majoritarian positions, according to what happens protecting fundamental rights of the individual against the violations proceeding from options referable to the will of the parliamentary majority (Rosenfeld 1995, 104).

On the other hand, the conclusion according to which the judicial interpretation of the laws is inevitably antidemocratic in consideration of the inherent subjectivity and the political force of the decisions of the judges (Unger 1983), it doesn't result in application to the European constitutional jurisdictions, in which the constitutional judge enjoys full constitutional legitimacy: the verification of its objectivity passes through the analysis of the methods of constitutional interpretation and particularly of the positive or reasonable explications of the constitutional jurisdiction offered by a multiplicity of doctrinal tides (Acosta Sánchez 1998, 367).

The category of the reasonable or possible explications of the constitutional jurisdiction is joined by the realist explication of V. Crisafulli that conceives the *dynamic* explication as a necessary alteration of the democratic-parliamentary scheme, that binds it to a new democratic paradigm, that of the continuous democracy, and finally the *contextual* explication, that sees the expansion and strengthening of constitutional jurisdictions as a result of the dynamics of the contexts, particularly of the social context.

3.2 Legitimation and Functions of Constitutional Justice Organs

The role and the functions of constitutional justice organs in contemporary democracies, and the reasons of their legitimation, can be evaluated in a partial and sectorial perspective (coinciding with the judgment of constitutionality of the laws) or in a systemic perspective, to embrace the functions of the organs themselves in their complexity.

If you adopt the function of constitutionality control of the laws as a parameter of reference, you can remark that the role developed by the constitutional justice organs is realized in the assumption to a different and further centre, in comparison to the political one, of the process of recognition and development of constitutional values, in the contribution given by the constitutional judge to the precise statement of the content of the constitutional norms through an hermeneutic work that, according to the different hypotheses, supports, integrates, amends or even replaces the choices of the legislator.

It is realized, in the described way, a complementary and subsidiary weighting of the affairs the society in comparison to every single material sphere that, in the most qualified hypotheses, it is converted in a sort of axiological drain by the constitutional judge, that contributes to the individualization of the fundamental principles and values to which necessarily has to conform the legislator that intends to regulate or update a certain subject. The organs of constitutional justice, on the other hand, propose themselves as custodians of the respect of the constitutional rules on which the consent is realized: the function developed by the constitutional judge in the described optics, therefore, is not entirely finalized until the realization of the consent, contrary to the preservation, to the safeguard and the consolidation of the consent around the rules themselves.

Favouring, completing or censoring the normative choices of the legislator, the constitutional justice organs exercise a function of legitimation of the content of legislative actions, whose verification by the constitutional judge is realized through a sort of *certification of constitutionality* in the hypotheses of constitutional review a priori (as in the French experience) or in the determination and attestation of the conformity to the Constitution of the normative proposition forged by the legislator, in other words in the legitimation of the content that characterizes the same proposition.

Such determination becomes particularly incisive where the constitutional sentences recognized law force. The constitutional justice organs own an articulated typology of decisions that allows the constitutional judge to modulate and vary the political impact of his/her own sentences, which become a tool used with different ductility according to the degree of interference inside the discretionary sphere of the legislator that the judge himself intends to reach. The morphology of the constitutional pronunciations results in an extremely variegated way and is characterized by the presence, in the arc whose extreme poles are represented by the sentences of mere acceptance or rejection of the constitutionality, of types of pronunciations that make the holders of the legislative power extremely elastic, the borders of effectiveness in their work of discipline or reform of the single subjects.

The availability of such ample instruments induces, on the other hand, the constitutional judge to conceive, similarly as supple and elastic, the principle of self-restraint and to see with a large sense of proportion the principle, to the first one tightly connected, of the abstention from pronunciations concerning or touching political questions of the legislator. The tendency followed by the constitutional justice organs is realized rather in the configuration by the same ones of hypothesis and alternative solutions for the legislator that intends to regulate or to the reform single matters, even if inside a framework determined by the constitutional judge and through the apposition of precise limits, usually accompanied by the warning to provide in the wished sense or by the threat to sanction in the constitutional trial different options eventually preferred by the legislator.

From the use of such ample jurisprudential instruments it seems to derive the intent of the constitutional judge to validate the role and the functions of moderation, criticism and decantation of the decisional process of minorities, groups of interest, exponential subjects of collective or diffused interests, that would otherwise be deprived of fundamental interlocutors, that find in the constitutional justice a centre of *representation* of their own requests. It is on the base of these observations that emerges the necessity to contemplate the constitutional jurisdictions not only as "negative custodians" of the Constitution, called to purify the legal order from the unconstitutional norms created by other powers of the State (Garlicki, Zakrzewski 1985, 31), that would have the tendency to underline only its static dimension, but also as active custodians, that in their dynamic dimension are called to develop a creative function of principles, values and constitutional rights, a function of arbitration of the conflicts intervening among constitutional subjects or organs, in general a function of rectification of the system as a whole finalized to the pursuit of two fundamental objectives: to fill the gap sometimes existing between law and society, and to protect the democracy (Barak 2006, 231). Such function of **bringing back law to justice** is realized through the censorship of the legislator's work, and is accompanied by the identification of constitutional principles, values and rights that updates and circumstantiates the options originally adopted by the constituent framers, coming if necessary to the necessary weighting and consequent balancing of the interests (concerning the dogmatic part, as well as the organizational one of the Constitutions) and is eventually integrated by the exercise of further functions altogether finalized to guarantee the perpetuation of the Constitution (resolution of inter-organic and inter-subjective conflicts, control on the political parties etc.). The source of legitimation of functions of such qualitative and quantitative entity necessarily has to be sought at the highest level and must be identified with the constituent power and with the Constitution that the same one has wanted. Constitutional justice enjoys democratic legitimation as contemplated in a democratic Constitution approved according to a democratic procedure. The constituents that – above all after 1945 – have adopted in the contemporary Constitutions one of the constitutional justice and constitutional judicial review models, have prospectively conceived the constitutional justice organs as commissioners for the future, conferring them the mandate, always revocable in case of an event qualifiable, according to the terminology of Ackerman as a *constitutional moment*, to protect, to adjust and to update the options followed adopting the founding act of the constitutional order. The organs of constitutional justice participate more from close up than other constituted powers of the typical nature of the constituent power.

The constituent framers recognize, starting from the second post-war period, the insufficiency of the traditional representative circuit to assure fit representation to the plurality of the emerging interests in the society and of the inadequacy of the law, become – as already Bachof and Forsthoff had warned – more and more contingent and exposed to the humoral aspirations of occasional minorities, to select them and to assure an appropriate guardianship, not withdrawing in front of the traditional canons of the generality and abstractness of the norms. Fragmented, lazy, procrastinating parliaments, incapable to offer fit technical declination to the represented interests, as well as the progressive attitude of the law as law-measure, are factors able to erode since its foundations the constitutional democratic and rule of law State.

The constitutional justice also arises in consequence of the deep identity and functional crisis in the law and the parliaments in contemporary democracies and from the will of the constituent framers to preserve ***democracy*** and ***justice*** beyond the transient contingencies that acquire the forms of a precarious law.

References

Acosta Sanchez, J.A. 1998. *Formación de la Constitución y jurisdicción constitucional.* Madrid: Tecnos.

Adamovich, L. 1987. Verfassungsgerichtsbarkeit und Gewaltentrennung. In *Festschrift für Wolfgang Zeidler*, W. Fürst, R. Herzog, and D.C. Umbach, (a cura di), 281–292. Berlin-New York: Walter de Gruyter.

Alexy, R. 1986. *Theorie der Grundrechte*. Frankfurt a. M.: Suhrkamp.

Bachof, O. 1963. *Jueces y Constitución*. Madrid: Taurus. (1959, Grundgesetz und Richtermacht. Tübingen: Mohr).

Barak, A. 2006. L'exercice de la fonction juridictionnelle vu par un juge: le rôle de la Cour suprême dans une démocratie. *Revue française de Droit constitutionnel*: 227–302.

Böckenförde, E.-W. 1991. *Recht, Staat, Freiheit. Studien zur Rechtsphilosophie, Staatsheorie und Verfassungsgeschichte*. Frankfurt a. M.: Suhrkamp.

Brewer-Carias, A.R. 1996. *Instituciones políticas y constitucionales. Tomo VI – Justicia constitucional.* Caracas: Editorial Jurídica.

Bryde, B.O. 1982. Verfassungsentwicklung, Stabilität und Dynamik im Verfassungsrecht der Bundesrepublik Deutschland, Baden-Baden: Nomos.

Chryssogonos, K. 1987. *Verfassungsgerichtsbarkeit und Gesetzgebung. Zur Methode der Verfassungsinterpretation bei der Normenkontrolle*. Berlin: Duncker & Humblot.

Ebsen, I. 1985. *Das Bundesverfassungsgericht als Element gesellschaftilicher Selbstregulierung – Eine pluralistische Theorie der Verfassungsgerichtsbarkeit im demokratischen Verfassungsstaat*. Berlin: Duncker & Humblot.

Favoreu, L. 1986. Europe occidentale. In *Le contrôle juridictionnel des lois,* L. Favoreu, and J.A. Jolowicz (a cura di). Paris: Economica.

Friesenhahn, E. 1976. Die Funktion der Verfassungsgerichtsbarkeit im Gesamtgefüge der Verfassung, In P. Häberle (a cura di), 355–366. Verfassungsgerichtsbarkeit.

Garlicki, L., and W. Zakrzewski. 1985. La protection juridictionnelle de la Constitution dans le monde contemporain. *Annuaire International de Justice Constitutionnelle.*

Häberle, P. 1980. *Verfassungsgerichtsbarkeit zwischen Politik und Rechtswissenschaft.* Königstein: Müller.

Häberle, P. 2005. *Lo Stato costituzionale*. Roma: Istituto della Enciclopedia Italiana Treccani.

Häberle, P. 2006. Verfassungsgerichtsbarkeit in der offenen Gesellschaft. In *Das Bundedsverfassungsgericht im politischen System*, R.C. van Ooyen, and M.H.W. Möllers (a cura di), 35–46. Wiesbaden: Verlag für Sozialwissenschaften.

Haltern, R.R. 1998. *Verfassungsgerichtsbarkeit, Demokratie und Misstrauen. Das Bundesverfassungsgericht in einer Verfassungstheorie zwischen Populismus und Progressivismus*. Berlin: Duncker & Humblot.

Hinkel, K.R. 1984. *Verfassungsgerichtsbarkeit zwischen Recht und Politik – Eine historische Betrachtung*, Herford: Maximilian.

Jekewitz, J. 1980. Bundesverfassungsgericht und Gesetzgeber – Zu den Vorwirkungen von Existenz und Rechtsprechung des Bundesverfassungsgerichts in den Bereich der Gesetzgebung. In 19/1980 *Der Staat*, 534–556.

Landfried, C. (a cura di). 1988. *Constitutional review and legislation: An international comparison*. Baden-Baden: Nomos.

Marcic, R. 1963. *Verfassung und Verfassungsgericht*. Wien: Springer.

Massing, O. 2005. *Politik als Recht – Recht als Politik*. Baden-Baden: Nomos.
Nogueira, H. 2004. *La jurisdicción constitucional y los tribunales constitucionales de Sudamerica en la alborada del siglo XXI*. México: Porrúa.
Rau, C. 1996. Selbst entwickelte Grenzen in der Rechtsprechung des United States Supreme Court und des Bundesverfassungsgerichts, Berlin: Duncker & Humblot.
Roellecke, G. 1980. Verfassungsgerichtsbarkeit, Gesetzgebung und politische Führung, in Verfassungsgerichtsbarkeit, Gesetzgebung und politische Führung – ein Cappenberger Gespräch, Köln, 24–42.
Rosenfeld, M. 1995. *Possibilité de la démocratie et deconstruction du droit*. Bruxelles: Bruylant.
Rousseau, D. 1995. De la démocratie continue, in *idem* (ed.), *La démocratie continue*, Paris: LGDJ. Bruxelles: Bruylant.
Rousseau, D. 1998. *La justice constitutionnelle en Europe*. Paris: Montchrestien.
Rousseau, D. 2006. *Droit du contentieux constitutionnel*. Paris: Montchrestien.
Sagüés, N. 2002. *Derecho procesal constitucional*. Buenos Aires: Astrea.
Schlothauer, R. 1979. *Zur Krise der Verfassungsgerichtsbarkeit*. Frankfurt a.M: Suhrkamp.
Schmitt, C. 1981. *Il custode della Costituzione*. A cura di Antonio Caracciolo. (*Der Hüter der Verfassung*). Milano: Giuffré.
Schneider, H.P. 1980. Verfassungsgerichtsbarkeit und Gewaltenteilung. Zur Funktionsgerechtigkeit von Kontrollmaβstäben und Kontrolldichte verfassungsgerichtlicher Entscheidungen, *NJW*: 2103–2111.
Smend, R. 1966. Verfassung und Verfassungsrecht. In *Id., Staatsrechtliche Abhandlungen*, 2a ed. Berlin: Duncker & Humblot.
Stern, K. 1980. *Verfassungsgerichtsbarkeit zwischen Recht und Politik*. Opladen: Westdeutscher Verlag.
Stern, K. 1997. Verfassungsgerichtsbarkeit und Gesetzgebung. In *Staatsphilosophie und Rechtspolitik*, B. Ziemske, T. Langheid, H. Wils, and G. Haverkate (a cura di). München: Beck.
Troper, M. 1998. *Per una teoria giuridica dello Stato*. Napoli: Guida.
Unger R. 1983. *The critical legal studies movement. Harvard Law Review* 96: 561–575.
Weber, A. 1986. La jurisdicción constitucional en Europa. *Revista española de derecho constitucional.*
Wendenburg, H. 1984. Die Debatte um die Verfassungsgerichtsbarkeit und der Methodenstreit der Staasrechtslehre in der Weimarer Republik, Göttingen: Schwartz.

Luca Mezzetti PhD in Constitutional law, full professor of Constitutional Law at the Faculty of Law of the University of Bologna (Italy). President of the Italian Section of the Iberoamerican Institute of Constitutional Law. Director of the High School of Legal Studies at the University of Bologna. Professor of Constitutional Law at the University "L. Bocconi" of Milan. Visiting professor at several foreign universities. Member of the scientific committee of several Italian and foreign law reviews. Member of the Italian Agency for Anticorruption.

Chapter 4
National Identity and Market Freedoms After the Treaty of Lisbon

Sinisa Rodin

Abstract The aim of this paper is to explore the balance between market freedoms and national regulatory autonomy following the entry into force of the Treaty of Lisbon, particularly in the light of the rephrased national identity guarantee under Article 4(2) TEU. The paper will discuss whether the newly established obligation of the European Union to respect the national identities of its Member States has any consequences in the case law of the European Court of Justice. Arguably, defining the proper scope of application of the national identity guarantee is relevant to the application of EU law, since it disturbs the previously established balance between European and national law. If defined too broadly, it can undermine the uniform application and effectiveness of EU law. If defined too narrowly, it would be devoid of any useful effect.

With this objective in mind, the paper will first clarify the concept of national identity and, more specifically, national constitutional identity. Second, it will discuss the case law of the CJEU preceding the entry into force of the Treaty of Lisbon. In this part, it will be suggested that the development of national identity law before the Treaty of Lisbon went through three evolutionary phases: a phase of early and implicit national identity law; a phase in which the CJEU developed the margin of discretion doctrine; and a phase in which the CJEU started to differentiate national constitutional rules and accord them different levels of scrutiny. In the third part, the paper will explore whether there have been significant developments in the

Judge, Court of Justice of the European Union. The paper is published with permission of the Croatian Yearbook of European Law and Policy. Views represented are personal opinions of the author writing in academic capacity and do not reflect positions of the CJEU.

S. Rodin (✉)
University of Zagreb, Zagreb, Croatia
e-mail: srodin@gmx.com

R. Arnold (ed.), *Limitations of National Sovereignty through European Integration*, Ius Gentium: Comparative Perspectives on Law and Justice 51,
DOI 10.1007/978-94-017-7471-0_4

national identity case law of the CJEU after the entry into force of the Treaty of Lisbon, and suggest that the general approach of the CJEU has not significantly changed. It will also be argued that the main developments related to Article 4(2) TEU have not taken place before the CJEU, but in national arenas, notably in France and Germany. In the fourth and final part, the paper will return to the issue of the differentiation of national identity claims and conclude that one category is understood by the CJEU as an ordinary justification of national measures restricting one of the market freedoms, while the other category of claims prompts the CJEU to defer to national authorities.

4.1 Introduction

The aim of this paper is to explore the balance between market freedoms and national regulatory autonomy following the entry into force of the Treaty of Lisbon, particularly in the light of the rephrased national identity guarantee under Article 4(2) TEU. The paper will discuss whether the newly established obligation of the European Union to respect the national identities of its Member States has any consequences in the case law of the European Court of Justice. Arguably, defining the proper scope of application of the national identity guarantee is relevant to the application of EU law, since it disturbs the previously established balance between European and national law. If defined too broadly, it can undermine the uniform application and effectiveness of EU law. If defined too narrowly, it would be devoid of any useful effect.

With this objective in mind, I will first clarify the concept of national identity and, more specifically, national constitutional identity. Second, I will discuss the case law of the CJEU preceding the entry into force of the Treaty of Lisbon. In this part, I will suggest that the development of national identity law before the Treaty of Lisbon went through three evolutionary phases: a phase of early and implicit national identity law; a phase in which the CJEU developed the margin of discretion doctrine; and a phase in which the CJEU started to differentiate national constitutional rules and accord them different levels of scrutiny. In the third part, I will explore whether there have been significant developments in the national identity case law of the CJEU after the entry into force of the Treaty of Lisbon, and suggest that the general approach of the CJEU has not significantly changed. I will also argue that the main developments related to Article 4(2) TEU have not taken place before the CJEU, but in national arenas, notably in France and

Germany. In the fourth and final part, I will return to the issue of the differentiation of national identity claims and conclude that one category is understood by the CJEU as an ordinary justification of national measures restricting one of the market freedoms, while the other category of claims prompts the CJEU to defer to national authorities.

4.2 Defining National Identity

As noted by Advocate General Maduro, national identity has been part of EU law from the beginning (ECR 2008). It has been present in the Treaties since the adoption of the Treaty of Maastricht, where it was introduced in Article F(1) of the TEU, which states that 'The Union shall respect the national identities of its Member States, whose systems of government are based on the principles of democracy'. The Article was subsequently renumbered and rephrased to become Article 6(3) of the Treaty of Amsterdam. The Amsterdam provision simply provided that 'The Union shall respect the national identities of its Member States.' Article I-5 of the Treaty establishing a Constitution for Europe rephrased the provision, the identical wording of which subsequently became paragraph (2) of Article 4 of the TEU.

According to Article 4(2) of the TEU:

> [t]he Union shall respect the equality of Member States before the Treaties as well as their national identities, inherent in their fundamental structures, political and constitutional, inclusive of regional and local self-government. It shall respect their essential State functions, including ensuring the territorial integrity of the State, maintaining law and order and safeguarding national security. In particular, national security remains the sole responsibility of each Member State.

When compared to earlier statements, Article 4(2) speaks about 'fundamental structures, political and constitutional, inclusive of regional and local self-government', while the earlier text generally referred to national identities. It would seem that an added value of the new wording, which is ascribed to the chairman of Working Group V of the European Convention, Mr Henning Christophersen, is the explicit reference to national constitutional identity, whatever this may be (von Bogdandy and Schill 2011, 1417).[1] In a

[1] The European Convention, which prepared the text of the Constitutional Treaty, discussed a number of proposals as to what should be explicitly mentioned as a part of national identity. Among the proposals, there were: 'constitutional and political structures including regional and local self-government and the legal status of churches and religious bodies' (Altmeier) and also 'language, national citizenship, military service, the educational systems, the welfare systems, including the public health systems, the

way, it was the semantic force of Article I-5 of the Constitutional Treaty that narrowed the discourse on national identity into discourse about national constitutional identity. The Treaty of Lisbon followed suit.

The Merriam-Webster dictionary defines identity as 'sameness in all that constitutes the objective reality of a thing' and 'the condition of being the same with something described or asserted'. In brief, identity can be described as a state of being the same as one thing and, at the same time, differentiated from everything else. The word 'national' refers to nation Member States of the European Union. The words 'shall respect' and 'inherent in their fundamental structures' imply a normative claim that in certain essential areas of regulation, defined as 'fundamental structures, political and constitutional', the regulatory powers of the Member States should enjoy immunity from the encroachment of EU law.

Taken together, the wording of Article 4(2) TEU would appear to protect the right of the Member States and their citizens[2] to define, independently of EU law, such elements of their constitutional and political order which make them unique and at the same time different from any other Member State or, indeed, from the European Union at large. Such essential elements constitute the specific content of what is referred to as *national constitutional identity.* In a certain sense, from the Lisbon Treaty onwards, national identity as a technical term under Article 4(2) TEU largely coincides with national constitutional identity. Therefore, I shall use the two terms interchangeably

system for personal taxation, the right of abortion'. See European Convention, Secretariat, Working Group V, Working Document 28, paper of the Chairman Mr Henning Christophersen on priority issues regarding complementary competence (circulated at the last meeting of WG V on 6 September 2002), Brussels 24 September 2002. Von Bogdandy and Schill name the clause, after the chairman of the Working Group, the Christophersen Clause.

[2] Von Bogdandy and Schill distinguish between an objective and subjective understanding of national identity, the former being based on objectively discernible criteria, such as a common language, history or political institutions, and the latter being defined by the 'will of individuals to belong to a community'. Von Bogdandy and Schill (n 2) 1430. The case law of the CJEU based on Article 4(2) TEU and its earlier forms appears to protect objective national identity as defined by national law and national institutions. If the interpretation were stretched to include the subjective element, the individual choice of belonging to a certain national identity would amount to an enforceable right under EU law.

4.2.1 Article 4(2) TEU Identity and Article 2 TEU Values

One part of the national identity of the Member States is construed as opposed to the rest of the World. Namely, by being a Member State of the EU, a State is differentiated from all non-EU states (Sadurski 2006, 7–8). Membership of the EU forms an inextricable part of the Member States' identity (von Bogdandy and Schill 2011, 1426). In normative terms, acceptance of certain EU-specific values contributes to what makes the national identities of the Member States unique. As a result of membership of the EU, the national identities of the Member States are understood to comprise the values of Article 2 TEU on which the EU is founded, in particular:

> values of respect for human dignity, freedom, democracy, equality, the rule of law and respect for human rights, including the rights of persons belonging to minorities ... in a society in which pluralism, non-discrimination, tolerance, justice, solidarity and equality between women and men prevail.

Respect for these values is a minimum requirement for EU membership. Once a State accepts these values by joining the EU, this respect becomes a rebuttable presumption that can be rebutted only subject to the procedure laid down by Article 7 TEU.

It can be said that Article 2 TEU defines those elements of national identity that are, at the same time, postulated by membership of the European Union and without which neither the Member States nor the European Union itself can claim legitimacy.

However, the concept of national identity is broader than the values enshrined in Article 2 TEU. Namely, the elements of national identity (constitutional identity included), such as Member States' fundamental political and constitutional structures, law and order, or national security, are construed independently at the national level. In other words, national identity and European values do not necessarily overlap. Nevertheless, it is a normative requirement of EU membership that even such elements of national identity which are constructed independently and regardless of the EU context, still have to comply with the values of Article 2 TEU. The history of the twentieth century teaches us that in the absence of this requirement, national 'fundamental structures, political and constitutional' would be capable of pursuing a variety of morally problematic ends.

That being said, one can conclude that not any kind of national identity would be tolerated within EU membership, but only the kind that promotes the values on which the Union is founded or which is at least neutral in respect of them.

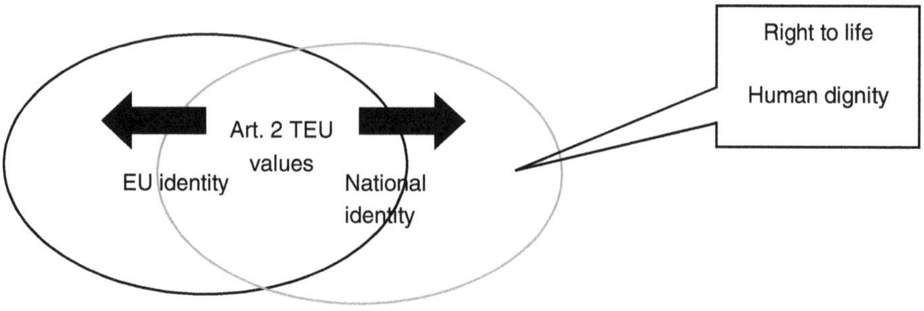

Fig. 4.1 Overlapping identities

In other words, the constitutional framework of the EU distinguishes between explicit 'good' and implied and dormant 'bad' national identities, the former being worthy of protection and the latter not. This was, after all, implicit in Article F(l) of the Maastricht Treaty, which linked respect for national identity to respect for the principles of democracy on the part of the Member States (Fig. 4.1).

4.2.2 National Identity and Other Treaty Values

A separate set of values, applicable to all areas of EU regulation, is laid down in Part I, Title II, Articles 9 and 10 of the TFEU. These provisions enshrine values that have to be respected in defining and implementing EU policies. They include a high level of employment, guaranteeing adequate social protection, fighting against social exclusion, providing a high level of education and training, protecting human health, and fighting against discrimination based on sex, racial or ethnic origin, religion or belief, disability, age or sexual orientation. The function of these provisions is anything but clear. The values enshrined therein may create restraints for supranational policy-making. Most of them have been granted constitutional protection at the national level and arguably may constitute part of national constitutional identity. The question, however, is whether reliance on Articles 9 and 10 TFEU may broaden the regulatory discretion of the Member States and change the balance between EU and national law.

Advocate General Cruz Villalon argued in his Opinion in *Palhota (*2008*)* that the CJEU should recognise broader discretion for the Member States in the pursuit of the values listed in Article 9 of the TFEU, such as a high level of employment, the guarantee of adequate social protection, the fight against social exclusion, and a high level of education, training and protection of human health. Accordingly, mandatory requirements justifying a departure from market freedoms should no longer be interpreted narrowly. For example, the social protection of workers should be taken into account in the performance of a proportionality test when assessing whether national measures restricting the free movement of services are justified. The result of such reasoning would be that a Member State is allowed to maintain its own understanding of social policy, for example providing adequate social protection in such a way that it could narrow the scope of application of, for example, the free movement of workers. This is essentially no different from claiming that a high level of social protection constitutes part of the national identity of certain Member States and justifies a departure from market freedoms.

In *Palhota,* the issue was raised whether a national measure requiring an employer, established in one Member State and posting workers to the territory of another, to send a prior declaration of posting can be justified in the context of the free movement of services. After having presented its proportionality analysis in paragraph 49, the CJEU went on to assess the appropriateness and necessity of the national measure. The CJEU found that there is a less restrictive measure for the employer, namely, 'to report beforehand to the local authorities on the presence of one or more deployed workers, the anticipated duration of their presence and the provision or provisions of services justifying the deployment' (Palhota 2008).

While the Advocate General's suggestion may have provided discretion to the Member State to choose from among equally effective measures, and select one which serves the protection of workers better, the CJEU maintained the traditional test of the least restrictive alternative for the free movement of services.

Palhota is the first and probably the most explicit (*Georgi Ivanov Elchinov v Natsionalna zdravnoosiguritelna kasa* 2009)[3] post-Lisbon case so far where the existing free-movement case law was challenged by an Advocate General and survived. Accordingly, a fully developed proportionality test remains applicable to situations where Member States invoke the mandatory requirements mentioned in Articles 9 and 10 TFEU. After the entry into force of the Treaty of Lisbon, the CJEU has even strengthened the level of scrutiny by requiring national legislation allegedly promoting a high level of protection of human health to be applied in a consistent and systematic manner (*José Manuel Blanco Pérez and María del Pilar Chao Gómez v*

[3] A similar suggestion that national courts should be granted more discretion was introduced by AG Cruz Villalon and ignored by the CJEU in a procedural context.

Consejería de Salud y Servicios Sanitarios (C-570/07) and Principado de Asturias 2007*)*.[4]

4.2.3 National Identity and Regulatory Competence

EU law restricts regulatory autonomy of the Member States in both the area of Union and Member State competence. The same holds for the national identity guarantee under Article 4(2) TEU.

First, as a part of Article 4 TEU, the national identity guarantee represents part of a more general system of co-operation between the Union and the Member States. Upon closer examination, Article 4 TEU lays down several different guarantees that have to be understood in the context of Article 5 TEU.

The first paragraph of Article 4 TEU is a competence rule.[5] It stipulates the residual powers of the Member States, and in this way complements the principle of conferral laid down by Article 5(1) TEU. The Union is based on the principle of conferred powers, the residue of which rests with the Member States. In this light, it is perfectly clear that, as a matter of competence, the national identity guarantee refers but, as I will shortly show, is not limited to the powers conferred on the EU. In its regulatory dimension, Article 4(2) TEU can be understood as a rule that delimits the exercise of the powers conferred. In other words, it can be interpreted as prohibiting the Union from acting even in areas where regulatory competences have been conferred, if the exercise of such competences would affect Member States' national identity. Arguably, the same would hold even in situations where the exercise of EU competence would 'genuinely have as its object the improvement of the conditions for the establishment and functioning of the internal market' within the meaning of paragraph 84 of the *Tobacco Advertising* case (*Federal Republic of Germany v European Parliament and Council of the European Union* 1998).

Furthermore, if national identity is to be distinguished from the principles of subsidiarity and proportionality enshrined in Article 5(3) and (4) TEU, then it cannot come under national parliaments' scrutiny under the Protocol on the application of the principles of subsidiarity and proportionality. A plausible interpretation would be that the national identity guarantee should be applicable even in cases where an act of the EU has already passed the

[4] For an analysis of consistency and coherence in the case law, see Mathisen 2010, 1021.

[5] Art 4(1) TEU: 'In accordance with Article 5, competences not conferred upon the Union in the Treaties remain with the Member States.'

national parliaments' muster, ie despite it being in compliance with the principle of subsidiarity.

Alternatively, it could be argued that since national identity construction pertains to the Member States, it represents an inherent part of the subsidiarity principle. A consequence of this approach would be that once national parliaments have not objected to the adoption of a rule on subsidiarity grounds, it is presumed that the rule in question respects national constitutional identity. There is no support for either interpretation in the parliamentary practice of the Member States so far.

Secondly, Article 4(2) TEU also plays a role in the area of Member State exclusive competence. While one could expect that in this area the national identity guarantee is uncontested by the very nature of exclusive competence, it is not the case. Namely, it is well established in the case law of the CJEU that even in areas where the Member States have exclusive competence, such as when regulating civil status (*Tadao Maruko v Versorgungsanstalt der deutschen Bühnen* 2006)[6] or higher education, their competence cannot be exercised against EU law. The most recent confirmation of this position can be found in *Rottman,* regarding the regulation of national citizenship (*Janko Rottman v Freistaat Bayern* 2010). As I will demonstrate below, in *Rottman,* which both the referring court and the Advocate General understood as a national identity case, the CJEU acknowledged the regulatory competence of the Member State concerned, but nevertheless asserted its case law, according to which the Member States are bound by EU law even in areas of their competence.[7] Thus, it becomes clear that Article 4(2) TEU is applicable in areas of Member State exclusive competence.

---

[6] 'Civil status and the benefits flowing therefrom are matters which fall within the competence of the Member States and Community law does not detract from that competence. However, it must be recalled that in the exercise of that competence the Member States must comply with Community law and, in particular, with the provisions relating to the principle of non-discrimination.' See also Case C-372/04 *Watts* [2006] ECR I-4325, para 92; Case C-444/05 *Stamatelaki* [2007] ECR I-3185, para 23; Case 120/78 *Rewe-Zentral AG v Bundesmonopolverwaltung für Branntwein* [1979] ECR 649, para 8; Case C-76/05 *Schwarz and Gootjes-Schwarz* [2007] ECR I-6849, para 70; Joined Cases C-11/06 and C-12/06 *Morgan and Bucher* [2007] ECR I-9161, para 24; and most recently, in the context of higher education, Case C-73/08 *Nicolas Bressol and Others and Céline Chaverot and Others v Gouvernement de la Communauté française,* (2010) ECR I-2735, para 28. M *Bressol* (n 13).

[7] *Rottman* (n 15) para 41: 'Nevertheless, the fact that a matter falls within the competence of the Member States does not alter the fact that, in situations covered by European Union law, the national rules concerned must have due regard to the latter'; and para 45: 'Thus, the Member States must, when exercising their powers in the sphere of nationality, have due regard to European Union law'. See also the case law cited therein.

The obligation of the Member States to respect EU law is also present with regard to national procedural law, where it is conventionally understood that the Member States enjoy national procedural autonomy subject to respect for the principles of effectiveness and equivalence. However, as Bobek rightly points out, such national autonomy does not really exist, since even national procedural legislation is subject to the scrutiny of the CJEU (Bobek 2011). Clearly any claims that certain features of national procedural law represent part of national constitutional identity are equally doomed to failure, (*Francesco Guarnieri and Cie* 2009)[8] as was demonstrated in *Elchinov* (*Georgi Ivanov Elchinov v Natsionalna zdravnoosiguritelna kasa* 2009)

A number of cases that deal with national identity values have been located in the sphere of Member State competence, such as the right to life, human dignity, the nationality of teachers and notaries, republican government, the use of national languages, the civic status of citizens and, indeed, the regulation of national constitutional procedures. Since national identity claims will typically be emphasised more in areas of Member States' exclusive competence, it can be reasonably expected that fine-tuning between market freedoms and national identity claims will take place along the lines sketched by Roman Herzog and Lüder Gerken in their comment published in 2008 following the contentious *Mangold (Werner Mangold v Rüdiger Helm* 2005*)* judgment of the CJEU (Herzog and Gerken 2008). The tension can be summarised as follows: either the CJEU will start to exercise self-restraint, or national constitutional courts will have to take the protection of national constitutional identity more seriously.

4.3 National Identity Before the Treaty of Lisbon

Roughly speaking, national identity jurisprudence before the Treaty of Lisbon went through three evolutionary phases. In the first phase, national identity was not claimed as such, but was recognised in an implicit way by means of national insistence on constitutional standards for the protection of

---

[8] However, the CJEU is prepared to allow an implicit margin of discretion. For a recent example, see Case C-291/09 *Francesco Guarnieri & Cie* (not yet reported), where the CJEU took the position that a national rule is 'purely procedural and its purpose is not to regulate trade in goods.' See para 16. Accordingly, the impact of the national procedural rule was 'too uncertain and indirect.' For the concept of an implicit margin of discretion see below in the text.

fundamental rights. The second phase followed in the early 1990s and was characterised by the development of a margin of discretion. The third pre-Lisbon phase resulted in the concession that national constitutional identity is not absolute. This third phase heralded a subsequent differentiation of national constitutional rules into two classes: fundamental constitutional provisions 'worthy' of deferring to national authorities and other constitutional provisions treated like ordinary justifications.

4.3.1 The 'Old' National Identity Law

Judicial reference to national constitutional identity is well discussed in legal scholarship. Two well-known references are the early *Solange* dialogue between the German Federal Constitutional Court and the CJEU (Solange I 1974, Solange II 1986, Maastricht), and the *Frontini* judgment of the Italian Constitutional Court establishing the theory of countervailing power to the supranational transfer of sovereignty, ie so-called *controlimiti* (*Frontini v Ministero delle Finanze* 1973). According to the *Frontini* reservation, the transfer of sovereignty, which is inherent in the Founding Treaties, cannot include the transfer of powers to Community institutions to 'violate the fundamental principles of the Constitution or the inalienable rights of man.'

German and Italian reactions were prompted by the evolving doctrine of supremacy, which after its inception in *Costa v ENEL*[9] was crystallised by the CJEU in the *Internationale Handelsgesellschaft* case where the Court boldly observed that:

the validity of a Community measure or its effect within a Member State cannot be affected by allegations that it runs counter to either fundamental rights as formulated by the constitution of that State or the principles of a national constitutional structure (*Internationale Handelsgesellschaft mbH v Einfuhr- und Vorratsstelle für Getreide und Futtermittel* 1970).

The CJEU followed the same line of reasoning in its subsequent case law. For example, in the Belgian Flemish Government case, (*Government of Communauté française and Gouvernement wallon v Gouvernement flamand* 2006) the Flemish government attempted to justify discrimination on the grounds of a lack of regulatory competence in the matter, which according to the Belgian constitution belongs to the federal government. The CJEU shunned the argument by reiterating its earlier case law, stating that 'a Member State cannot plead provisions, practices or situations prevailing in

[9] BVerfGE 37, 271, 2 BvL 52/71.

its domestic legal order, including those resulting from the constitutional organisation of that State, to justify the failure to observe obligations arising under Community law' (*Government of Communauté française and Gouvernement wallon* 2006).

Advocate General Sharpston rightly pointed to Article 27 of the 1969 Vienna Convention on the Law of Treaties, according to which '[a] party may not invoke the provisions of its internal law as justification for its failure to perform a treaty' (*Government of Communauté française and Gouvernement wallon* 2006*)*. It is now widely accepted that the Vienna Convention also refers to national constitutional law (de Hoogh 2011).[10] Nevertheless, German insistence on high standards of protection of fundamental rights prompted the development of significant fundamental rights case law and ultimately to the adoption of the Charter of Fundamental Rights of the EU.

4.3.2 Second Phase: Margin of Discretion

Margin of discretion is the power exercised by the Member States in areas of regulation falling within the scope of EU law. In such areas, Member States can justify derogations from EU law by demonstrating a broadly defined legitimate regulatory aim (Hohfeld 1916–1917, 710, 711).[11] To justify the aim as legitimate, a Member State can rely on a variety of self-defined interests that need not be shared by other Member States. However,

[10] Concerning national constitutional law, André de Hoogh draws attention to the drafting history of Article 27 of the Vienna Convention which 'confirms that the reference to internal law comprises the constitution of a State party. In fact, the amendment proposed by Pakistan initially claimed "[e]very treaty in force is binding upon the parties to it and must be performed by them in good faith, and no party may invoke the provisions of its constitution or its laws as an excuse for its failure to perform this duty" (Vienna Conference 1969, 145; adopted: 55 in favor, none against, 30 abstentions (Vienna Conference 1969, 158)). Though certain hesitations may be observed on the part of the participants in the Vienna Conference in 1968–1969 to support the resulting provision (adopted: 73 in favour, 2 against, 24 abstentions; Vienna Conference 1969, 54), as to this particular point, the provision did find favor and only two States (Venezuela and Iran) expressed their opposition suggesting the primacy of their constitutional law over treaties. Two States (Venezuela and Guatemala) specifically attached reservations on this point, against which objections have been raised by certain other States'.

[11] In areas that fall outside the scope of EU law, one cannot speak about discretion, but Member States are still under an obligation to 'have a due regard to EU law'. In Hohfeldian terms, one could say that Member States enjoy immunity from application of EU law in areas where the EU has exercised its regulatory competence.

such interests must not run against the values of EU law and must pass the proportionality test. Margin of discretion started to play a more significant role in the early 1990s following the judgment of the CJEU in *SPUC v Grogan* (*The Society for the Protection of Unborn Children Ireland Ltd v Stephen Grogan and others* 1990).

For the purpose of the present discussion, it is useful to distinguish between two different types of discretion.

The first type is the discretion that Member States exercise in the implementation of EU law, notably, directives. Such discretion may pertain to the legislative authorities (*Georgios Orfanopoulos and Others and Raffaele Oliveri v Land Baden-Württemberg* 2001) or to the national courts when interpreting national law (*ITC Innovative Technology Center GmbH v Bundesagentur für Arbeit* 2007).[12] The *Van Duyn* situation, where national public authorities had to interpret public policy justification, also falls within this type. This first type of discretion does not give the Member States a licence to depart from compliance with EU law but, on the contrary, discretion to interpret national law in line with EU law (*Yvonne van Duyn v Home Office* 1974; *Regina v Pierre Bouchereau* 1977).

The second type of discretion is of constitutional significance and concerns potentially competing national and European values. In a case where a European and national rule or value does not coincide, one of the two has to give way to the other. In such situations, both the EU and Member State have normative claims that the European or national rule or value should control the other. When the two rules or values are allowed to co-exist without an imminent resolution, one can speak about either an implied or an explicit margin of discretion.

The CJEU has so far recognised margin of discretion in explicit and implied ways. Examples of an explicit margin of discretion are *Schmidberger (Eugen Schmidberger, Internationale Transporte und Planzüge v Republik Österreich* 2003*)* and *Omega (Omega Spielhallen- und Automatenaufstellungs-GmbH v Oberbürgermeisterin der Bundesstadt Bonn* 2004*)*. Implicitly, the CJEU granted a margin of discretion in *SPUC v Grogan* and *Melki and Abdeli (The Society for the Protection of Unborn Children Ireland Ltd v Stephen Grogan and others* 1990*)*.

Implied margin of discretion is best illustrated in *SPUC v Grogan* where the CJEU had to address the tension between a national constitutional rule defining the right to life and the free movement of services. As is commonly known, the tension was resolved on jurisdictional grounds and Community law was found to be inapplicable.

[12] The CJEU allowed the discretion of the national court to be used to interpret national law in line with EU law.

The significance of *SPUC v Grogan* is in highlighting the fact that national constitutional values may escape the scrutiny of EU law, as long as they are outside its scope. Nevertheless, soon after the case had been decided, Ireland was able to introduce a specific protocol to the Maastricht Treaty, which granted immunity and according to which nothing 'in the Treaty on European Union, or in the Treaties establishing the European Communities, or in the Treaties or Acts modifying or supplementing those Treaties, shall affect the application in Ireland of Article 40.3.3 of the Constitution of Ireland'.[13]

The Protocol amounts to a constitutional amendment, the purpose of which was to prevent the Grogan situation from re-emerging in an economic context and not being resolved by functional reasoning.

Indeed, jurisdictional rules may relieve the CJEU from passing its judgment on highly sensitive national constitutional choices, such as the prohibition of the public display of communist symbols in the *Attila Vajnai* case (*Criminal proceedings against Attila Vajnai 2005)*. While it is easy to agree that the prohibition of the red star represents part of Hungarian post-communist identity, constructed against negative historical experiences, the non-economic nature of the activity put the case outside the scope of EU law.

Implied margin of discretion is, as one can see, of a jurisdictional nature, and the CJEU controls it through functional concepts such as *economic activity, undertaking, official authority* or *internal situation.*

A more complicated situation arises when a conflict cannot be avoided by jurisdictional means. In such situations, one value has to prevail over the other. The CJEU has already dealt with such situations in *Schmidberger, Omega* and *Kücükdeveci (Seda Kücükdeveci v Swedex GmbH & Co KG 2010)*. In all such situations, the following general rule applies: once a case is brought within the scope of EU law, either by direct application of a Treaty rule or by a directive, a rule or general principle of EU law can have exclusionary effects. This is also an instance where the concept of national identity can have an impact and possibly restrict the exclusionary effects of EU law. *Hic Rhodus, hic salta!*

The three mentioned cases are, however, different as to the nature of the protected national values. In *Schmidberger,* it was freedom of assembly as a fundamental right, in *Omega* it was human dignity as a fundamental constitutional value, while in *Kuçukdeveçi* it was an instrument of social policy.[14] Moreover, while freedom of assembly is a value endorsed by the EU and all

[13] Protocol annexed to the Treaty on European Union and to the Treaties establishing the European Communities.

[14] *Kügükdevegi* (n 41) para 36.

the Member States, human dignity, was, before the entry into force of the Charter of Rights of the EU,[15] a specific characteristic of the German constitutional order that was compatible with EU values[16] but not necessarily recognised at the constitutional level by other Member States. The case is similar to social policy measures, where the Member States, by the very nature of the area and Treaty-entrenched choice, exercise wide discretion. Do these differences have any significance in respect of the breadth of the margin of discretion?

In all three cases, the CJEU insisted on the legitimate aim of national regulation.[17] As long as that aim is juxtaposed with a market freedom, it is legitimate, as it is compatible with the broader referential framework (general principles) of EU law. In two out of the three mentioned cases, this was the case, as national measures were found to be compatible or at least, reconcilable with general principles of EU law.[18] In *Kuçukdeveçi,* the national measure was found to be in accordance with the social policy justifications provided for by Directive 2000/78,[19] but not in accordance with a broader referential rule: the general principle of non-discrimination. In other words, there was no compatibility between national law and EU law at the level of the broader referential framework of the EU, and so the national law had to be set aside.

If Article 4(2) TEU has an effect, it should be tested in situations where an element of national identity does not coincide with the broader referential value framework of the EU. Neither *Schmidberger* nor *Omega* is such a case, bearing in mind that the protection of fundamental rights is an important element of identity of both the EU and its Member States.

Nor is *Kuçukdeveçi,* though for different reasons. Policy, including social policy, is a variable of national government. It is at the discretion of the executive branch to formulate and implement various policies, and for that reason there can be no equation between policy and national constitutional identity. EU law does not prescribe any given direction in which Member States should frame their social policy and does not interfere with Member States' choice to constitute themselves as a welfare state. A genuine conflict

[15] The Charter guarantees human dignity in Article 1.

[16] *Omega* (n 36) para 34.

[17] *Schmidberger* (n 35) paras 79 and 80; *Kügükdevegi* (n 41) para 36; *Omega* (n 36) para 35.

[18] *Schmidberger* (n 35) paras 71–73; *Omega* (n 36) para 34.

[19] *Kügükdevegi* (n 41) para 36. See Article 6(l) of Council Directive 2000/78/EC of 27 November 2000 establishing a general framework for equal treatment in employment and occupation, OJ L 303, 2 December.2000, 16–22.

between EU law and national constitutional identity would emerge only if EU law touched upon the fundamental constitutional choice of a Member State, for example, to constitute itself within a certain socio-economic or political framework.[20]

To conclude, the second period in which the national identity guarantee was framed did not bring about a meaningful definition of national identity or consequently a resolution of the tension between national identity and internal market freedoms.

4.3.3 Third Phase: Differentiation of Constitutional Rules

It was only after the signing of the failed Constitutional Treaty that the national identity guarantee was linked directly not to a vague concept of national identity but to a somewhat more concrete concept of constitutional identity. It was only after the entry into force of the Treaty of Lisbon that this linkage obtained legal significance.

Parallel with Treaty incorporation, an awareness emerged that not every national constitutional claim automatically represents a constituent part of national constitutional identity. While AG Maduro suggested in *Michaniki* that a contested rule of the Greek constitution should be understood as an element of national identity, the CJEU simply assessed the contested rule according to the usual proportionality test (Kosta 2007). Its legitimacy depended on the extent it pursued the interests of transparency and equal treatment, which at the same time are principles defined by EU law.

The approach of the CJEU in *Michaniki* led Besselink to suggest that: more trivial provisions of national constitutional law – those which do not form part of the constitutional identity of the Member State – are not granted such priority [over EU law], and the normal *Costa* doctrine of the priority of directly effective EU law prevails (Besselink 2010, 36, 49).

Von Bogdandy and Schill hold the same and suggest that 'only fundamental structures of the Member States are relevant' (von Bogdandy and Schill 2011, 1431). If this interpretation is correct, then the function of Article 4(2) TEU would be to create a referential framework for the CJEU when making a distinction between essential and non-essential elements of

[20]Arguably, such a conflict would emerge if a Member State opted to abandon a market economy, which is a condition of EU membership.

national constitutions. The described approach would require different intensities of judicial scrutiny.

In the case of non-essential elements, the CJEU would perform a proportionality test under which a national identity claim would not be an automatic justification for departure from economic freedoms. Provided a regulatory aim is legitimate, a national measure will still need to be appropriate and necessary, regardless of whether it can be characterized as an element of national identity or not.[21] Member States will enjoy a margin of discretion, however, only insofar as their measures can be reconciled with the broad referential framework of EU law.[22] In cases where essential elements are concerned, the CJEU would defer the decision to the national judicial or legislative authorities, with *(Omega)* or without *(SPUC v Grogan)* reserving a proportionality test for itself.

In support of such an interpretation is the fact that so far the CJEU has been more generous in granting a margin of appreciation in cases involving fundamental right guarantees and national constitutional values than in cases involving ordinary national law, even in cases of well-established national civil law principles (*Traghetti del Mediterráneo SpA v Repubblica Italiana* 2006).[23]

AG Maduro himself implicitly recognised in paragraph 33 of his Opinion in *Michaniki* that some constitutional rules are capable of triggering the national identity guarantee under Article 4(2) TEU, while some are not.[24]

---

[21] *Schmidberger* (n 35) paras 82–87; *Kuçukdeveçi* (n 41) para 37; *Omega* (n 36) para 36.

[22] As far as margin of discretion is concerned, in *Kuçukdeveçi* ((n 41) para 38), the CJEU restated its well-established position that Member States enjoy a wide margin of discretion in framing their respective social policies. In *Schmidberger* ((n 35) para 89), a broad margin was allowed to national authorities in striking a balance between a fundamental right and market freedom. In *Omega* ((n 36) para 31), again, the margin was decided as being broad.

[23] In *Traghetti del Mediterráneo,* the CJEU ruled that EU law precluded the application of a national law which excludes state liability for damages for breach of EU law for damage caused to individuals by an infringement attributable to a court adjudicating in the last instance, or which restricts liability for damages arising from erroneous application of EU law by a national court to cases of intentional fault, serious misconduct and denial of justice. In such a case, the Simmenthal mandate is fully applicable and the national court has to set the national legal rule aside. Case C-173/03 *Traghetti del Mediterráneo SpA v Repubblica Italiana* [2006] ECR I-5177, para 46.

[24] See paragraph 33 of the Opinion: 'It is, nevertheless, necessary to point out that that respect owed to the constitutional identity of the Member States cannot be understood as an absolute obligation to defer to all national constitutional rules.' The wording 'all national constitutional rules' implies that there may be some constitutional rules which automatically trigger deference.

The same thought was introduced by AG Kokkot in *UGT-Rioja (Unión General de Trabajadores de La Rioja (UGT-Rioja) and Others v Juntas Generales del Territorio Histórico de Vizcaya and Others* 2006*)*, where she interpreted the CJEU's position concerning the balance between respect for national constitutional principles and observance of EU Law (*Portuguese Republic v Commission of the European Communities* 2006). According to AG Kokkot, while the CJEU respects local autonomy as defined by national constitutions, 'the Member States cannot hide behind their constitutional order and circumvent the prohibition on aid under Article 87 EC through a purely formal transfer of legislative powers' (*Portuguese Republic v Commission of the European Communities* 2006). Whether this was the case or not was left to the national court to decide.[25]

As far as the CJEU is concerned, as early as 1996, in *Commission v Luxembourg (*1996*)* the CJEU recognised national identity as a legitimate aim, though subject to the application of a proportionality test. Accordingly, a Member State may not invoke national identity in order to derogate from a market freedom as long as there is a less restrictive alternative to freedom of movement.

More recently, the CJEU supported the differentiation thesis in *Rottman,* decided in March 2010, (Rottman v Freistaat Bayern 2010) where the referring court suggested that 'the effect of assuming that there existed, in European Union law, an obligation to refrain from withdrawing naturalisation obtained by deception would be to strike at the heart of the sovereign power of the Member States'.

In his Opinion in *Rottman,* AG Maduro suggested that the power to deprive a person of Member State citizenship represents an 'essential element' of a Member State's national identity, since it affects the composition of the national body politic. Accordingly, making national citizenship dependent on EU citizenship would contravene Article 6(3) TEU (now 4(2) TEU). This, however, follows, not from the national identity provision alone, but from the very architecture of Union citizenship, which is explicitly made secondary to national citizenship. Accordingly, the CJEU ignored the Advocate General's argument and decided the case on the grounds of the exclusionary effects of EU citizenship law (Rottman v Freistaat Bayern 2010).[26]

Even more recently, national identity was claimed as derogation in the 'Notaries' Cases', decided in May 2011 (*Commission v Belgium, France,*

[25] *UGT-Rioja* (n 57) para 144.

[26] However the CJEU deferred the proportionality test to the national court.

Luxembourg, Austria, Germany, Greece and Portugal 2008). The argument introduced by the Grand Duchy was that:

since the use of the Luxembourgish language is necessary in the performance of notarial activities, the nationality condition at issue is intended to ensure respect for the history, culture, tradition and national identity of Luxembourg within the meaning of Article 6(3) EU

(which was applicable at the material time) (*Commission v Luxembourg* 1996). However, the CJEU was not impressed by the argument, and invoked its earlier position according to which national identity can be 'effectively safeguarded otherwise than by a general exclusion of nationals of the other Member Sates' (*Commission v Luxembourg* 1996). What is noteworthy is that the CJEU, in paragraph 124 of the judgment, spoke about Article 4(2) TEU of the Treaty of Lisbon, but relied on the reasoning expressed in its 2006 judgment, indicating that there was no substantial change between the Maastricht, Amsterdam and Lisbon positions.

On balance, national identity claims had limited success in the pre-Lisbon era. On the one hand, Member States were successful in what can be called implied margin of discretion cases, where the CJEU refused to rule on national value choices on jurisdictional grounds. However, on the substantive count, justification on the grounds of national identity was argued a number of times in order to justify restriction of market freedoms but with limited success. When it comes to substantive conflicts, the CJEU treated national identity as a general justification and balanced it against market freedoms or other values of EU law.

4.4 National Identity and the Treaty of Lisbon

As I have already mentioned in the introduction, the national identity provision was first introduced as part of Article I-5 of the Constitutional Treaty and was subsequently transposed into Article 4(2) of the TEU.

While the first Treaty defined the concept only in vague terms, Article I-5 of the Constitutional Treaty and the subsequent Article 4(2) TEU added some clarity to the concept, defining it as national 'fundamental structures, political and constitutional'. Looking into the legislative history of the European Convention that originally framed the text of what has today become Article 4(2) TEU, Working Group V 'Complementary Competences', in its final report to the European Convention,[27] emphasised that 'the provision was not a derogation clause' and that 'the Member States will remain

[27] CONV 375/02 REV1 WG V 14, Brussels, 4 November 2002.

under a duty to respect the provisions of the Treaties.' Instead, the Working Group explained that the purpose of the provision is 'that the Union, in the exercise of its competence, is under an obligation to respect the national identities of the Member States', which is subject to the interpretation of the CJEU, which is the 'ultimate interpreter of the provision if the political institutions went beyond a reasonable margin of appreciation.'[28]

In addition, the newly phrased Article 4(3) TEU has introduced a more balanced approach to the duty of loyal co-operation. According to the new wording, pursuant 'to the principle of sincere cooperation, the Union and the Member States shall, in full mutual respect, assist each other in carrying out tasks which flow from the Treaties'.

This is not quite the same as the former Article 10 TEC, according to which the addressees of the duty of loyal co-operation were only the Member States. A long line of cases based on Article 10 TEC fashioned the provision so as to create concrete obligations on the part of Member States, such as the obligation of EU-friendly interpretation (*Sabine von Colson and Elisabeth Kamann v Land Nordrhein-Westfalen* 1984) or the obligation to make good damages for breach of EU law (*Andrea Francovich and Danila Bonifaci and others v Italian Republic* 1990). Now, for the first time, the duty of co-operation has become reciprocal, that is, binding on the EU and on the Member States at the same time.

Reading paragraphs (2) and (3) of Article 4 TEU together, two questions arise. First, to what extent can these provisions, taken together, be interpreted as creating an enforceable obligation for the EU to interpret national law while taking into account national identity? Second, to what extent do they authorise the Member States to derogate from EU law on the grounds of national identity?

4.4.1 Court of Justice of the European Union

There are two cases referring to national identity which were decided after the entry into force of the Treaty of Lisbon: *Sayn Wittgenstein,* decided on 22 December 2010 (*Ilonka Sayn-Wittgenstein v Landeshauptmann von Wien* 2009), and *Runevic-Vardyn,* decided on 12 May 2011 (*Malgozata Runevic-Vardyn and Lukasz Pawel Wardyn v Vilniaus miesto savivaldybes administracija and Others* 2009). In both cases, the situation involved a tension between national constitutional identity on the one hand and freedom of

[28] CONV 375/02 REV1 WG V 14 (n 69) 11.

movement under Article 21 TFEU and the right to privacy (*Ilonka Sayn-Wittgenstein v Landeshauptmann von Wien* 2009) on the other.

Sayn-Wittgenstein concerned an Austrian-born, German-adopted woman with Austrian citizenship, claiming the right to have her title (Fürstin von Sayn-Wittgenstein), acquired from her adoptive father, entered into the Austrian register of civil status. It was claimed that, as she was an estate agent, the impossibility of using the title of *Fürstin* would impair her freedom to provide services.

According to the Austrian government, allowing registration of a noble title would be incompatible 'with the fundamental values of the Austrian legal order, in particular with the principle of equal treatment enshrined in Article 7 of the Federal Constitutional Law and implemented by the Law on the abolition of the nobility' (*Ilonka Sayn-Wittgenstein v Landeshauptmann von Wien* 2009).

While the CJEU recognised that national identity may be taken into consideration in a proportionality analysis, it clarified that reliance on national identity should be treated as a public policy justification that, in accordance with earlier case law, has to be interpreted strictly as a 'genuine and sufficiently serious threat to a fundamental interest of society' (*Ilonka Sayn-Wittgenstein v Landeshauptmann von Wien* 2009).

In addition, the CJEU allowed a margin of discretion, in accordance with paragraph 31 of its reasoning in *Omega*. Finally, in paragraph 93, the CJEU performed the balancing test itself and concluded that Austria acted proportionately in pursuance of a legitimate constitutional aim. The CJEU paid attention to the right to privacy under the Charter and the Convention, but the issue was not discussed further.

Runevič-Vardyn concerned the case of a woman who wanted to have the spelling of her family name amended in her birth and marriage certificates with letters not existing in the Lithuanian alphabet.[29] The CJEU first emphasised in paragraph 66 that a 'person's forename and surname are a constituent element of his identity and of his private life', protected both under the Charter and the Convention, and continued by finding that the free movement guarantee under Article 21 TFEU applied to the case.

However, protection of a State's national language, as a part of national identity protected by Article 4(2) TEU, is a value that the European Union must respect (paragraph 86). Accordingly, national identity had to be balanced with both free movement and the right to private life.

[29] It follows from paragraph 22 of the judgment that the name 'Malgozata Runevic' was to be changed to 'Malgorzata Runiewicz', and on the marriage certificate from 'Malgozata Runevic-Vardyn' to 'Malgorzata Runiewicz-Wardyn'.

With regard to the first point, the tension between the Article 21 TFEU free movement guarantee and Article 4(2) TEU national identity provision, the CJEU followed the *Sayn Wittgenstein* argumentation. If it is within the scope of Article 21, a national restriction on the freedom of movement can be justified only subject to a proportionality test. However, unlike in *Sayn-Wittgenstein,* where the CJEU performed the balancing itself, in *Runevič-Vardyn* the proportionality test was deferred to the national court.[30]

With regard to the second point, the CJEU ruled on the relationship between individual rights and national identity. Again, it is upon the national court to establish whether the national rule leading to the refusal of amending a personal name in a person's relevant documents 'causes serious inconvenience to them and/or their family, at administrative, professional and private levels'. Accordingly, the national court will have to decide whether a fair balance between the interests at issue has been struck.[31]

As can be seen, in both cases, which now appear to be settled case law, the national identity guarantee was interpreted narrowly but remained an element of the balancing analysis. The question remains why, in the former case, the balancing was performed by the CJEU, while it was left to a national court in the latter. One of the obvious reasons lies in the fact that a republican form of government is not a negotiable issue and it would not be reasonable to expect from the national court to set it aside on account of freedom of movement. On the other hand, while language does indeed represent an element of national identity, it is not unthinkable for a national court to allow for exceptions in the case of personal names. However, when it came to the assessment of a fundamental right against national constitutional identity, the CJEU deferred to the national court.

What appears to have come out of the two mentioned cases is that the CJEU will either recognise national constitutional identity itself or defer the final judgment to a national court.

While in preliminary reference cases the CJEU has a choice either to balance national identity and an EU freedom itself or to defer to a national court, in infraction proceedings there is no such choice. Deference in infrac-

[30] *Runevic-Vardyn* (n 74) para 83: 'In the event that the national court finds that the refusal to amend the joint surname of the applicants in the main proceedings constitutes a restriction of Article 21 TFEU, it should be noted that, according to settled case law, a restriction on the freedom of movement of persons can be justified only where it is based on objective considerations and is proportionate to the legitimate objective of the national provisions (see, *inter alia, Grunkin and Paul,* paragraph 29, and *Sayn-Wittgenstein,* paragraph 81).' However, in civil law tradition, it is questionable to what extent a national court will be prepared to interpret black-letter law.

[31] *Runevic-Vardyn* (n 74) para 91.

tion proceedings would entail leaving the final judgment to national legislative authorities and solving the case in favour of a Member State.

However, as we have seen from cases involving Luxembourg official authorities (*Commission v Luxembourg* 1996), the CJEU has preferred to do the job on the grounds of it being the least restrictive alternative (*Commission v Luxembourg* 1996). In both cases, just as in *Sayn-Wittgenstein* and *Runevič-Vardyn,* national identity was understood as a legitimate aim which, as an exception to the freedom of movement, had to be interpreted restrictively and subject to a proportionality test.

In addition, it has to be recognised that both the pre-Lisbon Luxembourg cases discussed above dealt with the exercise of official authority, an area of law in which the CJEU insists on a uniform approach. Being an exception from market freedoms, the official authority exception not only has to be interpreted narrowly, but also has to be given 'uniform interpretation and application throughout the Community and cannot therefore be left entirely to the discretion of the Member States' (*Colegio de Oficiales de la Marina Mercante Española* 2001).

It would appear that the approach of the CJEU has not changed and still relies on a narrow interpretation of official authority, even in the face of national identity arguments. Preliminary reference cases dealing with the concept of official authority also follow this pattern (*Josep Peñarroja Fa 2011*). Such a position would appear to confirm Besselink's claim that constitutional identity, though inherently national, is in fact a concept of EU law.[32] In other words, Article 4(2) TEU has made the discourse about the relationship between EU law and national constitutional law a part of EU constitutional law. While it is easy to agree with von Bogdandy and Schill that '[t]here is now a common European discourse on this most sensitive issue' (von Bogdandy and Schill 2011, 1441), it is still less clear who, if anyone, has the final say. Or to put it in Paul Feyerabend's terms, the unresolved and possibly unresolvable puzzle lies in the fact that the common European constitutional discourse does not take place in the form of a guided exchange (Feyerabend 1978, 29).[33]

Admittedly, the CJEU has no jurisdiction to interpret national law, even less so national constitutional law (Feyerabend 1978, 29). On the other hand, national constitutional courts do not have jurisdiction to interpret Article 4(2) TEU. Besselink suggests a solution according to which national

[32] Besselink (n 51) 37.

[33] According to Feyerabend, guided exchange is a form of communication in which 'some or all participants adopt a well specified tradition and accept only those responses that correspond to its standards.'

constitutional courts would first determine the substance of national constitutional identity, while the CJEU would determine the meaning of the relevant EU law. Indeed, national identity is primarily (Young 2011)[34] constructed at the national level, not only as a matter of law but also as a matter of common sense (*Cristiano Marrosu and Gianluca Sardino v Azienda Ospedaliera Ospedale San Martino di Genova e Cliniche Universitarie Convenzionate* 2006).[35]

This does not make national identity absolute. If this were the case, application of the Article 4(2) TEU guarantee could be triggered by a mere claim that a certain value represents a part of national identity, in which case the CJEU would have to exercise self-restraint. In other words, it would provide for the immunity of national law from the application of EU law, which is obviously not the case.

There are only a few hints so far that the CJEU is prepared to defer to national authorities. Most recently, this was the case in *Runevič-Vardyn,* where the CJEU left it to the national court to balance individual rights against national constitutional identity. An earlier example can be found in *UGT-Rioja,* which was discussed above.[36]

This may be a signal indicating the approach of the CJEU in future cases. Namely, apart from national identity cases, the CJEU is in the habit of leaving it to national courts to establish the relevant facts and balance their finding with a relevant national regulatory interest. An example of such practice is well illustrated by *Familiapress (Vereinigte Familiapress Zeitungsverlags- und vertriebs GmbH v Heinrich Bauer Verlag* 1997*),* where freedom of the press and press diversity stood in the way of the application of national and

[34] Iris Marion Young has demonstrated how a dominant culture can impose its identity on minority social groups, thus creating a phenomenon of double identity. Therefore it does not seem unthinkable that national identity can be constructed by external actors.

[35] The national authorities, in particular the constitutional courts, should be given the responsibility to define the nature of the specific national features that could justify such a difference in treatment. Those authorities are best placed to define the constitutional identity of the Member States which the European Union has undertaken to respect. 'The CJEU, however, ignored the argument.

[36] *UGT-Rioja* (n 57) para 144: 'It is for the national court, which alone has jurisdiction to identify the national law applicable and to interpret it, as well as to apply Community law to the cases before it, to determine whether the Historical Territories and the Autonomous Community of the Basque Country have such autonomy, which, if so, would have the result that the laws adopted within the limits of the areas of competence granted to those infra-State bodies by the Constitution and the other provisions of Spanish law are not of a selective nature within the meaning of the concept of State aid as referred to in Article 87(1) EC.'

EU competition rules. Therefore, *Runevič-Vardyn* looks rather like a continuance of earlier practice than a venture into a new one.

4.4.2 National Developments

As can be seen, the CJEU firmly defends the position that the national identity guarantee under Article 4(2) TEU may not preclude the application of EU law, even in cases of conflict with national constitutional rules. If national identity does prevail, it prevails only because the CJEU has forged the balance in such a way. The same rule, (according to which States may not invoke their constitutional rules in order to justify their failure to comply with a treaty) which is based on the Vienna Convention on the Law of Treaties, holds in infraction proceedings[37] and preliminary reference cases.

Yet, constitutional identity has become a beloved theme in the legal orders of certain Member States. Interestingly, the battlefield on which the supremacy of EU law over national constitutional rules was challenged took place not on substantive, but on procedural grounds. In this way, the dilemma has been transformed from the question of which rule prevails to that of who decides, or even better, who decides last.

It is probably too simple to ascribe a revival of national constitutional identity awareness to the new wording of the national identity clause in Article I-5 of the Constitutional Treaty and the subsequent entry into force of the Treaty of Lisbon. In fact, the involvement of France, which has recently elevated the national identity idea to the status of a constitutional principle, was modest at the time when the provision was discussed within the European Convention. As can be seen from the documents of the Secretariat of the European Convention (CONV 574/1/03 REV 1 2003), the proposed amendments to the then definition of national identity included that 'national identity comprises, as appropriate, the Constitutional "structures/organisation of public authorities at local and regional level/selection

[37] For a good example of how a national constitution may not justify non-implementation of a directive, see Case C-323/97 *Commission v Belgium* [1998] ECR I-4281, para 8: The Court has consistently held that a Member State may not plead provisions, practices or circumstances existing in its internal legal system in order to justify a failure to comply with the obligations and time-limits laid down in a directive (see, in particular, Case C-107/96 Commission v Spain [1997] ECR I-3193, para 10).

of languages/local autonomy/status of churches."' However, French input was negligible.[38]

Michel Troper suggests that French constitutional doctrine was directly triggered by the concept of constitutional identity, as introduced by the Constitutional Treaty and later on embraced by the Treaty of Lisbon (Troper 2009, 2561, 2573).[39] It would appear that the French constitutional reform of 1 March 2010 was motivated by an intention to insulate the French constitution against European law having the last say (Kostadinov 2011).[40] Again, Troper puts it succinctly. Since EU law prevails over national constitutional law, 'a French court wishing to avoid acknowledging the supremacy of European law must use another argument than the fact that some principle of French law is a constitutional norm. This is where "constitutional identity" comes into play' (Troper 2009, 2572).

The doctrine was also embraced by the *Conseil Constitutionnel,* which in 2006 adopted a position according to which 'transposition of a directive may not run counter to a rule or principle inherent to the constitutional identity of France, except when the constituting power consents thereto.'[41]

In order to avoid repeating the emerging literature on the point (Fabbrini 2008, 1297; Rodin 2011), suffice it to say that the main effects of the French constitutional reform and, in particular, the newly established abstract constitutional review and 'priority preliminary reference' to the Constitutional Council, run against the well-established supremacy law of the CJEU. First, if a law is declared unconstitutional by the *Conseil Constitutionnel* as being contrary to EU law, the power of an ordinary court judge to disapply it is

[38] According to the Summary provided by the Secretariat, the amendments were introduced by 'Mr Michel + 5 Belgian members of the Convention + observers + Lopes + Hübner + Einem + Kiljunen + Vanhanen + Cushnahan + Olesky + Tiilikainen + Peltomäki + Costa + 3 Portuguese + Santer + 2 Luxembourgers + Lequiller + Frendo + B onde + 8 members of the Convention + Wittbrodt + Fogler + Brok + 12 EPP members of the Convention + Katiforis + Serracino-Inglott (+ Inguanez) + Chabert (observer) + 5 members of the Convention (observers)'.

[39] This is also confirmed by Josso, who writes that before the Constitutional Council's decision, there were no other statements of any specific elements of national constitutional identity; S Josso, 'Le caractère social de la République, principe inhérent à l'identité constitutionnelle de la France', report to the Paris Congress of Association française de droit constitutionnel.

[40] Kostadinov refers to Bernaud and Fatin-Rouge Stéfanini 2008, 190.

[41] Constitutional Council decision no 2006-540 DC, July 27, 2006, JO '[L]a transposition d'une directive ne saurait aller à l'encontre d'une règle ou d'un principe inhérent à l'identité constitutionnelle de la France, sauf à ce que le constituant y ait consenti.' In such a case, it would be the national law implementing the directive that would be held unconstitutional.

pre-empted. Second, an ordinary judge is instructed not to address a preliminary reference to the CJEU before the *Conseil Constitutionnel* has spoken on the matter.

The answer of the CJEU came in *Melki and Abdeli,* and not surprisingly follows the existing case law. The CJEU took the effort to explain in great detail what requirements a national interlocutory constitutional review has to meet in order to be compatible with EU law. As the CJEU clarified in paragraph 57 of the judgment, Article 267 TFEU precludes national legislation establishing an interlocutory constitutional review, insofar as the procedure prevents 'all the other national courts or tribunals from exercising their right or fulfilling their obligation to refer questions to the Court of Justice for a preliminary ruling.'

In this way, the CJEU maintained the judicial dialogue with ordinary courts, and rendered the legal opinions of the *Conseil Constitutionnel* adopted in interlocutory constitutional review procedures irrelevant from the perspective of the supremacy of EU law (*Rheinmühlen-Düsseldorf* 1974; *Cartesio Oktatö es Szolgältatö bt* 2008).[42]

The main problem of the French approach to constitutional identity is that it sweeps too broadly and fails to provide for its protected core.

Germany has a long record of dialogue with the CJEU. The German Federal Constitutional Court (BVerfG) triggered the evolution of the protection of fundamental rights in the EU by insisting on standards of protection substantially comparable to those under the Basic Law.

However, so far, the BVerfG has, until recently never addressed a preliminary reference to the CJEU.[43] Instead, its influence has always been exerted through its position as the 'court of last say' in the European judicial dialogue. Namely, even after the CJEU has spoken on a matter of EU law, the BVerfG is still in a position to pass judgment on issues of national constitutional law, and in that way protect national constitutional identity.

In 1992, in its decision in the *Maastricht* case,[44] the BVerfG resorted to two powerful devices: the essential contents guarantee, under which the BVerfG acts as guardian of the core of fundamental rights under Article 19(2), which are also protected by the constitutional eternity clause under Article 79(3) of the Basic Law, and the *ultra vires* doctrine, according to

[42] It should be noted that the judgment in *Melki and Abdeli,* similar to the judgment in *Elchinov,* supports the *Rheinmühlen* case law, according to which a referring court is not bound by the legal interpretation of the national appellate court. This is an important procedural element of the supremacy of EU law.

[43] The first reference and only one so far is pending before the CJEU. See C-62/14 Peter Gauweiler and Others v Deutscher Bundestag.

[44] BVerfGE 89, 155.

which it can review and refuse to apply acts of the Union which exceed the transferred powers (Mahlmann 2010, 1407).[45] According to the BVerfG in *Lisbon* (inferring from the *Maastricht* judgment), constitutional identity is guaranteed by Article 79(3) of the Basic Law, and 'the constituent power has not granted the representatives and bodies of the people a mandate to dispose of the identity of the constitution.'[46] As the BVerfG clarified:

The obligation under European law to respect the constituent power of the Member States as the masters of the Treaties corresponds to the non-transferable identity of the constitution (Article 79.3 of the Basic Law), which is not open to integration in this respect. Within the boundaries of its competences, the Federal Constitutional Court must review, where necessary, whether these principles are adhered to.[47]

Accordingly, any act of the Union which would impinge on national constitutional identity would be *ultra vires* and thus inapplicable in Germany,[48] and it is for the BVerfG to refuse to apply it.[49]

In July 2010, the BVerfG significantly narrowed the *ultra vires* doctrine in the *Honeywell* judgment (Möllers *Honeywell'* 2010),[50] where it held that before an act of the EU can be scrutinised on *ultra vires* grounds, the CJEU should be given an opportunity to rule on the matter, either in an annulment action or as a matter of preliminary reference. When it comes to a constitutional review, the BVerfG can declare an act of the EU *ultra vires*. However: the act of the authority of the European Union must be manifestly in violation of competences and … the impugned act is highly significant in the structure of competences between the Member States and the Union with regard to the principle of conferral and to the binding nature of the statute under the rule of law (Möllers *Honeywell'* 2010).

While the BVerfG has only once addressed a preliminary reference to the CJEU, paragraph 60 of the *Honeywell* decision indicates that it is prepared to do so. No less importantly, a national court is under a constitutional obligation to refer to the CJEU, and failure to do so may lead to a violation of the constitutional right to a lawful judge under Article 101(1) of the Basic Law (Möllers *Honeywell'* 2010).

---

[45] The BVerfG applied this doctrine in BVerfGE 58, 1 (30–31); 75, 223 (235, 242); 89, 155 (188), and notably in the *Lisbon* judgment, BVerfG, 2 BvE 2/08 of 30.6.2009.

[46] *Lisbon* (n 106) para 218.

[47] *Lisbon* (n 106) para 235.

[48] *Lisbon* (n 106) para 241.

[49] no *Lisbon* (n 106) para 240.

[50] BVerfG, 2 BvR 2661/06 of 6.7.2010.

In short, the BVerfG has linked German constitutional identity to the eternal and entrenched status of fundamental rights and the core of their protection under Article 79(3) of the Constitution. By doing so, it has ensured it has the last say in cases involving fundamental rights but, at the same time, it has allowed enough space for the CJEU to rule on the interpretation and validity of EU law. Importantly, the BVerfG has wrapped its doctrine in the principle of sincere co-operation under Article 4(3) TEU and maintained its doctrine of cooperation between the two courts and also a doctrine of friendliness to EU law.[51] Being fully aware of the CJEU's position, according to which national identity can justify a departure from market freedoms only if it cannot be safeguarded in any other way (Commission v Luxembourg 1996), the BVerfG has reserved its position as protector of national constitutional identity for situations in which fundamental political structures 'cannot be safeguarded in any other way'.[52]

4.5 Conclusion

The identities of the Member States are older than the Founding Treaties and exist separate from and regardless of EU law. Moreover, just as individual or group identities continue to exist in different settings of governance, the national identities of the Member States will continue to exist regardless of what form or substance the EU takes in the future. In this sense, Article 4(2) TEU reiterates the truism that national identities do exist. Having said that, it begs an answer to the question of what the legal consequence is of such a recognised existence of national identities.

The Treaty of Lisbon has not significantly affected the national identity jurisprudence of the CJEU. Even before its entry into force on 1 December 2009, the CJEU had developed a main interpretative strategy how to address Member States' constitutional claims. As I have demonstrated above, the pre-Lisbon case law can be grouped into three evolutionary phases. As a result, the CJEU developed its doctrine of margin of discretion, implied and explicit, and made it clear that national identity cannot be absolute. The CJEU also made a distinction between claims that can be called *national identity small,* which are treated like ordinary public policy justification, and claims which can be called *national identity large,* that trigger some kind of deference to national judicial or regulatory authorities. Accordingly, a viable

[51] *Lisbon* (n 106) para 240.

[52] *Lisbon* (n 106) para 240.

national identity claim makes a regulatory aim legitimate *per se,* which in national identity small cases results in the application of the least restrictive alternative test, and in national identity large cases leads to deference.

The Treaty of Lisbon has added more clarity to the concept of national identity. As far as the Treaties are concerned, the Treaty of Lisbon was the first one to make clear that national identity refers to national constitutional and political structures. In a way, Lisbon accommodated national claims to the Vienna Convention rule that States may not claim an internal law in order to justify a violation of a treaty.

The situation is quite different if a treaty itself allows some discretion to the States, and this is exactly what Article 4(2) TEU did. However, the question remains: what counts as a viable national identity claim? Is national constitutional identity, as Besselink puts it, a concept of EU law, or is there a plurality of national concepts which have to be respected as a matter of law? A plausible first-hand answer would be that a viable national constitutional identity claim has to rely on an entrenched constitutional rule, value or fundamental choice. It must not be a mere policy choice, or grant of jurisdiction to local authorities, but has to be essential for the recognition of a national constitutional order, and differentiated from other constitutional orders.

The post-Lisbon era has brought about developments at both the European and national level. While the Treaty has not significantly affected the approach of the CJEU described above, France and Germany have started to increasingly rely on constitutional identity, challenging the claim that it is an exclusive concept of EU law.

In the national identity small cases, the CJEU has maintained its public policy approach, combined with the least restrictive alternative test. Under this approach, national identity cannot justify restriction of market freedoms if there is an alternative, less restrictive, way to protect national identity. This is well illustrated by the *Commission v Luxembourg* cases, which although decided in different stages of European integration, follow the same pattern of analysis.

The situation is different in national identity large cases, where the CJEU has shown a readiness either to recognise a national identity claim out of hand *(Sayn-Wittgenstein)* or defer to the national court *(Runevič-Vardyn).* What qualified the two last mentioned cases as national identity large cases? In the first case, it appeared to be a fundamental constitutional choice of a republican form of government. In the latter case, it was the recognition of the CJEU that a national court is better equipped to do the balancing test in a sensitive language case. This approach, however, is not prompted by the Lisbon Treaty, but follows the same line of reasoning and deference which the CJEU adopted in *UGT-Rioja* back in 2008.[53] Arguably, as early as 2008, the same provision was already present in the aborted Constitutional Treaty and was an anticipated part of the incoming Treaty of Lisbon. However, it remains unclear whether deference to the national court is motivated by the wish to defer a value choice or by a more practical reason, that is, to allow a national court to establish the relevant facts, as the CJEU did, for example, in *Familiapress*[54]*

Another tendency that can be seen in cases decided by the CJEU is that it will be less ready to concede a national identity claim in cases where there is a well-established interpretation and a need for uniform interpretation of EU law.[55]

More substantive developments have taken place on the side of the Member States, notably in France and Germany. France implemented a constitutional reform that resulted in a Kelsen-like system of interlocutory constitutional review. The new mechanism was introduced in an attempt to give the *Conseil Constitutionnel* a voice at the European level and possibly preempt conflicts between French and EU law before they reached the CJEU in the form of a preliminary reference. However, by focusing on a procedural instrument of interlocutory constitutional review, the newly introduced system not only set a collision course with the well-established preliminary reference case law of the CJEU,[56] but also fell short of defining the substantive core of a French constitutional identity that could serve as a countervailing force in Article 4(2) TEU cases.

The German approach appears to be more sober. It is based on the principle of cooperation and a clearly defined constitutional identity core. The relationship with EU law is understood as one of co-operation, and the role of the BVerfG is a complementary and subsidiary one. National constitutional identity is asserted, but dormant, allowing the BVerfG the final say in critical cases, but not interfering in national identity small situations.

Article 4(2) TEU has arguably created the potential for a new balance between national identity and market freedoms, and Article 4(3) TEU has re-defined the duty of loyal (or sincere) co-operation. Under the new provision, the obligation of sincere co-operation has become reciprocal, and it is

[53] *UGT-Rioja* (n 57).

[54] *Familiapress* (n 94).

[55] *Colegio de Oficiales de la Marina Mercante Española Supra* (n 75), and the case law cited therein.

[56] *Rheinmühlen-Düsseldorf* (n 104); more recently, see *Cartesio Oktató és Szolgáltató bt* (n 104) paras 93–97.

for the Union and Member States to assist each other in the performance of the Treaties.

In the context of Article 4(2) TEU, this can mean that Member States are at liberty to define the core of national constitutional identity, while the CJEU retains the power to interpret the broader normative framework within which national identity operates in the EU. Too extensive an interpretation of the national identity clause has the potential to block or even reverse the course of European integration. On the other hand, too narrow an interpretation would render Article 4(2) devoid of its useful effect.

The role of Article 4(2) TEU is twofold. As a competence rule, it imposes limits on EU regulation, even in cases where such regulation would otherwise be permissible. As an interpretative rule, it provides guidance for the CJEU and national courts on how to interpret the relationship between EU and national law.

As the law appears to stand today, the Member States are under an obligation under Article 2 TEU not to construe national identity in a way that is in confrontation with the fundamental rules, principles and values of the EU. On the other hand, the CJEU, within the limits of its jurisdiction, determines to what extent the Treaties are to be interpreted as allowing a margin of discretion in national identity claims, or as treating such claims as an ordinary public policy justification. Certainly, national constitutional courts retain the right to rule on the application of national constitutional law even after the CJEU has spoken, and this can lead to a collision between national constitutional and EU law. However, we have not witnessed such a development yet.

References

Andrea Francovich and Danila Bonifaci and others v Italian Republic. 1990. Joined Cases C-6/90 and C-9/90. ECR I-5357.

Bernaud, V., and M. Fatin-Rouge Stéfanini. 2008. La réforme du contrôle de constitutionnalité une nouvelle fois en question? Réflexion autour des articles 61–1 et 62 de la Constitution proposé par le comité Balladur. *Revue française de droit constitutionnel*: 2008/5 (HS n°2): 190.

Besselink, F.L.M. 2010. National and constitutional identity before and after Lisbon'. *6 Utrecht L Rev*: 3.

Bobek, M. 2011. Why there is no principle of "Procedural Autonomy" of the Member States. In *The European court of justice and the autonomy of the Member States*, ed. B. de Witte and H. Micklitz. Cambridge: Intersentia.

Cartabia, M. 1989. Nuovi sviluppi nelle "competenze comunitarie" della Corte costituzionale, nota a sentenza n. 232 del 1989.

Cartesio Oktatö es Szolgältatö bt. 2008. C-210/06. ECR I-09641.

Case C-328/04 Criminal proceedings against Attila Vajnai [2005] ECR I-8577.
Case C-555/07 Seda Kü.ükdeve.i v Swedex GmbH & Co KG [2010] ECR I-365.
Cases C-47/08, C-50/08, C-51/08, C-53/08, C-54/08, C-61/08 and C-52/08 Commission v Belgium, France, Luxembourg, Austria, Germany, Greece and Portugal.
Case C-213/07 Michaniki AE v Ethniko Symvoulio Radiotileorasis and Ypourgos Epikrateias [2008] ECR I-9999, Opinion of AG Maduro, para 31.
Colegio de Oficiales de la Marina Mercante Española. 2001. Case C-405/01. ECR I-10391.
Commission v Luxembourg. 1996. Case C-473/93 *Commission v Luxembourg.* ECR I-3207.
CONV 574/1/03. 2003. Reactions to draft Articles 1 to 16 of the constitutional Treaty – Analysis, REV 1, Brussels.
Cristiano Marrosu and Gianluca Sardino v Azienda Ospedaliera Ospedale San Martino di Genova e Cliniche Universitarie Convenzionate. 2006. C-53/04. ECR I-7213.
de Hoogh, A. 2011. The relationship between national law and international law in the report of the Georgia Fact-Finding Mission. *EJIL: Talk.* Accessible at http://www.ejiltalk.org/the-relationship-between-national-law-and-international-law-in-the-report-of-the-georgia-fact-finding-mission/
Eugen Schmidberger, Internationale Transporte und Planzüge v Republik Österreich. 2003. Case C-112/00. ECR I-5659.
Fabbrini, F. 2008. Kelsen in Paris: France's constitutional reform and the introduction of *A Posteriori* constitutional review of legislation. *German Law Journal* 9(10).
Federal Republic of Germany v European Parliament and Council of the European Union. 1998. Case C-376/98. ECR I-8419.
Feyerabend, P. 1978. *Science in a free society.* London: NLB.
Francesco Guarnieri & Cie. 2009. Case C-291/09.
Frontini v Ministero delle Finanze in A Oppenheimer (ed), *The relationship between European Community law and national law: The cases.* 1973. Italian Constitutional Court. Case no 183/73.
Georgi Ivanov Elchinov v Natsionalna zdravnoosiguritelna kasa. 2009. Case C-173/09.
Georgios Orfanopoulos and Others and Raffaele Oliveri v Land Baden-Württemberg. 2001. Joined Cases C-482/01 and C-493/01. ECR 5257.
Government of Communauté française and Gouvernement wallon v Gouvernement flamand. 2006. Case C-212/06 22008. ECR I-1683.
Herzog, R., and L. Gerken. 'Stop the European Court of Justice', Zentrum für Europäische Politik, Freiburg 2008. Published originally in Frankfurter Algemeine Zeitung (8 September 2008). See also EUobserver, 11 September http://euobserver.com/9/26714. Accessed 8 Aug 2011.
Hohfeld, W.N. 1916–1917. Fundamental legal conceptions as applied in judicial reasoning. *26 Yale LJ.*
Ilonka Sayn-Wittgenstein v Landeshauptmann von Wien. 2009. Case C-208/09.
Internationale Handelsgesellschaft mbH v Einfuhr- und Vorratsstelle für Getreide und Futtermittel. Case 11/70 21970.
ITC Innovative Technology Center GmbH v Bundesagentur für Arbeit. 2007. Case C-208/05. ECR I-18.
Janko Rottman v Freistaat Bayern. 2010. Case C-135/08. ECR I-1449.
Joined Cases C- C-372/09 and C-373/09 Josep Peñarroja Fa ECLI:EU:C:2011:156.

José Manuel Blanco Pérez and María del Pilar Chao Gómez v Consejería de Salud y Servicios Sanitarios and Principado de Asturias. 2007. Joined Cases C-570/07 and C-571/07.

Kosta, V. 2007. *Michaniki AE v Ethniko Simvoulio Radiotileorasis, Ipourgos Epikratias.* Case C-213/07.

Kostadinov, B. 2011. Prethodna pitanja ustavnosti u nacionalno pravu i pravo EU. In *Prethodni postupak u pravu Europske unije*, eds. T. Capeta, I. Goldner Lang, S. Rodin, 89. Maastricht: BVerfGE, Narodne novine.

Mahlmann, M. 2010. The politics of constitutional identity and its legal frame: The ultra vires decision of the German federal constitutional court. *12 German LJ*: 11(12): 11.

Malgozata Runevic-Vardyn and Lukasz Pawel Wardyn v Vilniaus miesto savivaldybes administracija and Others. 2009. Case C-391/09.

Mathisen, G. 2010. Consistency and coherence as conditions for justification of Member State measures restricting free movement. *47 CML Rev*: 47(4): 1021.

Möllers, C. 2010. Constitutional *Ultra Vires* review of European acts only under exceptional circumstances. *7 Eur Const L Rev:* 7(2011): 161–167.

Omega Spielhallen- und Automatenaufstellungs-GmbH v Oberbürgermeisterin der Bundesstadt Bonn. 2004. Case C-36/02. ECR I-9609.

Palhota. 2008. Case C-515/08.

Portuguese Republic v Commission of the European Communities. 2006. Case C-88/03. ECR I-7115.

Regina v Pierre Bouchereau. 1977. ECR 1999.

Rheinmühlen-Düsseldorf. 1974. C-146/73. ECR 139.

Rodin, S. 2011. Back to square one: The past, the present and the future of the Simmenthal mandate. In *Constitutional challenges in the light of the recent case law of national constitutional courts*, ed. Beneyto, and Pernice. Baden-Baden: Nomos.

Sabine von Colson and Elisabeth Kamann v Land Nordrhein-Westfalen. 1984. Case 14/83.

Sadurski, W. *European constitutional identity?* EUI working papers, Law No 2006/33, 7–8.

Solange I. 1974. BVerfG vol. 37, 271.

Solange II. 1986. BVerfGE vol. 73, 339.

Tadao Maruko v Versorgungsanstalt der deutschen Bühnen. 2006. Case C-267/06. ECR I-1757.

The Society for the Protection of Unborn Children Ireland Ltd v Stephen Grogan and others. 1990. Case C-159/90 31991. ECR 4685.

Traghetti del Mediterráneo SpA v Repubblica Italiana. 2006. Case C-173/03.

Troper, M. 2009. Sovereignty and Laïcité. *L Rev 6* 30(6).

Unión General de Trabajadores de La Rioja (UGT-Rioja) and Others v Juntas Generales del Territorio Histórico de Vizcaya and Others. 2006. Joined Cases C-428/06 to C-434/06. ECR I-6747.

Vereinigte Familiapress Zeitungsverlags- und vertriebs GmbH v Heinrich Bauer Verlag. 1997. Case C-368/95. ECR I-03689.

Vienna Conference. 1969. United Nations Conference on the Law of Treaties, Official Records. http://legal.un.org/diplomaticconferences/lawoftreaties-1969/vol/english/confdocs.pdf.

von Bogdandy, A., and S. Schill. 2011. Overcoming absolute primacy: Respect for national identity under the Lisbon Treaty. *48 CML Rev*: 1417.

Werner Mangold v Rüdiger Helm. 2005. Case C-144/04. ECR I-998E.

Young, I.M. 2011. *Justice and politics of difference.* Princeton: Princeton University Press.

Yvonne van Duyn v Home Office. 1974. Case 41/74. ECR 1337.

Sinisa Rodin University of Zagreb, Faculty of Law, Ph.D. University of Michigan Law School, L.L.M. Harvard Law School, Fulbright Fellow and Visiting Scholar (2001–2002), tenure track and tenured professor at University of Zagreb, Faculty of Law. Jean Monnet Chair since 2006 and Jean Monnet Chair ad personam since 2011. Cornell Law School Visiting professor 2012. Member of the Croatian Constitutional Amendment Committee, President of the working group on EU membership (2009–2010); of the Croatian EU membership negotiating team (2006–2011). Judge at the Court of Justice since 4 July 2013.

Chapter 5
The European Union in the Constitutional Framework of Member States: The Italian Case

Diana-Urania Galetta

Abstract The position of the Italian Constitutional Court on the requirement of protecting fundamental principles and rights of a national system related to the European Union (EU) has its origins in a ruling of 1965 in which, for the first time, it referred to the existence of a nucleus of Italian constitutional norms resistant to Community norms (*controlimiti*). At a later time a mutual understanding between the Courts arose in the name of the autonomy/separation of the two systems which were nevertheless 'coordinated with one another'. After the adoption of the Treaty of Lisbon a 'communitarization' of the counter-limits' has taken place. The question of the introduction of a specific provision into the Italian Constitution about the European Union arises, therefore, once again and with more force. *If sovereignty in Europe is limited by European integration*, the insertion of an 'Europa-Klausel', permitting a major opening of the Italian Constitution, would in fact be the only adequate instrument to curb its progressive erosion.

English translation (by Samuel Cross, Oxford) of the text published in Spanish in FORO. Revista de Ciencias Jurídicas y Sociales, Nueva Época, 2013/2. We thank Prof. Ricardo Alonso García very much for the friendly permission to publish it in this book.

D.-U. Galetta (✉)
Dipartimento di Diritto pubblico italiano e sovranazionale, Università degli Studi di Milano, Via Festa del Perdono 7, 20131 Milan, Italy
e-mail: diana.galetta@unimi.it

R. Arnold (ed.), *Limitations of National Sovereignty through European Integration*, Ius Gentium: Comparative Perspectives on Law and Justice 51,
DOI 10.1007/978-94-017-7471-0_5

5.1 The Origins of Constitutional Jurisprudence on Counter-Limits (*controlimiti*)

The position of the Constitutional Court on the requirement of protecting fundamental principles and rights of a national system related to the European Union (EU) has its origins in a ruling of 1965, in which the jurisdictional competence of the European Court of Justice (ECJ) was disputed. In actual fact, what was brought into question was the compatibility of the law which had made the 'Treaty establishing the European Coal and Steel Community' (the 'ECSC Treaty') executive with the Italian Constitution, more specifically the section which had the effect of guaranteeing to a European Community judge an exclusive jurisdiction over the appeals against the executive actions of the Community High Authority. In particular, it was assumed that there was a contrast between those norms and a series of fundamental principles of the Italian constitutional system, including the allocation of jurisdiction to ordinary judges put in place and regulated by the national judicial rules and regulations, the prohibition of the installation of Courts of Exception (*Tribunali Straordinari*) or specialised judges, the guarantee to every citizen of a complete protection of their rights and legitimate interests (interessi legittimi) in face of the activity of public administration. By that point, the Court had, however, admitted that, although within its jurisdictional scope, competencies previously assigned to the State could be attributed to the Community, provided this transferral is done *"without prejudice to the right of the individual to effective judicial protection, as far as this right is one of those inviolable rights of the person, which the Constitution guarantees in Article 2 of the same document"*.

The reference to the existence of a nucleus of Italian constitutional norms resistant to Community norms came after developments in the subsequent case of '*Frontini*'. In this case, the Italian Constitutional Court observed that, in fact, *"on the basis of Article 11 of the Constitution, the limitations on sovereignty consented to were assented to only in order to achieve the goal of accession to the European Union: and must therefore be excluded that such limitations... can at any rate bestow unto the EEC an impermissible power to violate the fundamental principles of our constitutional law, or the protection of inalienable rights afforded to human beings."* If this were to occur, *"...the jurisdictional control of this Court would always be guaranteed above the continuing compatibility of the Treaty with the fundamental principles referred to above"*.

This limitation to the opening of the Italian system to that of the Community was confirmed in a literal manner in a following ruling of the

Court in the case of *Granital* and, also, in decisions No. 1146 of 1988 and No. 203 of 1989.

5.2 Counter-Limits from the Decision in *Granital* until the Charter of Fundamental Rights of the European Union

The landmark decision in *Granital* of the 8th June 1984 fulfilled the difficult task of mediation between two apparently irreconcilable options (the monistic one of the European Court of Justice and the dualist option espoused by the Italian Constitutional Court).

In fact, the Constitutional Court didn't renounce the basic premise of the separation of Community and national system, in so far as it defined the two systems as *"autonomous and distinct, even though coordinated, according to the repartition of competence established and guaranteed in the Treaty"*. Instead the Court concentrated all of its attention on the necessity of identifying the norm which was applicable in the case before it. As a matter of fact, the Court, once it proceeded on the basis of the direct effect of the Community norms, would not have been able to contemplate the conflict between Community norms and national norms even on a hypothetical level – the Community norm being the only norm (based on the system of the division of powers) capable of controlling the relationship between the two and therefore the applicable one in cases of this type. The inapplicability of the national norm to the dispute rendered the question of constitutionality inadmissible for lack of jurisdiction. On the other hand, however, the Constitutional Court affirmed that the presence of a Community norm which was directly applicable could not determine the invalidity of the contrasting national norm. As far as the status of those national norms is concerned, which are in clear contrast with EU provisions possessing the necessary characteristics to exert a direct effect, such norms will remain valid and with legal force, although not applicable until – and only in so far as – the competence in the subject matter belongs to the European Union. This is in line with the reasoning consistently proposed by our Constitutional Court.

The mutual understanding between the Courts actually arose in the name of the autonomy/separation of systems which were nevertheless coordinated with one another, and the reference to the existence of counter-limits (re-establishing the jurisprudence of *Frontini*) seemed to be a sufficient safeguard for national sovereignty.

Nevertheless, it is true that some years later the Italian Constitutional Court, resorting once more to the concept of counter-limits, did not hesitate to issue a clear warning to the Community judges with the pivotal decision of *Fragd*. In fact, it pronounced that the question of constitutionality brought before the Court was inadmissible. This didn't, however, prevent it from asserting that a complete retroactivity of Declaratory Judgements about the invalidity of a Community Regulation would be incompatible with the inviolable right to legal protection and, accordingly, unconstitutional. Only a limitation on the temporal effects of such judgements would be constitutional.

The Constitutional Court was therefore suggesting (although only on a theoretical level) the idea of a potential control of its own over provisions contained in the Treaty which would be to the detriment of inviolable rights[1]; this was to be through control over the national legislation which enforced the Treaty of Rome.

The political consequences of the (in reality never enforced) statements of principle contained in the judgement were evident, before the legal consequences were even taken into account. However, in almost 25 years since case No. 232 of 1989, the *controlimiti* remain unused in constitutional jurisprudence in an actual case, despite repeated declarations in a similar vein on a theoretical level. Yet if the debate about the *controlimiti* has resurged with vigour recently, after the coming into force of the Charter of Fundamental Rights of the European Union, that debate has taken place in negative terms. Many commentators, indeed, have begun to question whether if it is of any use to continue asserting the existence of such counter-limits, given that the European Union has also formally recognised its own body of fundamental rights. As a matter of fact, in the context of the growing focus of the ECJ jurisprudence on the protection of fundamental rights, it is easy to understand the scepticism with which the doctrine surrounding counter-limits has been greeted and the temptation to abandon once and for all this controversial element of relations between Member State and the European Union.

5.3 The Opening of a Direct Dialogue with the Court of Justice: The First Reference for a Preliminary Ruling of the Italian Constitutional Court

Subsequently, in 2008, the Italian Constitutional Court opened the way for direct dialogue with the European Court of Justice, referring its first preliminary ruling.

[1] In particular Articles 189 and 177 (using the old referencing of the Treaty of Rome).

The rest of the story is well known. In the wake of an appeal brought by the State against a Sardinian law[2] which had introduced regional taxes levied only against non-residents of Sardinia (the so-called 'tax on luxury'), the Constitutional Court, after the resolution of the majority of the issues – including those which had various aspects of 'Community illegality' – decided to suspend the proceedings and apply for a preliminary ruling from the European Court of Justice. This referral only in relation to the taxes on the stopover of air and maritime freight, in order to verify if they were detrimental to the principle of the free movement of services and goods or of the prohibition of State aids established on a Community level.[3]

This was, without any doubt, an historical decision of the Italian Constitutional Court and most commentators recognized in it the beginnings to a new phase in the "Community journey" of the Italian Constitutional Court. Indeed in the past, not only had it rigorously abstained from referring to the ECJ for a preliminary ruling, but it had also steadily denied possessing those judicial functions necessary to be considered as a *court or tribunal for the purposes of the* Treaty in order to be able to refer for a preliminary ruling to the European Court of Justice.

The Constitutional Court actually had appeared to have definitively decided the question, affirming, in clear wording, that *"in the Constitutional Court, 'national court' in the sense of Article 177 EEC [now Article 267 TFEU] does not exist, as it cannot be included amongst other divisions of the judiciary, whether they are ordinary or special courts, as the differences between the function assigned to the former ... and those historically attributed to courts are great and profound"*. For this reason, Ruling No. 103/2008 can be considered, in certain aspects, as completely revolutionary, much more so for the fact that it affirms – in an evident antithesis with what the Constitutional Court asserted in 1995 – that *"The Constitutional Court, still in the unique position of highest judicial body, for the purposes of Article 234 EC [now Article 267 TFUE] is a national court and, in particular, a court of last instance"*, and can therefore refer for a preliminary ruling to the ECJ.

Its historical importance is not reduced on the basis that the question was asked in the ambit of a dispute arising from Article 127 of the Italian Constitution, in which the Constitutional Court is the only Court with competence to answer the question (*giudizio in via principale*). What really matters is that the Constitutional Court, through the referral of its first preliminary

[2] Regional Law No. 4/2006.

[3] Order No. 103/2008.

ruling to the ECJ, had actually opened a direct dialogue with the European Court of Justice.

A dialogue which has been confirmed by a later ruling of the Italian Constitutional Court: the Order of 3rd July 2013[4] in which the Constitutional Court has opened the way to its reference for a preliminary ruling to the ECJ even for those cases where the Constitutional Court is also deciding in the context of a reference for preliminary ruling stemming from a lower Court (*giudizio in via incidentale*).

5.4 *Controlimiti* in the Case Law of the Ordinary Courts: From *Federfarma* to the Present Day

The topic of counter-limits did not remain confined just to the ambit of the jurisprudence of the Constitutional Court. It has been dealt with repeatedly by ordinary courts, who on multiple occasions have tried to apply to the case before them that which has been affirmed and reaffirmed – though only ever on a theoretical level – by the Constitutional Court since the decision in *Frontini* onwards. As such, there has thus been a diffusion of the idea that it is possible for an ordinary court to judge over compliance of EU law with the so called counter-limits.

The most notorious case is certainly that of *Federfarma* of the Council of State,[5] in which the Council of State applied in an actual case (the first!) the theory of counter-limits, declining to ask for a preliminary ruling from the ECJ beforehand.

To put it very concisely, the reasoning of the Council of State in the case of *Federfarma* consisted of saying that, given that the controversial national norm had the objective of protecting the fundamental right to health care, it is altogether useless to send a preliminary ruling to the ECJ as, in any case, it would not be possible to take into account its decision.

The Constitutional Court reacted immediately to this statement of the Council of State, through an order of 2006,[6] with which it expressly excluded the possibility of a general application of the counter-limits on the part of an ordinary Court, and reiterated that where there is a doubt such as that which had arisen in the case of *Federfarma*, the judge should ask for a preliminary ruling from the Constitutional Court instead. Only the Constitutional Court

[4] Order No. 207/2013.

[5] 8th August 2005, No. 4207.

[6] Order of the 28th December 2006, No. 454.

would be able to judge the difference between the norm enshrined in Community Law and the inalienable right of human beings or the fundamental principles of our Constitution.

Despite the clear position of the Italian Constitutional Court, which was evidently contrary to the idea of a generalised application of the counter-limits, there exist examples of application of them on the part of the ordinary courts. In particular, it is worth noting these two cases:

(1) Case No. 16542 of 2006 of the Criminal Appeals Division of the Court of Cassation.[7] With this judgement the ordinary court refused, although without referring expressly to the concept of counter-limits, to raise the question of Community (and constitutional) legitimacy of a norm of national law which prohibited the extradition of an individual after a European arrest warrant in a case unforeseen in the EU Framework Decision. The reason given was that such a norm *"reproduced a constitutional norm (Article 13 of the Constitution, last paragraph)"*, which evidently prevails over EU law. In this way, the Court of Cassation had assumed the function of deciding for itself whether national legislation in the field of preventive detention, interpreted in light of the counter-limits, constituted a fundamental principle of the judicial system, instead of limiting itself to place doubt on the question, referring it to the Constitutional Court for decision

(2) On the contrary, on the topic of recuperation of State aids judged to be incompatible with Community Law, the Fiscal Division of the Court of Cassation, whilst in this case recognising the unquestionable necessity to "disapply" Article 2946 of the national Civil Code, in fact wanted to question the improbable nature of counter-limit of the provision in question, where it provides for a limitation period. It grasped the opportunity to state that *"the theory of counter-limits had reasonable justifications in the 1970s and 1980s ... now it appears in plain contradiction with the very concept of integration ... at this point the conflict between Community and State law does not appear thinkable in a truly legally integrated Europe."*[8]

---

[7] (In turn overturned by the Criminal Appeals Court with ruling No. 4614 of 2007).

[8] Court of Cassation No. 23418 of 2010; ultimately No. 7659 of 2012.

5.5 The Counter-Limits After the Treaty of Lisbon

One could certainly maintain that, after the adoption of the Treaty of Lisbon, a sincere and appropriate 'communitarization of the counter-limits' had taken place. In actuality the new Article 4, Paragraph 2 of the Treaty on the European Union expressly declares that *"The Union shall respect the equality of Member States before the Treaties as well as their national identities, inherent in their fundamental structures, political and constitutional, inclusive of regional and local self-government."*. Meanwhile, Article 53 of the Charter of Fundamental Rights of the European Union, which, after the Treaty of Lisbon, was rendered legally binding and applicable (it has the same legal force as the Treaties themselves), says that *"Nothing in this Charter shall be interpreted as restricting or adversely affecting human rights and fundamental freedoms as recognised, in their respective fields of application, by Union law and international law and by international agreements to which the Union or all the Member States are party, including the European Convention for the Protection of Human Rights and Fundamental Freedoms, and by the Member States' constitutions."*

These important normative innovations do little except demonstrate the true fact of the matter which existed well before the coming into force of the Treaty of Lisbon (it is sufficient to cite for this purpose the case of *Omega* in the European Court of Justice (C-36/02),[9] in which the guarantee of the free circulation of goods and services was said to be opposed to the protection of human dignity). Yet they certainly serve to reiterate how, at this moment in time, it is probably of little value to talk of counter-limits in the way in which they have been discussed until now.

In this context, the firm position adopted by the ECJ in the case of *Melloni*[10] over the question of counter-limits also is of particular relevance. Responding to a reference for a preliminary ruling presented by the Spanish Constitutional Court, which was based on the assumption that *"Article 53 of the Charter authorises in a general manner a Member State to apply the standard of protection of fundamental rights guaranteed by its Constitution when it is higher than that afforded by the Charter, and to resist the application of the provisions of the European Union under such circumstances"*, the ECJ clarified explicitly that it *"cannot embrace this interpretation"*, for the reason that *"said interpretation of Article 53 of the Charter would diminish the principle of the primacy of European Union law, and would permit a Member State to put up obstacles to the implementation of Union law which*

[9] 11th October 2004, Case C-36/02.

[10] 26th February 2013.

plainly conforms with the Charter, if they do not respect the fundamental rights guaranteed by the Constitution of that State."[11]

The question of if the introduction of a specific provision into our national Constitution about the European Union would be convenient and necessary therefore appears once again at this point, and with more force. This is especially the case seeing as the provision of Article 3 of the Italian Constitution – in its 2001 amended version – without doubt has not resolved the problem.

In my opinion, a specific constitutional provision about the European Union would be very useful, only if it were of adequate enough content to allow, once and for all, for the resolution of internal debates about the relationship between legal systems (between the separation and the integration), as well as the interminable debate over the meaning and the significance of counter-limits. If it were, therefore, a *'Europa-Klausel'* which would permit a major opening of our Constitution, in a similar manner to the *'Verfassungsverbund'*, which defended the more advanced doctrine, with full awareness that the europeanisation of national constitutions is, in fact, the only adequate instrument to curb the erosion of national constitutions.

5.6 Conclusions

In conclusion, it is important to reiterate how, in the present day, it probably doesn't make any sense to persist with the discussion of counter-limits any more in the manner in which they have, until now, been analysed. The more so, as the theory of counter-limits was already born with an ambivalence at its heart. If, on the one hand, the *controlimiti* were developed as an instrument to guard the prerogatives of the national legislation, on the other this instrument has served instead to render acceptable the recognition of the primacy of Community law, including over constitutional norms. In any case, it must be emphasised that in the most recent developments of the theory of counter-limits, judges, as we have seen, have shown themselves to be in favour of a diffuse/generalised application of counter-limits. This contrasts with what was consistently repeated by the Italian Constitutional Court in the ruling of 28th December 2006,[12] which expressly denied the possibility of a general application of counter-limits by an ordinary court. In reality, the result of the application of the theory of counter-limits on the part of ordinary courts, without passing through the filter of the Constitutional Court, is what has replaced the latter in its relation with the European Court

[11] European Court of Justice, 26.02.2013, C-399/11, sections 56–58.

[12] Ruling No. 454.

of Justice, impeding thereby the Constitutional Court continuing the dialogue which had worked so effectively throughout the course of the previous decades. Direct application of the theory of counter-limits by the ordinary judge, reveals its undisguised ambition to replace the constitutional judge, turning itself into the primary agent in the dialogue between the courts.

Essential Bibliographic References

On the Protection of Fundamental Rights in the EU

Alonso García, R. 2012. *Sistema Jurídico de la Unión Europea*. Cizur Menor (Navarra): Thomson Reuters.

Chalmers, D., G. Davies, and G. Monti. 2010. *European Union law*. Cambridge: Cambridge University Press.

Conforti, B. 2000. Note sui rapporti tra diritto comunitario e diritto europeo dei diritti fondamentali. *Rivista Internazionale dei Diritti dell'Uomo*, 423.

Daniele, L. 2009. La protezione dei diritti fondamentali nell'Unione europea dopo il Trattato di Lisbona: un quadro d'insieme. Il diritto dell'Unione Europea, 652.

Morbidelli, G. 2006. Corte Costituzionale e Corti Europee: la tutela dei diritti (dal punto di vista della Corte di Lussemburgo). *Diritto processuale amministrativo 2006/2:* 285.

Schwarze, J. 2012a. Der Schutz der Grundrechte durch den EuGH. In *Europarecht. Strukturen, Dimensionen und Wandlungen des Rechts der Europäischen Union. Augewählte Beiträge*, ed. J. Schwarze. Baden-Baden: Nomos.

Schwarze, J. 2012b. Grundrechte der Person im Europäischen Gemeinschaftsrechts. In *Europarecht. Strukturen, Dimensionen und Wandlungen des Rechts der Europäischen Union. Augewählte Beiträge*, ed. J. Schwarze. Baden-Baden: Nomos.

Tizzano, A. 2005. I diritti fondamentali e le Corti in Europa. *Il diritto dell'Unione Europea 2005/4*: 839.

von Danwitz, Th. 2010. Über die Integrationsverantwortung des Gerichtshofes der Europäischen Union. *Das Europäische Verwaltungsrecht in der Konsolidierungsphase. Die Verwaltung*. Beiheft 10, 241.

On the Impact of EU Law on National Sources and the Counter-Limits Doctrine

Barone, A. 2006. A proposito della sentenza Federfarma: fra tutela del consumatore e tutela costituzionale dei diritti fondamentali il Consiglio di Stato smarrisce la retta via?. *Il diritto dell'Unione europea*, 201.

Celotto, A. 1999. Le "modalità" di prevalenza delle norme comunitarie sulle norme interne: spunti ricostruttivi. *Rivista italiana di diritto pubblico comunitario 1999/6*, 1473.

Celotto, A. 2005. I controlimiti presi sul serio. In Morbidelli, G. 2005. Controlimiti o contro la pregiudiziale comunitaria?. *Giurisprudenza costituzionale*, 3404.
Chieppa, R. 2007. Nuove prospettive per il controllo di compatibilità comunitaria da parte della Corte Costituzionale. *Il diritto dell'Unione europea 2007/3*, 493.
Chiti, M.P. 2011. *Diritto amministrativo europeo*. Milano: Giuffré.
Daniele, L. 2006. La protection des droits fondamentaux peut-elle limiter la primauté du droit communautaire et l'obligation de renvoi prejudiciel. *Cahiers de droit européen*, 67.
Galetta, D.U. 2001. La previsione di cui all'articolo 3, comma 1, cpv. 1, della legge di revisione del titolo V della costituzione come definitivo superamento della teoria dualista degli ordinamenti. In *Problemi del federalismo*, ed. E. De Marco and P. Bilancia. Milano: Giuffré.
Greco, G. 2007. I rapporti tra ordinamento comunitario e nazionale. In *Trattato di diritto amministrativo europeo*, vol. II, ed. M.P. Chiti and G. Greco. Milano: Giuffré.
Pernice, I. 2000. *Kompetenzabgrenzung im Europäischen Verfassungsverbund*. Berlin: Humboldt-Universität.
Tesauro, G. 2009. Costituzione e norme esterne. *Il diritto dell'Unione europea*, 195.
Tizzano, A. 2010. Der italienische Verfassungsgerichtshof (Corte Costituzionale) und der Gerichtshof der Europäischen Union. *Europäische Grundrechte Zeitschrift*, 1
Uccello Barretta, L. 2013. La Corte costituzionale e il rinvio pregiudiziale nel giudizio in via Incidentale (nota a Corte cost. ord. n. 207/2013). *Osservatorio dell'Associazione Italiana dei Costituzionalisti*, 1.

Diana-Urania Galetta Full Professor of Administrative Law and European Administrative Law at the Law Faculty of the "Università degli Studi" of Milan, Italy. She is a member of several national and international associations, amongst those, the Italian and the German associations of Public Law Professors and the "Societas Iuris Publici Europaei". She is a member of several international research groups, including the "Network on European Administrative Procedural Law" (ReNEUAL), within which she is a member of the Steering Committee as well as the Team Leader of WG 4.

Chapter 6
Limitation of Sovereignty by the European Integration – The Polish Approach

Translated by Timothy Adam Wojewódka

Bogusław Banaszak

Abstract Nowadays, the constitution treats the nation as the creator of statehood, the subject of state authority and, in a political understanding, as the community, which decides either directly on its affairs or via its representatives. In Poland the adoption of the principle of sovereignty of a nation has an external aspect. This arises from the accentuation of values such as independence and the inviolability of the territory of Poland and the security of its citizens. The Republic of Poland can, on grounds of an international agreement, delegate to an international organisation or to an international institution competences of state institutions in some matters (Art. 90 of the Constitution). Even in the case that Poland transfers the competence to pass laws on the grounds of an international agreement with an international organisation or institution, the polish constitution still remains the highest law of Poland. This has been emphasised by the constitutional court of Poland.

Keywords Limitation of Sovereignty by European Integration • European Integration • Nation • Competences transfer • EU Law

B. Banaszak (✉)
Faculty of Law and Administration, University at Zielona Góra,
Zielona Góra, Poland
e-mail: bbanaszak@o2.pl

R. Arnold (ed.), *Limitations of National Sovereignty through European Integration*, Ius Gentium: Comparative Perspectives on Law and Justice 51,
DOI 10.1007/978-94-017-7471-0_6

6.1 Introduction

The constitutional amendment of the 29th of December 1989 rejected, at the threshold, the political transformation of the principle of sovereignty of the working class and stated that the people of Poland constitute the 'subject of the highest authority' in Poland. The constitution from the 2nd of April 1997 did not change anything in this regard and proclaimed the principle of sovereignty of the people, stating in Article 4 of the constitution that the highest authority belongs to the people and that it is the people who wield the authority either unmediated or through its representatives. In this way, it has unequivocally referred to the traditional polish constitutional law principle of sovereignty, which dates back to the constitution of 3rd May.

To characterise the meaning of the principle of the people's sovereignty we need to look back to the legacy of polish juridical thought. Furthermore, we need to consider the judicature of polish courts before the adoption of the new constitution. The constitution of 1921 provoked a lively discussion about the understanding of the principle of sovereignty of the people in the newly revived state. This discussion contained opinions, which were part of the study of constitutional law of other contemporary democratic European states. On the one hand, there were opinions that stated that the nation, from a legal point of view, is a personalized fiction, because there was no institution in the state apparatus that could fully realise its power (cf. Jaworski 1921, 116). On the other hand, attempts have been made to define the notion of the sovereign positively. It has been equated to various subjects including: the ethnic people, the electoral corps, and the totality of the inhabitants. In the theory a belief that refers to the French constitutional law doctrine was promulgated. According to that belief, the nation is a political community comprising of all citizens, regardless of their ethnic affiliation. This definition of the sovereign had supporters even after the proclamation of the constitution of the Polish People's Republic. In the constitution it was clearly recognised that the working people are the sovereign. However, the constitution concurrently underscored the national character of the country, emphasising that the nation is a subject of the authority of the state.

6.2 The Contemporary Constitutional Conception of Sovereignty

Nowadays, the constitution treats the nation as the creator of statehood, the subject of state authority and, in a political understanding, as the community, which decides either directly on its affairs or via its representatives.

Furthermore, the constitution sees the nation as the creator of state institutions, which derive their legitimacy to act from the nation. Thus,"a nation is a group of people, linked together in a political sense, who are different from other people, aware of these differences and who act according to this awareness. The will of the nation in institutional-establishing issues does not reflect the will of every single person, but rather the common will, understood according to the definitions of *J. J. Rousseau*. The question arises, whether one can identify the nation, understood as just described, in accordance with the traditional perception of the entirety of the citizens. The phrasing found in the preamble of the constitution enforces this perception: "We, the polish people – all citizens of the Republic (...) establish the constitution (...)". Moreover, this seems to be the only possible positive definition of the sovereign. However, such an understanding gives rise to the peril that the law-maker, in determining the obtainment and loss of citizenship, would be able to determine the subjective scope of the community of citizens. In this way, it would not be the community that created the state, but rather the creator of the constitution or the legislator, who shaped the institution of citizenship that became the subject of state authority. Therefore, opinions arise, that the constitution cannot define in this way, or in any other, the notion of the sovereign (cf. Sarnecki 1997, 19). On the other hand, it might be regarded as misleading to equate the nation with the community of citizens, because aside from individuals, who are entitled to participate in political activities, the nation encompasses individuals, who hold polish citizenship, but are either underage or deprived of their freedom and thus not permitted to participate in public affairs. These individuals are part of the community comprising the state, "are also classified as the nation and take part in the exercise of authority, say at least for the reason, that their goods have to be also (perhaps even above all: children) realised in the state of that nation" (Tuleja 1995, 33).

In the constitution the nation is not divided into ethnic categories, although the unclear phrasing in the preamble, cited above, could give rise to such doubts, since it mentions the "polish nation" as well as Article 6 par. 1 which states, that Poland creates conditions for the availability and equal access to cultural goods, being the source of the identity of the "polish nation", in addition to Article 5 which states, that Poland guards its "national heritage". As a matter of fact, however, these phrasings do not reference the notion of an ethnic nation. The topicality of the thesis of the Constitutional Court, which came into existence during the transformation period, that the using of the phrasing "polish nation" in Article 8 in the then in force constitution corresponds to the people living in Poland and does not differ in any way from the phrasing "nation" (without the adjective "polish") as the subject of sovereignty (cf. Grzybowska 1990, 4). The Constitutional Court, which came into existence during the transformation period, ruled that the phrasing "polish nation" in Article 8, of the constitution of the time, corresponded to the people living in Poland and did not differ in any way from the phrasing "nation" as the subject of sovereignty, without the adjective "Polish."

Such a conception of a nation is interlinked with the principle of self-determination of a nation – meaning the right to become a legal subject on the international level and to found an independent state on the internal level, thus becoming the subject of the highest authority in the country (the sovereign). From this principle, one can also derive the prohibition for one state to act against the independence of another state. The Charter of the UN phrases the principle of self-determination of a nation as the fundamental principle of friendly and peaceful relations among nations. This principle is being realised by way of: elections, plebiscites and wars for national liberation, to name a few.

Referring to the communal subjectivity of sovereignty in Article 4 of the Polish constitution, one feels compelled to wonder whether, on the grounds of this Article, one could attempt to narrow down the scope of individual rights. The nation as the subject of authority is not, after all, the sum of the individuals of which it consists of. However, the constitutional regulations referring to the legal status of the individual give grounds to dispel such fears. Constitutional regulations in this sphere guarantee the citizen the real possibility to take part in political life and to thereby direct public affairs by deciding upon issues concerning the state either personally or through elected representatives. It needs to be highlighted, that the constitution does not treat the individual as a means to realise the aims of the state, but rather as a benchmark for the actions of the public authorities and the State.

It is also worth mentioning, that the adoption of the principle of sovereignty of a nation has an external aspect. This arises from the accentuation of values such as independence and the inviolability of the territory of Poland and the security of its citizens, which are stated in Article 5.

6.3 Delegation of the Competence of Organs of State Authority to an International Organisation or Institution, in Relation to Certain Matters, as Limitation of Sovereignty

From the point of view of the principle of sovereignty, Article 90 par. 1 of the polish constitution contains an extraordinary crucial regulation. The Article reads:

1. The Republic of Poland can, on grounds of an international agreement, delegate to an international organisation or to an international institution competences of state institutions in some matters.
2. The regulation endorsing the ratification of the international agreement, mentioned in par. 1, may be enacted by Parliament with a majority vote of 2/3 in the presence of at least half of the statutory number of deputies, as well as by the senate with a majority vote of 2/3 in the presence of at least half of the statutory number of senators.
3. The ratification of such an agreement may also be endorsed by a nation-wide referendum, according to the Article 125.
4. The act concerning the selection of the endorsement procedure of the ratification may be enacted by parliament with an absolute majority of votes in the presence of at least half of the statutory number of deputies.

This regulation is specific, insofar that it refers to the procedure of endorsing the ratification of the transfer of competences from state institutions to international subjects. It is, however, too general in its reference to the meritum of the issue. The regulation does not even mention the word sovereignty, although from the wording of the regulation it is clear that it affects this matter. Neither does the regulation name the competences that may be transferred. Due to the fact that the object of the transfer of competences can, "in some matters" be the competences of state institutions, one must conclude, that it is not permissible to renounce the sovereignty as well as to transfer the totality of a state institution's competences. The limitation of the exertion of sovereignty, which is possible according to Article 90, may not be equated in any circumstances with the limitation of sovereignty.

K. Działocha has correctly mentioned, that: "The regulation of the constitution referring to transferring (can be transferred) [transferral] of the competences of state institutions in some areas, to an international organisation or institution, denotes an act through which the Republic of Poland resigns from the exclusivity of its power in the specified field and scope, thus granting permission to the application of legal acts of international organisations or institutions, in the specified field and scope of its internal relations" (Działocha 2007, 3).

Even in the case that Poland transfers the competence to pass laws on the grounds of an international agreement with an international organisation or institution, the polish constitution still remains the highest law of Poland. This has been emphasised by the constitutional court of Poland: "The transfer of competences «in some areas» has to be understood as a prohibition to transfer the totality of competences of a given institution, to transfer the entire competences in a given field, as well as to transfer competences of a given state institution touching the remit of that institution. Thus, it is essential to painstakingly define the areas and the range of the competences that are being transferred. There are no grounds to believe that it would be enough to live up to this requirement by keeping competences in a few areas at the constitutional institutions, say just for semblance. Transfers that would undermine the sense of existence or function of any of the institutions of the Republic of Poland would be in clear conflict with Article 8 par. 1 of the polish constitution. Article 91 par. 2 of the constitution of Poland guarantees precedence of application of international agreements, which have been ratified on grounds of statutory authorisation or a nation-wide referendum (according to Article 90 par. 3), therein: agreements about the transfer of competences «in some areas» – before the resolutions of those regulations that cannot be co-practised – does not lead to (in any scope) the acknowledgement of the analogical precedence of these agreements before the resolutions of the constitution. – The constitution thus remains – by virtue of its special authority – «the highest law of Poland» in relation to all binding international agreements. This refers also to ratified international agreements on the transfer of competences «in some areas». By virtue of the imperative nature of the constitution, resulting from Article 8 par. 1 of the constitution of Poland, the constitution takes advantage of the precedence of application and prevalence" (Constitutional Court 2005, pos. 49). It should not be forgotten, that, as is being emphasised in polish legal studies, "the transfer of competences does not mean (…) a loss of sovereignty of the country in relation to the transferred competences. The transfer does not have absolute in character and can always be withdrawn. If such a withdrawal takes place in violation of an international agreement, then the withdrawing country runs afoul of breaking international law as well as its own constitutional law" (see Jaskiernia 2002, 10).

Because of the weight of the polish legislator's authority, the transfer of competences is tantamount to the supersession of the polish legislator by the EU legislator, the consequence of which is the full application of the appropriate EU regulations. This does not only pertain to the situation, in which the regulation in question refers to EU law *sensu stricto*, but also to regulations from beyond this system, to which the EU law remands. Thus, there is no possibility for a polish institution to ascertain that it is bound only by polish law and the law of the international organisation or institution to which the Republic of Poland has transferred legislative competences in a given area, but that it denies the application of regulations formed by another, to which the Polish or EU legislator remands.

To cut a long story short – if one says A one also has to say B. If we have submitted to the acknowledgement of the legislative competences of EU institutions in a given area of social relations – then, we must also accept all consequences thereof, including even the acknowledgement of the precedence over EU law of certain regulations from other systems, if this is the will of the EU legislator. As a side note, it is important to mention that the remittal to other regulations or systems of law is not reprehensible. Remittals are justified by the principle of rationality of legislative actions, which derives from the principle of a democratic law state (see the comment to Article 2). If an issue has been, in the opinion of the legislator, regulated in a satisfactory way (that is, if it falls within the aims of the regulation, which the legislator aims to issue) in a regulation, then he has the choice between repeating the regulation in an act issued by himself or remanding to the already existing regulation.

The ratification of an agreement named in Article 90 par. 1 of the polish constitution depends on the personal decision of the President. However, he is only allowed to ratify such an agreement after the parliament has assented to the act. Unarguably the act of assent can, and even should, contain regulations defining the moment of its coming into effect. The act could also contain regulations delineating the direction of the interpretation of the regulations in an international agreement. These cannot be, however, too detailed, in order not to encroach on the principle of separation of powers. In the parliament's act of assent there cannot be any conditions, which have to be met, in order for the President to ratify the agreement (i.e. all or some of the other states have to ratify the agreement prior to the own ratification. The act of assent for the ratification of an international agreement should also not contain any additional regulations indemnifying the durability of all or some regulations of that agreement. Such additional guarantees could encroach on the principle of the separation of powers.

It should not be forgotten, that it is the President's decision whether or not to ratify an international agreement, and the parliament's assent only enables him to realise his competences. If the President's decision depended on additional conditions, the principle of separation of powers will have been breached. If the parliament believes the fulfilment of some conditions to be crucial, then it can wait] with the enactment of the act. However, if the parliament gives its assent then the President has to be able to realise his competences in the range of the ratification processes without any conditions, i.e. referring to the interpretation of the conditions contained in the act.

At this point it is worth mentioning, that the parliament should be able to express its point of view concerning a change in the scope of the already binding agreement in the same manner in which it gave its assent for the initial form of the agreement. This would amount to the realisation of the constitutional conception of the principle of separation of powers (Article 10 of the constitution) and at the same time mark out the content of the nation of conducting internal and external politics of Poland by the government (Article 146 par. 1 of the Constitution). This is clearly about the accentuation of its executive character. The parliament, providing its assent for the ratification of international agreements, in accordance with Articles 89 and 90 of the constitution, demarcates a line for the realisation of tasks laid down in the given area in the international agreement. Thereafter, the government realises them using the means and tools an administration has. The acceptation of this obvious principle gives the legislator two possibilities. For every change of an already binding ratified agreement, the legislator must either require ratification according to the procedure laid down in Article 89 or 90 of the constitution, or he permits – for changes that do not constitute, on the basis of merit, modifications of the agreement – the repetition of its assent, and makes way for the adoption of an act which does not contain abstract and general regulations. In this way, the procedure of giving assent for the change in scope of an already binding agreement will be the same as in the event of the original agreement and the act giving such an assent, would in fact have the character of a supplemental act. This ensures the full control of the parliament over the actions of the executive authority and at the same time it ensures the realisation of the principles in Articles 89 or 90 of the constitution. The second solution is more rational and compatible with the principle of rationality of the legislator, constituting a crucial element of the constitutional (Article 2) principle of a democratic law state.

6.4 Assent for the Ratification

Article 90 of the constitution regulates the procedure of passing an act to give assent for the ratification of an international agreement, restricting the execution of sovereignty. In this context, one should have the following ruling of the constitutional court in mind: "Article 90 may be interpreted, as follows: the parliament has the possibility to issue an act, concerning the referendum procedure, in order to pass the power to directly decide upon the act of assent to the sovereign if the assent act that enables the President to ratify an agreement falls through, because of a failure to obtain the qualified majority of votes." (Constitutional Court 2003). The result of the referendum in the matter of giving assent for the ratification of an agreement is binding, if more than half of those authorised to vote take part in it. The solution (assent or otherwise) that receives the most votes is the one the sovereign will choose. If the majority of the votes have been given in favour of the ratification, the President of the Republic of Poland obtains the assent to ratify an agreement, if not, he will not be allowed to do so. Since the referendum has a binding character, the President should not have the option to question the outcome. The dependence of the ratification on the President's personal agreement is abolished, in favour of the principle of the sovereignty of the nation. In such a situation the act of ratification by the President is just an act of confirmation of the will of the sovereign.

However, the possibility exists for one more situation to occur, namely in the event of a minority taking part in the referendum. Such a situation means that the constitutionally requested condition (Article 125 par. 3) will not have been met. The effect of such an outcome of the referendum is that it only has a consultative character. Thus, it is *de facto* not formally binding as there is lack of an official decision. In the case of an important matter such as the ratification of an agreement on the grounds of Article 90, such an eventuality would lead to many institutional difficulties. This is why the legislator (in the act from 14th March 2003 on the nation-wide referendum; Dz.U. (Off. J.) Nr 57, pos. 507 with changes)[1] decided to pass the resolution, that in such an event; the parliament is permitted to, again, try to pass an act of assent for the ratification of that agreement. Thus, we are back at the starting point, meaning that the parliament can again postulate for a referendum in order to receive the assent for the ratification and the entire procedure will be repeated. "The legislator (…) adopted a technical measure, which is not, however, a normative novelty, referring to Article 90 of the constitution which foresees the reversion-mechanism to the parliamentary procedure, insofar as the parliament acknowledges the need for such a procedural act. This procedure is indispensable for the realisation of the fundamental aim, which is the President's legal right to accomplish the ratification of an international agreement" (Constitutional Court 2003, pos. 43).

References

Constitutional Court of Poland. 2003. Judgment of 27th May 2003, K 11/03, OTK-A 2003, Nr. 5.

Constitutional Court of Poland. 2005. Judgement of 11th May 2005, K 18/04, OTK-A 2005, Nr 5.

Działocha, Kazimierz. 2007. Art. 90, par. 3. In *Konstytucja Rzeczypospolitej Polskiej.* Komentarz. Tom V. 2007, ed. Leszek Garlicki. Warsaw: wydawnictwo Sejmowe.

Grzybowska, K. 1990. Obywatelstwo i narodowość – konstytucyjna koncepcja. *Rzeczpospolita,* 14.2.1990. Warszawa: Warsaw (Warszawa).

[1] English: Journal of Laws of the Republic of Poland, abbreviated Dz. U.

Jaskierna, Jerzy. 2002. Akcesja do Unii Europejskiej a konstytucyjny system stanowienia prawa. In *Akcesja do Unii Europejskiej a Konstytucja Rzeczypospolitej Polskiej*, ed. H. Zięba-Zalucka and M. Kijowski. Rzeszów: Wy. Sejmove.

Jaworski, W.L. 1921. *Prawa Państwa Polskiego*, vol. 2. Kraków: Krakowska Spółka Wydawnicza.

Sarnecki, P. 1997. Idee przewodnie konstytucji Rzeczypospolitej Polskiej z 2 kwietnia 1997 r. *Przeglad Sejmowy*, 5/1997. Warszawa: Warsaw (Warszawa).

Tuleja, P. (ed.). 1995. *Prawo konstytucyjne*. Warszawa: C.H. Beck. Dziennik Urzędowy, Nr 57, 14 marca 2003.

Bogusław Banaszak Prof. Dr. Dr. h.c. mult. Bogusław Banaszak, Dean of the Faculty of Law and Administration at the University at Zielona Gora. Holder of the Chair of Constitutional Law at this University, former (2006–2010) President of the Legislative Council of Poland, Professor at the University Viadrina/Frankfurt/Oder (1998–2008) and at university of Wroclaw (1977–2014), International Awards, Author of numerous publications, such as *Konstytucja Rzeczypospolitej Polskiej – Komentarz (Constitution of Republic of Poland-Commentary)*.

Chapter 7
The Transfer of Sovereignty in the Case Law of the Hungarian Constitutional Court

Péter Kovács

Abstract The author analyzes the jurisprudence of the Hungarian Constitutional Court vis-à-vis the deepening of the supranational integration of the European Union.

After having recognized the *sui generis* nature of European law in some "minor" cases, the Constitutional Court had to pass a decision also on the comprehensive reform of the *Treaty of Lisbon* and examined also some procedural aspects of the ratification of the *Treaty on fiscal stability*. In these decisions, the importance of the *a priori* parliamentary control was emphasized but no inherent limit has been set based on national constitutional identity.

Since 2012, Hungary has lived under a new constitution called the 'Fundamental Law', replacing the Constitution which was in force between 1949 and 2012 but which underwent major changes in 1989, the time of the regime change, in order to respect the rule of law.

This article will be restricted to the presentation of the case law of the Constitutional Court in relation to European law in the old and new contexts.

Péter Kovács was a judge at the Constitutional Court of the Republic of Hungary (2005–2014) and is professor of international law at the Péter Pázmány Catholic University. (The opinions expressed herein are made within an academic capacity and do not reflect the opinions of the Constitutional Court). Currently, he is a judge at the International Criminal Court.

P. Kovács (✉)
Péter Pázmány Catholic University, Budapest, Szentkirályi u. 28, 1088 Hungary
e-mail: profpeterkovacs@hotmail.com

R. Arnold (ed.), *Limitations of National Sovereignty through European Integration*, Ius Gentium: Comparative Perspectives on Law and Justice 51,
DOI 10.1007/978-94-017-7471-0_7

In order to cover the situation *ex ante*, it is necessary to recall that Article 7(1) of the former Constitution was drafted according to the Austro-Germanic tradition of dualism, even if there is some underlying uncertainty in the wording used.

Article 7 of the Constitution stipulates as follows:

> "*Article 7–1. The legal system of the Republic of Hungary accepts the universally recognised rules of international law, and shall ensure conformity between its obligations assumed under international law and its domestic law.*"

Article Q of the Fundamental Law takes the same concept in the spirit of a 'receptive' approach.[1]

According to Article Q of the Fundamental Law,

> "*(2) In order to satisfy the obligations assumed under international law, Hungary shall ensure the compatibility of its domestic law with international law.*"
>
> "*(3) Hungary accepts the universally recognised rules of international law. Other sources of international law are incorporated into Hungarian law by official publication in a legal work.*"

(*Nota bene:* the official English translations show a greater difference between the wordings than the Hungarian text.)

With regard to the clause on European integration, its first version was adopted in 2002 in the preparatory phase of Hungary's accession to the European Union and was numbered as Article 2/A. The question of transfer of sovereignty was duly settled by the aforementioned measure but the measure was silent as to the status of European law (and secondary law in particular). This lacuna has been constantly criticised in academic debate, underlining that a possible reference to the clause on international law would pose problems in light of the *sui generis* legal nature of European Union law. Moreover, the text in Article 7(1), cited above, refers to treaties and customs yet mentions absolutely nothing on the binding norms adopted by international organisations authorised to do so.

The text in Article 2/A was as follows:

> "*(1) For the purpose of its participation as a member state within the European Union and pursuant to an international treaty, the Republic of Hungary may exercise certain competences deriving from the Constitution in conjunction with other member states, to the extent required for the exercise of the rights and the fulfilment of the obligations stipulated by the founding treaties of the European Union and the European Communities – hereinafter 'the European Union' – respectively. The exercise of this competence may be achieved independently or through the institutions of the European Union.*"

---

[1] Author's note: This is to be distinguished from the 'transformative' approach, which only gives effect to international law through domestic legislation; the 'receptive' approach incorporates international law directly.

In the Fundamental Law, the European clause has been taken up with only a minor grammatical modification but has been supplemented by a reference to Community legislation in paragraph 3.

Numbered as Article E, the European clause thus stipulates that:

> "*(2) Hungary, as a member of the European Union, may, pursuant to a treaty, exercise certain constitutional competences in conjunction with other member states to the extent required for the exercise of rights and obligations under the founding treatise of the European Communities and the European Union; these competences are exercised apart from, as well as through, the institutions of the European Union.*
>
> *(3) The law of the European Union – in the framework of paragraph (2) – may stipulate general rules which are binding.*
>
> *(4) The authorisation required for the ratification and the enactment of a treaty referred to in paragraph 2 shall be subject to a two-thirds majority vote in the national assembly.*"

(As above, it should be noted that the official English translations of Article 2/A and Article E show a greater difference than the Hungarian versions).

The case law of the European Court of Justice has been followed by the Constitutional Court, which was swift to conclude that, contrary to conflicts that have emerged between national and traditional international law, the examination of the compatibility between a domestic legal norm and the law of the European Union does not fall within its competence. In this way, the Constitutional Court has aimed to avoid being overwhelmed by a mass influx of technical matters which have no legal importance. (It should be noted that during this very period, the procedure of constitutional control could be triggered by anyone and without real interest, as a result of the *actio popularis* system. Even if the examination of a conflict between international and national law could escape the *actio popularis*, it could nevertheless easily be triggered: a single Member of Parliament was entitled to do so…)

Furthermore, the preservation of judicial sovereignty has not as a result been undermined, as the Constitutional Court did not need to refer preliminary questions to the European Court of Justice and the rules on the division of competences between the Court in Luxembourg and the national tribunals have also been observed.

Despite this, the Constitutional Court has not always been able to avoid dealing in detail with questions of major importance on European integration, as we shall see.

7.1 The Constitution and an Insight into the Problem of the Transfer of Sovereignty in the Case Law of the Constitutional Court

7.1.1 Recognition of the Sui Generis Nature of European Law

Like all other new member states of the European communities, Hungary has also had to define the position of European law (Community law) in the Hungarian legal system (Várnay et al. 2006).[2] For this exercise, the legislator and the Constitutional Court have their own responsibilities in order to reach a result which is compatible with the constitution and conforms to the inherent logic of cooperation within the European Union.

The distance covered so far has been long and some contradictions have arisen.

The initial difficulty was that, at the time of the major constitutional reform relating to the regime change in 1989/1990, the constituents had not yet considered that it would be necessary to include a European clause in the Constitution. We did, however, incorporate the above-cited Article 7 into the Constitution on the basis of international law and Hungarian law.

Created in 1989, the Constitutional Court was given certain competences relating to the compatibility of domestic law and international obligations. Thus, the following fall within the competence of the Constitutional Court: the *a priori* examination of constitutionality of international treaty provisions (which may take place before the definitive international obligation arises), as well as the examination of incompatibility between international treaties and bodies of law and other judicial measures from the State Administration.

During the preparation for the accession to the European Union, the National Assembly supplemented the Constitution with a European clause, the above-mentioned Article 2/A.

Yet the legislator did not supplement the law on the Constitutional Court and thus, the text remained without clear indications as to the existence (or non-existence) of the Court's competence in the event of a contradiction between the Constitution and Community law, as well as a conflict between Community obligations and sub-constitutional domestic law.

It should also be noted that academic debate has at the same time drawn attention to a certain ambiguity in the new constitutional article, or at least a certain lacuna: whilst the question of the transfer of sovereignty is correctly resolved in this formula, the hierarchical position of Community law within

---

[2] For a detailed analysis of this development, and an explanation of the contradictions.

the Hungarian legal system has not been clarified. This position should be sub-constitutional, but hierarchically superior (or at least, given priority above) domestic law, taking into account the specific characteristics of the different forms of Community legislation and the consequences of the primacy and direct applicability of Community law etc.

Academic debate has also noticed some ambiguity in the constitutional case law relating to the problem of Community law: in some resolutions, the Constitutional Court treated Community law "as a foreign law" (ABH 1998, 232) [3] – of course, before the accession to the European Union -, whilst other resolutions applied an amalgam of Community law and international law and cited Article 7(1) of the Constitution.[4] Most frequently, the Constitutional Court tried to avoid ruling on the nature of Community legislation altogether (ABH 2004, 297).[5]

It is in this context that the Constitutional Court encountered Community law once again (ABH 2006/II. 1824–1831).

This case related to gambling bets on the Internet which were only permitted for companies located in Hungary and given a licence by the competent national authority. Hungary imposes an absolute prohibition in this area on companies that have their headquarters in a foreign country. According to § 7 of Article 2 of the Law XXXIV/1991 on betting, "it is forbidden to exercise any activity of sale, organisation, mediation for participation in a game of betting organised abroad, as well as publicity- or propaganda-related activities relating to a game of betting abroad." As regards the violation of the prohibition on publicity, the director, the provider and the person distributing the publicity, are responsible.

---

[3] ABH is the acronym for the Yearbook of the Constitutional Court, – in Hungarian "Alkotmánybíróság Határozatai" – edited and published by the Court.

[4] In a manner logical in itself, resolution n° 72/2002 (XII.19) considered the agreement of association between Hungary and the European Communities (1991) as a treaty of international law (ABH 2002, 438). In resolution n° 17/2004 (V.25.), surprisingly, Hungary's agreement of accession was considered as an ordinary international treaty: it is true that the key issue of the decision (whether a law, on the stockpiling of sugar produce conforming to certain Community rules, was constitutionally compatible) was aimed at the final days prior to the entering into force of the accession when *pro forma* this instrument could have been regarded as a body of international law.

[5] In resolution n° 17/2004 (V.25.), after having presented at length the contents of the agreement of accession and of certain rules relating to the sugar reserves, the Constitutional Court arrived at the conclusion that, in the decision, the question was not the compatibility of Community law with the constitution, but rather the compatibility of Hungarian legislation with the Constitution. Here, the Court stated that the legislation in question contained elements which lacked Community empowerment.

It is further true that Hungary is not by any means the only country, among the other member states of the European Union, to have closed its electronic lottery market. States have a desire to maintain its monopoly insofar as possible, on the one hand because of the obvious financial interests, but on the other hand, because of concerns about ensuring the protection of the legitimate interests of those who gamble, as well as protecting this very delicate market from the influence of organised crime. Another reason often invoked is the need to ensure that children and adolescents are kept away from games which could be harmful to their psychological and mental development. States consider that they are only able to enforce the necessary control within their country and, as long as there is no uniform or common regulation, we cannot abolish the barriers.

All of this is taking place during a period when community institutions were unable to definitively adopt a directive on services and when large lottery companies were actively lobbying for this major market to open up to Europe, in a situation where a Gambling Directive would not only ensure access, but also precise arrangements for the presence of gambling.

During previous years, the Court of Justice of the European Communities has interpreted on several occasions the question of national restrictions on electronic bets (also known as bets online). In the famous preliminary ruling of the *Gambelli* case (Verbiest 2006; Scaramozzino 2006),[6] the CJEC, ruling on the question submitted to it by the Tribunale di Ascoli Piceno by order of that Court of 30 March 2001, asserted that a « national rule which prohibits and makes subject to criminal penalties the pursuit by any person in any place of the activities of taking, accepting, booking and forwarding bets placed, in particular on sporting events, without obtaining the prior authorization and licence required by domestic law, pursuant to Article 43 and Article 49 TEC on the freedom of establishment and the freedom to provide cross-border services respectively. It falls within the referring court's jurisdiction to verify whether such a rule, with regard to the specific arrangements of its application, truly meets the objectives that are able to justify it and whether the restrictions imposed by the rule do not appear disproportionate in light of those objectives. »

The claimant – who was none other than the powerful British firm Sportingbet Ltd – submitted that the Hungarian legislation went against Community obligations and in particular the principles of the freedom to provide cross-border services, such as those enshrined in Article 49 and related articles. It also argued that the Hungarian legislation went against the interpretation adopted by the Court of Justice of the European Communities.

[6] Preliminary ruling delivered on 6 November 2003, in the C-243/01 case.

It stated that the current state of affairs was the equivalent of a constitutional deficit on the part of the National Assembly.

The Constitutional Court rejected this claim with an argument based essentially on the fact that a constitutional deficit presupposes the existence of a specific obligation, which was not present on the facts of the case. Moreover, the claimant did not specify which article of the Constitution could have been violated by the supposed deficit. According to the Court, we cannot interpret Article 2/A as if it contained a specific obligation to legislate. The claim was therefore unfounded.

However, the Constitutional Court stated that "the accession clause contained in the above-mentioned Article 2/A defines the conditions and framework of the Republic of Hungary's participation, as well as the position of Community law in the system of sources of Hungarian law." Furthermore, the Court made an important step when it stated that "despite their conventional origin, the founding treaties of the European Union (or the treaties modifying them) shall not be considered as international treaties." (ABH 2006/II, 1828).

Certainly, the resolution of the Constitutional Court has not shed light on all of the interesting aspects of the decision. The message should be clear: in the case of an alleged violation of a community obligation, it does not fall within the Constitutional Court's jurisdiction to take up a position. On the contrary, it is well and truly the Court of Justice of the European Communities which is entitled to decide the case *in merito*, either directly (if the conditions inherent in the referral are met), or indirectly through referrals for a preliminary ruling by ordinary courts. Such recourse should be regarded as a given, especially in a decision where the inconsistency between national law and community law seems *prima facie* manifest.

It should be noted that the separate opinion annexed to the resolution proposes the adaptation of techniques prepared by the German Bundesverfassungsgericht (BVerfG 2005, 1–201) and the French Conseil Constitutionnel (CC 2004, n° 2004–496 DC), and adds that it is only in the case of a direct threat to a right protected in the Constitution that the Constitutional Court could take up a position on the constitutionality of an obligation deriving from primary or secondary legislation.

The Constitutional Court has therefore ruled that Community law should be treated as a *sui generis* law, and not as international law: the Court closed the familiar debate and resolved it in the same way as other member states of the European Union.

7.1.2 A Second Step Forward: An Image of Secondary Legislation in the Constitutional Case Law

On 12 December 2006, the Constitutional Court adopted its resolution n° 72/2006 (XII.15.) AB with regard to a number of claims which challenged the constitutionality of Hungarian legislation relating to the calculation of the working hours of doctors and nurses in hospitals (Raisz 2007).

In terms of the system applied in Hungary, it was relatively similar to that in France (Abdelkader Dellas and Others v. Premier ministre and Others 2005): the amount of time spent monitoring within the hospital after the doctor's normal working day is multiplied by different coefficients[7] according to the shifts and the difficulty of night-shifts for doctors. The hospital can impose upto six monitoring sessions on a doctor each month: in general, three or four can be considered as normal, including at least one long session, that is, on a weekend.

As for specific legislation, certain articles of the Labour Law Code,[8] the law on the status of public employees[9] and a government regulation[10] relating to the implementation of stipulations of the aforementioned law within health services, were applicable. The Court's resolution (ABH 2006, 819–869) rejected the claims concerning conformity of the different articles of the Code and the law with the Constitution, but nevertheless annulled several articles in the regulation. As regards the motives underlying the Court's rejection, these were primarily based on the absence of significant judicial links with the rather insubstantial articles[11] of the Constitution. The annulment of the articles

[7] Between 55 et 130 % on the condition that the collective policy of the hospital does not guarantee a superior sum.

[8] The XXII law from 1992.

[9] The XXXIII law from 1992.

[10] The government regulation 233/2000. (XII. 23.)

[11] (Unofficial translation by the author)
"Article 35: (1). The Government shall (…) b) ensure the implementation of laws;"
"Article 35: (2) 2. In performing its duties, the Government shall issue decrees and pass resolutions. They will be signed by the Prime Minister. Government decrees and resolutions may not conflict with the law. Government decrees shall be promulgated in the Official Gazette."
"Article 54: (1). In the Republic of Hungary, every person has the inherent right to life and to human dignity; no one shall be arbitrarily deprived of these rights."
"Article 70/A: (1). The Republic of Hungary shall guarantee the human and civil rights of all people residing in the territory, without any form of discrimination on race, colour, gender, religion, political or other opinion, national or social background, financial status, birth or any other situation. (2). The law shall provide strict sanctions for any harmful discrimination falling under Paragraph (1). (3). The Republic of Hungary shall

in the regulation was based, on the other hand, on the fact that here, the limitation of a constitutional clause was taking place at a lower level of law[12] and was therefore unconstitutional in the Hungarian legal system.

The most interesting aspect, however, was the reference made in some claims to the relevant Community legislation and in particular, to the interpretation of the Court of Justice of the European Communities: the claims were making references namely to the Directive 93/104/CE and in particular the interpretation given to it by the CJEC in the famous *Jaeger* decision (Landeshauptstadt Kiel v. Norbert Jaeger 2003).

Some of the claims were lodged prior to Hungary's accession to the European Union – thus during the period of Hungary's associated status – when the Constitution did not yet contain a specific article (Article 2/A) on Community law. In this way, these claims based their argument on the conflict of relevant Hungarian rules with international law. Furthermore, the Constitutional Court waited several years before finally expounding – in the aforementioned Sportingbet decision – the only acceptable formula, stating that Community law is not subject to the criteria of international law, but rather a *corpus juris sui generis.*

It is in this context that the Constitutional Court thus encountered the challenge of the potential applicability of a Community directive. This

support the attainment of equality of rights by implementing measures aimed at suppressing unequal opportunities."

"Article 70/B: (1). In the Republic of Hungary, every person has the right to work, and to freely choose his job and profession. (2). Every person, without any discrimination, has the right to equal remuneration for equal work. (3) Every worker has the right to remuneration conforming to the quality and quality of work performed. (4) Every person has the right to free time, to leisure time and to regular paid holidays."

"Article 70/D: (1) Those persons living on the territory of the Republic of Hungary have the right to the highest possible level of physical and mental health."

"Article 70e: 1. The citizens of the Republic of Hungary have the right to social security; in the case of old age, illness, disability, being widowed or orphaned or becoming unemployed through no fault of their own, they have the right to the social security benefits necessary for their well-being."

[12] "Article 2: (1) The Republic of Hungary is an independent and democratic state which abides by the rule of law."

"Article 8: (1) The Republic of Hungary recognises fundamental, inviolable and inalienable human rights; the respect for and protection of these rights are a primary obligation of the State. (2) In the Republic of Hungary, the regulations relating to fundamental laws and obligations are fixed by the law; nevertheless, this law may not restrict the substantive content of a fundamental right."

occurred in a situation where the CJEC finally made the decision to declare certain parts of it as directly applicable.[13]

The Constitutional Court observed (ABH 2006, 860–861) that one of the claimants wished to argue the incompatibility between Directive n° 93/104/CE on the reading together of Articles 2/A and 7(1) of the Constitution, using the argument that a directive could also indirectly provide a base of competence, since underlying a directive, it is always possible to discern the Treaty of Rome which must be considered – according to the Treaty itself – as an international treaty *stricto sensu.* In this way, the Court should base its decision on Article 7(1). According to the claimant, the Court could therefore use its competences relating to the examination of the harmony between domestic law and international obligations.

However, the Court recalled its *dicta* from the Sportingbet decision taken 6 months previously, and once again stated that with regard to the Constitutional Court's competence, these treaties [the Treaty of Rome and the other treaties of primary law – P. Kovács], as a source of primary law and the Directive, as a source of secondary law by virtue of its being Community law, forms part of domestic law, because since 1 May 2004, the Republic of Hungary is a member of the European Union. With regard to the competence of the Constitutional Court, Community law cannot be considered as international law. Now, the claimant – in his claim – has not alluded to any other treaty which could be regarded as an international treaty (ABH 2006, 861). The Constitutional Court therefore rejected the claim.

The Court thus reaffirmed its refusal to assimilate primary and secondary law into traditional international law.

---

[13] As the CJEC stated in its decision of 5 October 2004 in the joint cases of C-397/01 to C-403/01 (request for a prelimary ruling from the Arbeitsgericht Lörrach (Germany)): Pfeifer et al c. Deutsches Rotes Kreuz, Kreisverband Waldshut eV, in paragraph 120:

"in light of the aforementioned developments, it is necessary to respond to the third question that: Article 6, point 2, of Directive 93/104 must be interpreted, in circumstances such as those in the main proceedings, as precluding legislation in a Member State the effect of which, as regards periods of duty time ('Arbeitsbereitschaft') completed by emergency workers in the framework of the emergency medical service of a body such as the Deutsches Rotes Kreuz, is to permit, including by means of a collective agreement or works agreement based on such an agreement, the 48-h maximum period of weekly working time laid down by that provision to be exceeded.

The said provision satisfies all the necessary requirements to produce direct effect; this conclusion is repeated in the final part of the decision."

7.1.3 *Abandoning Independence or Transferring Sovereignty? The Law on the Treaty of Lisbon before the Constitutional Court*

On 12 July 2010, the Constitutional Court, in its resolution n° 143/2010. (VII.14.) AB, rejected a claim submitted by an individual and directed at the Law on the promulgation of the Treaty of Lisbon (Act CLXVIII de 2007). The claim asserted that the rules and new mechanisms of the Treaty of Lisbon threatened the existence of the Republic of Hungary as an independent and sovereign State (ABH 2010, 708).

The Constitutional Court observed that the claimant's reasoning and examples were more or less the same as those debated before other constitutional courts in Europe in the framework of an *a priori* examination of the constitutionality of the Treaty of Lisbon, performed at the request of national governments, members of Parliament, senators or heads of State.[14] The Constitutional Court scrupulously studied these *dicta* and the academic criticisms directed at some of them (ABH 2010, 699).

Even if the *a priori* examination of the constitutionality of treaties also exists in Hungary, its instigation has been reserved for the government or Head of State: in 2007, neither one nor the other brought this subject before the Constitutional Court.

The Constitutional Court first of all verified its competence relating to the law of promulgation (ABH 2010, 700–701) and arrived at the conclusion that even if the Treaty of Lisbon has already entered into force, modifying the treaty on European Union and the treaty establishing the European Community (the title of which has been changed to the Treaty on the Functioning of the European Union), this does not mean that the law of promulgation should be treated in a different manner to ordinary laws and other legislation which may be challenged by individuals, in the spirit of an *actio popularis* action guaranteed by the law on the Constitutional Court (ABH 2010, 700–701).

Yet the Constitutional Court warned that in the framework of *a posteriori* control of the law, particular attention is due, given that Hungary is a member state of the European Union. This is why a resolution which would have – hypothetically – found unconstitutionality, could not threaten the scrupulous execution of obligations relating to membership within the

[14] Cf. In particular the decisions of the German Federal Constitutional Court (Decision 2BvE 2/08, delivered on 30 June 2009) and the Czech Constitutional Court (Decision Pl. US 19/08, delivered on 28 November 2008 and the decision Pl. US 29/09, delivered on 3 November 2009).

European Union. According to the Constitutional Court, in this case, Parliament should act in order to create a situation where the European obligations can be executed without the Constitution being affected (ABH 2010, 703).

Further on this point, the Constitutional Court did not want to be as explicit as it had been at the time of the adoption of resolution n° 4/1997. (I.22.) AB.[15] The formula used clearly demonstrates the origin of this resolution, but the Court made sure not to suggest obligations, the fulfilment of which would be almost impossible. The characteristics of the legal system of the European Union were also taken into account at the time of editing the formula inherited. In the hypothesis in question, the burden was therefore on the legislator to decide whether the government should act on a diplomatic European level or, as the case may be, a constitutional revision would be the appropriate solution for the conflict.

In terms of clear warnings for the future, the Constitutional Court underlined that in the case of such important treaties, the competent authorities should take advantage of their powers and instigate the procedure of examining constitutionality *a priori* (ABH 2010, 705). The Court stated that the deliberation on the present case is closely linked to the fact that the examination of constitutionality *a priori* had not been solicited (ABH 2010, 705).

The Constitutional Court recognised that the authentic interpretation of European treaties and other Community legislation falls within the competence of the European Court of Justice (ABH 2010, 703).

The Constitutional Court nevertheless took advantage of the acte clair doctrine, which is why it did not need to have recourse to the European Court of Justice as it was evident that the arguments relied upon by claimants contesting the constitutionality of the law of promulgation, were based on an erroneous and superficial reading of the Treaty of Lisbon (ABH 2010, 703–704). This is why recalling the complete text of Article 49/A (now Article 50) of the Treaty on European Union is sufficient in itself to see that, contrary to claimants' assumptions, no State may be obliged to remain in the European Union if it does not wish to (ABH 2010, 704).

---

[15] "A resolution of the Constitutional Court which finds an issue of constitutionality, should not have any effect on the international obligations of the Republic of Hungary. Following this resolution by the Constitutional Court, the legislator must ensure harmony between international obligation and domestic law: by the fact that the Republic of Hungary denounces the part of the international treaty which contradicts the Constitution, or by the fact that the text of the treaty is modified or – if needed – it is the constitution which must be modified. The Constitutional Court has the power to suspend the determination of the date of annulment in a timely manner, until the said harmony has been achieved" (ABH 1997, 52).

Again following the acte clair doctrine, the Constitutional Court has considered that in order to reject the remaining parts of the claim, it is sufficient to have regard to obvious information within public knowledge on the European Union as it is presented after Lisbon (ABH 2010, 708–709): for example, the attribution of a legally binding character to the Charter of Fundamental Rights or the extension of powers of control of national parliaments, in light of protocol n°2 on subsidiarity and proportionality, etc. All of this demonstrates that the claimant's arguments on the dangers of the Treaty of Lisbon are without foundation (ABH 2010, 7010).

The Constitutional Court also interpreted the relevant articles[16] of the Constitution on sovereignty, democracy, the rule of law and European cooperation (ABH 2010, 706–707). It observed that the European clause cannot be interpreted as depriving the clauses on sovereignty and rule of law of their substance (ABH 2010, 708) (contrary to the German and Czech Constitutional Courts, the Hungarian Constitutional Court did not mention any point of no return, or limit implicit in European integration, or some exclusive domain to be always reserved for national legislation).

The Constitutional Court recalled from its established case law that the holder of sovereignty – in effect, Parliament – is entitled to limit the exercise of attributes of sovereignty (ABH 2010, 707).

The Constitutional Court underlined that the material and procedural rules were observed when the law of promulgation was adopted and when Parliament thus freely assented to the adoption of the contents of the Treaty of Lisbon (ABH 2010, 709).

The Constitutional Court reached the conclusion that even if the reforms of the Treaty of Lisbon are of significant importance, they did not modify the situation whereby Hungary maintains its independence, its conformance to the rule of law and its sovereignty. As a result, the claim was rejected in its entirety (ABH 2010, 710).

[16]Article 2: "(1). Republic of Hungary is an independent and democratic state which abides by the rule of law. (2) In the Republic of Hungary, all power belongs to the people, who exercise popular sovereignty through their elected representatives, as well as directly."

Article 2/A of the Constitution: (aforementioned)

Article 6: (…) (4) The Republic of Hungary shall contribute to the achievement of European unity in order to attain the freedom, well-being and security of European citizens."

7.2 The Fundamental Law and an Insight into the Problem of the Transfer of Sovereignty in the Case Law of the Constitutional Court

In the new context, the Constitutional Court was requested by the government to interpret Article E of the Fundamental Law with a view to clarifying whether the ratification of the Treaty on fiscal stability required a qualified or simple majority.

It is necessary to recall that Article E(4) contains a reference to a two-thirds majority and several years ago, in its resolution 143/2010. (VII. 14.) adopted on the Treaty of Lisbon, the Constitutional Court asserted – on the basis of Article 2/A of the Constitution – that the two-third majority is required not only for the ratification of the treaty of accession but also for all of the future European treaties which entails additional transfers of sovereignty.

Thus, the Parliament – as holder of sovereignty – is entitled to monitor the government leading (and having led) negotiations and it will be able to decide whether it is ready to accept a complex institutional reform of such scope. (Contrary to treaties transferring sovereignty, the ratification of ordinary treaties can be attained by a simple majority.[17])

The Constitutional Court confirmed that "the ratification of an international treaty, concerning the modification or amendment of rights and obligations deriving from founding treaties, requires a two-thirds majority subject to the condition that it also concerns the common exercise of competences guaranteed in the Fundamental Law. Such a treaty may, in particular, be an international treaty whereby Hungary – as a member of the European Union – is a contracting party with other member States when this treaty governs areas covered by the founding treaties or if its goal relates to the execution of the founding treaties or their control. The ratification of an

[17] Article 19, para. 3/f and 4 of the Constitution:
para. 3. "In exercising this competence, the National Assembly:
f) shall conclude major international treaties from the perspective of relations external to the Republic of Hungary;"
para. 4. "The adoption of the provided decisions at points g, h, i and j of paragraph 3 require a two-thirds majority vote by the Members of Parliament."
(NB: As subparagraph (f) is not enumerated in paragraph 4, *a contrario* it is the principle of simple majority which applies to treaties.)
Article 1 of the Fundamental Law:
"(2) The National Assembly: (d) permits the recognition of the binding, legal nature of international treaties falling under its competence;"
(NB: The Fundamental Law also omits to list the ratification among the questions relating to the two-thirds majority.)

international treaty does not require a two-thirds majority if this treaty does not concern the common exercise, with institutions of the European Union or its member-states, of new competences deriving from the Fundamental Law." (ABH 2012, 10–21.

The underlying problem of the question posed by the government was that the Treaty on fiscal stability effectively entails a new transfer of sovereignty for members of the Euro zone. This obligation for countries in the Euro zone is only an option for member states of the European Union which are still outside of the Euro zone, as this is notably the case for Hungary. Furthermore, the government also declared that it would not strive for the acceptance of these options before the country enters into the Euro zone in its own right.

This was precisely the reason why the Constitutional Court asserted that compliance with the aforementioned rules on the transfer of sovereignty is nevertheless inevitable in the decision "since an international treaty is only ratified once. This is why a solution, which only requires a simple majority at the time of the ratification, as a result of a delayed or conditional enforcement of the transfer of sovereignty but which, once the additional obligations come into force, would necessitate a two-thirds majority of votes of the members of Parliament, cannot be considered as constitutional." [18]

Further Reading

BVerfG. 2009. 2 BvE 2/08, 30 June 2009.

Blutman, László, and Nóra Chronowski. 2011. Hungarian constitutional court: Keeping aloof from European Union law. *Vienna Online Journal on International Constitutional Law* 3: 329–348.

Constitution of Hungary. 2011.

CzCC. 2008. Pl. ÚS 19/08, 28 November 2008.

CzCC. 2009. Pl. ÚS 29/09, 3 November 2009.

ECJ. 2003. Landeshauptstadt Kiel v. Norbert Jaeger, 9 September 2003, C 151/02.

ECJ. 2004. *Pfeifer et al v. Deutsches Rotes Kreuz*, 5 October 2004, joint cases of C-397/01 to C-403/01.

ECJ. 2005. *Abdelkader Dellas and Others v. Premier ministre and Others*, 1 December 2005, C 14/04.

Kovács, Péter. 2011. *Introduction à la jurisprudence de la cour constitutionnelle de la République de Hongrie: approche thématique*, Entwicklungen im europäischen Recht. Regensburg: Universitätsverlag.

[18] Resolution n° 22/2012. (V. 11.) AB, p. 18, § 52 (In 2012, the Constitutional Court introduced the numbering of paragraphs in its resolutions.)

Kovács, Péter. 2013. La loi sur le traité de Lisbonne devant la Cour Constitutionnelle de Hongrie Hungarian Yearbook of International Law and European Law, 397–401.
Kovács, Péter, and Diána Mecsi. 2014. Hungarian national report at the XVI th congress of the conference of European constitutional courts. In Proceedings of the XVI th congress of the conference of European constitutional courts, ed. Gerhart Holzinger, Vienna, 3–4 May, 2014. http://www.vfgh.gv.at/cms/vfgh-kongress/downloads/landesberichte/LB-Hongerie-EN.pdf.

References

ABH. 1997. Resolution 4/1997. (I.22.) AB.
ABH. 1998. Resolution 30/1998 (VI.25).
ABH. 2002. Resolution 72/2002 (XII.19) AB.
ABH. 2004. Resolution 17/2004, adopted 25 May 2004.
ABH. 2006/II. Resolution 1053/E/2005, adopted 16 June 2006.
ABH. 2010. Resolution 143/2010. (VII.14.) AB.
ABH. 2012. Resolution 22/2012 (V 11.)AB.
BVerfG. 2005. 2 BvR 2236/04, 18.7.2005.
Conseil constitutionnel. 2004. n° 2004–496 DC of 10 June 2004, *Journal officiel de la République française.*
Raisz, Anikó. 2007. The Hungarian constitutional court challenged by direct applicability of a directive. *Miskolc Journal of International Law* 4(1): 113–127.
Scaramozzino, Yannick-Eléonore. 2006. L'affaire Gambelli – Position de la Cour de Justice des Communautés sur les paris sportifs. Cabinet scaraye legal news. www.scaraye.com/article.php?rub=1&sr=2&a=335.
Thibault, Verbiest. 2006. Jeux et paris en ligne: l'arrêt Gambelli est-il pertinent pour la France?. JusData: http://www.jusdata.info/v2/index.php?detail[id]=283&detail[lang]=FR&pr[lang]=FR&pr[rub]=1. Accessed Dec 2007.
Várnay, Ernő, and Allan F. Tatham. 2006. A new step on the long way: How to find the proper place of community law in the Hungarian legal order? *Miskolc Journal of International Law* 3(4): 76–84.

Péter Kovács judge at the International Criminal Court. Professor of international law at the Peter Pazmany Catholic University of Budapest. He published numerous articles and books on minority protection, human rights, international and constitutional jurisprudence. He was elected to serve as judge of the Constitutional Court in 2005 for a nine year term. He was visiting professor at the following universities: Montpellier I, Paris II, Paris XI, Nantes (France), Regensburg (Germany) and Denver (United States).

Chapter 8
An 'Entirely-Specific' Situation or a Routine Limitation of the National Autonomy? *Slovak pensions XVII* of the Czech Constitutional Court

Jiří Zemánek

Abstract The article identifies the reasons which moved the Czech Constitutional Court to declare the judgment of the European Court of Justice in C-399/09 *Landtová* concerning the application of social security schemes in unprecedented way as an ultra vires act and to deprive it of binding force within the domestic legal system. The author argues that a more express ECJ's pronouncement about persons discriminated contrary to the respective EC Regulation, its more careful understanding of what exactly the Czech Court's case law was saying and – in particular – a reference by the Czech Court for preliminary ruling concerning the interpretation of the EC Regulation could avoid the unfortunate outcome of the case. The limitation of Member States's sovereignty by the European integration requires to make lines between the scope of competences conferred on the EU and the national ones also in the area of judicial power more transparent. This is what the article tries to do: to review the national reservations towards primacy of EU law as questionable, if their justification has not been cleared before by the ECJ.

J. Zemánek (✉)
Faculty of Law, Charles University, nam. Curievych 7, 11640 Praha 1,
Czech Republic
e-mail: zemanek@prf.cuni.cz

R. Arnold (ed.), *Limitations of National Sovereignty through European Integration*, Ius Gentium: Comparative Perspectives on Law and Justice 51,
DOI 10.1007/978-94-017-7471-0_8

8.1 The Euro-dedicated Earlier Case Law of the Court (With Some Reservations)

When the Court of Justice of the European Union (ECJ) in the case *Landtová* (Landtová v. Czech Social Security Administration 2011) proclaimed the case law of the Constitutional Court of the Czech Republic (the CzCC, the Court) on compensation allowances for some Czech pensioners, who were employees in the former Czechoslovak federation, as discriminatory on the grounds of nationality under the Union law, hardly anybody could have anticipated the reaction from the Czech side. This unexpected and bitter came soon, as the ECJ answered the preliminary question submitted by the Supreme Administrative Court (SAC) and confirmed the view of the latter, opposing the case law of the CzCC (CzCC 2012). According to the ECJ, all pensioners working as employees before dissolution of the Czechoslovak federation at the end of 1992 for an employer residing in the territory of the present-day Slovak Republic, must be treated equally under Union law,[1] regardless of their nationality. However, in the view of the CzCC, the ECJ accidentally overlooked the entirely specific historical situation connected with the dissolution of Czechoslovak federation. This situation should not have to be considered – for the purpose of calculating pension benefits – as a period of employment abroad, since it had been lacking cross-border movement (movement of workers within internal market of the EU), which is a prerequisite for the application of Union law. Therefore, the Court continued to insist on its case law, found the Union legislation on co-ordination of social security systems inapplicable in the instant situation and, as a result, declared the ECJ's judgment *Landtová* ultra vires.

This self-assured position of the CzCC contrasted with its case law precedent of adopting the doctrine of primacy of European law as an autonomous body of legal provisions applicable besides the Czech legal order (Zemánek 2007). In *obiter dictum* on *Sugar quotas* (CzCC 2006a) the Court

[1] The regulation no. 1408/71 on the application of social security schemes to employed persons and their families moving within the Community (Regulation); under Article 7 para 2 c/ it does not affect conventions on social security concluded between Member States, which shall continue to apply – as an exception - in so far as they are ensuring a more favourable treatment for beneficiaries or reflect for a limited time specific historical circumstances, subject to their inclusion in Annex III. Persons resident in the territory of one of the Member States to whome this Regulation applies shall be subject to the same obligations and enjoy the same benefits under the legislation of any Member State as the nationals of that State (Article 3 para 1). Safe as provided in Annex III, conventions which remain in force persuant to Article 7 para 2 c/ shall apply to all persons to whom this Regulation applies (Article 3 para 3).

confirmed its established view, that the conferral of some state powers on the Union is conditional. The original possessor of sovereignty and the powers flowing therefrom still remains the Czech Republic, whose sovereignty is founded upon its Constitution. The conditionality of this delegation is manifested on two planes: the formal plane and the substantive plane. This means that the transfer of powers[2] may persist only so long as these powers are exercised in a manner which is compatible with the preservation of the foundations of state sovereignty of the Czech Republic and in a manner which does not threaten the very essence of the substantive law-based state (so called 'material core'of the Constitution). In such determination the Court is obliged to protect constitutionalism (Article 83 Const.). According to Article 9 par. 2 Const., lowering the essential attributes of a democratic state governed by the rule of law remains even beyond the reach of the Constituent Assembly itself.

In other words, the transfer of powers of state bodies to the Union can not go so far as to violate the very essence of the republic as a democratic state governed by the rule of law, founded on respect for the rights and freedoms of human beings and of citizens, and establish a change of the essential requirements of a democratic state governed by the rule of law. If the Union could continue to change its powers at will and independently of its members, as if a constitutional competence (competence-competence) were transferred to it, this would be a transfer inconsistent with the Constitution. Such a Union legal act could not be binding in the Czech Republic. In accordance with this, the Court also intends to review, as ultima ratio, whether Union legal acts remain within the bounds of the powers that were provided to them. In this regard, the Court basically agreed with certain conclusions of the German Federal Constitutional Court (FCC), stated in its Maastricht decision, which concludes that the principle of loyalty to the Union has its limits in the constitutional principles and elementary interests of the Member States (CzCC 2008).

In spite of the thesis that constitutional courts maintain their role of supreme guardians of constitutionality, even in the realms of the Union against potential excesses on the side of Union bodies, it was hoped that such rhetoric could not lead to a rebellion, before the criteria of reference, outlined only in general terms ('material core' of the Constitution), were elaborated upon in detail. In addition, the readiness of the CzCC to submit

---

[2] The CzCC calls it 'delegation', which is not correct enough: the transfer of powers cannot be taken back on a unilateral basis any more. A retraction would require a common agreement of all Member States at the level of primary law (i.e., a revision of the Treaty) or a withdrawal of the Member State from the Union (subject to Art. 50 TEU).

questions for preliminary ruling to the ECJ remained reserved, but not hopeless. In this respect the Court followed an earlier path of the German FCC, upheld until its *Honeywell* decision (FCC 2010, 2661/06). It also accepted the broad understanding of the doctrine of indirect effect (Euro-constitent interpretation of national law) of Union law (CzCC 2006a, b).

The CzCC used the occasion also to demonstrate a balanced approach to the question of limits of integration, emancipating itself boldly from its German partner. In the Court's opinion, it is the task of a concrete and positive political decision of the legislature, seeking the best satisfaction of the sovereign's, i.e. the citizens' aspirations – on formation of peaceful and welfare conditions of their lives – outside of the state jurisdiction. Thus, it can not be a matter of an abstract and negative judicial decision, prejudicing satisfaction of these aspirations in policy areas of 'high sensitivity' by an action exclusively within the state jurisdiction. The Court did not admit a right for the judicial branch to define, a priori, a minimum level of specific powers of the state, which would allow it to remain sovereign. The state cannot be deprived of its sovereignty so long as it has not been authorized by the Constitution-maker to waive its competence-competence, which is an ultimate limit *de constitutione lata*. The Court, acting in the capacity of ultima ratio, must – in an extreme cases only – prevent the state from draining its constitutional responsibility through a total waiver of its powers. The lack of express constitutional criteria for the transfer of powers cannot be substituted by a judicial decision. This demonstrated the large confidence of the Court in the Parliament's decision on the limits of transfer, which can be made on a case-by-case basis only, not in advance by a statement on the finality of the process of European integration. In this way, the Court did not follow the defensive approach of the German FCC, which expressly determined that some areas of the country-specific, national identity-building *domaine reservée*, were fully closed or largely resistant to integration (FCC 2009, para 252; Thym 2009; Zwingmann 2012).

The self-restrained judicial behaviour of the CzCC, considering the limits of European integration, admitted an open-ended process rather than a comprehensive, integration-proof catalogue of Union powers; 'immune to immediate political pressures and *ad hoc* interpretations influenced by cases at issue at a particular time"(CzCC 2009, para 110). The refusal of a catalogue of vital state powers demonstrated not only the Court's awareness of real limits of parliamentary discretion, but of the need to look for other constitutive prerogatives other than the substantive essence of powers, which make the state a sovereign entity. The traditional understanding of a sovereign state as an exclusive possessor of the highest and omnipotent power in a demarcated territory, an independent and equal partner in international relations, is no longer sustainable in the contemporary world. In the globalized world, the centers of power are regrouped according to factors other than the simple power and will of individual sovereign states. A joint (collective) governance, entrusted with the execution of certain sovereign powers, is the only way to ensure the effective protection and enforcement of common European values vis-à-vis newly emerging world superpowers, where it is difficult to guess the future priorities to which they will be willing to subordinate the building of a new order in the globalized world (CzCC 2008, para 102). The adequate comprehension of sovereign statehood is a dynamic one, ready to re-consider its notion by taking seriously the changed environment of state existence. Its main attribute is the plurality of sources legitimating public power at any level it needs, to serve the people – of the state (all residents regardless of nationality) and internationally (Union citizens). Sovereignty becomes divided between state and supranational entities:

> It may seem paradoxical that the key expression of state sovereignty is the ability to dispose of one's sovereignty (or part of it), or to temporarily or even permanently cede certain competences. (CzCC 2009, para 104)

The consequence of this is the emergence of a concept of 'pooling' sovereignty between the Member States and the European Union. On this basis, the Court rejected suspicions about the decline of sovereign statehood.[3] The notion of 'pooled' sovereignty prevents the understanding of the state as the only legitimate, formative source of people's identity (even though the Court did not elaborate on this notion). It is composed of national (incl. infranational) as well as supranational elements (Zemánek 2011, 45).

However, in the judgment on *Slovak pensions XVII* the CzCC largely dropped the above mentioned self-restrained approach, appreciated by reviewers (Albi 2007; Ley 2010; Wendel 2011), as well as foreseeability of its decision-taking as the pre-condition of legal certainty. Instead of starting a multi-level dialogue on the scope of application of the respective Union Regulations, the Court inflicted an escalation of its controversy with the SAC, in detriment of the concerned person.

[3] Decision Lisbon I (Pl. ÚS 18/09) para 108: "The transfer of certain state powers that arises from the free will of the sovereign and will continue to be exercised with sovereign's participation in a manner that is agreed on in advance and that is reviewable, is not a conceptual weakening of the sovereignty of a state, but, on the contrary, can lead to strenghtening it within the joint actions of an integrated whole."Para 209: "In a modern, democracy-based state, state sovereignty is not an aim in and of itself, in isolation, but a means of fulfilling (…) fundamental values, on which the construction of a constitutional, law-based state stands."

8.2 The ECJ's Reasoning in the *Landtová* Case

Under the international arrangement agreed between both successor states at the time of dissolution of the former Czechoslovakia,[4] the criterion for determining the pension system relevant for the calculation of future pension claims was the last employer's place of residence during the time of federation. The Czech pensioners, having worked before the end of 1992 for an employer residing in the Slovak part of the former federation, were paid out of the Slovak social security scheme and vice versa, regardless of their factual place of work. However, Slovak pensions – due to a divergent economic development in the successor states – became noticeably lower than the Czech pensions. Czech pensioners in the above mentioned position were dissatisfied, since an incidental fact – the seat of their former federal employer – damaged their social status, as compared with other Czech citizens, whose employers had had residence in Czech territory. They brought actions, first, to administrative courts against the decisions of the Czech Social Security Administration (CzSSA), and later to the CzCC, against the violation of their fundamental right of equal treatment[5] and their right to adequate material security in old age.[6]

The CzCC found these consequences to be unjust, and after interpreting Art. 20 of the Cz-Sk Treaty, with respect to the principle of equality of citizens, deduced that the State had a duty to pay Czech pensioners the so called compensation allowance, in the amount corresponding to the amount that the person in question would have been eligible for, had all periods of work performed in the former Czechoslovak federation, been considered under Czech law and within the Czech pension system. As the Court argued, otherwise 'unjust discrimination' of a group of Czech citizens would occur.

But, the practice of applying this interpretation on an ad-hoc basis by the CzSSA was neither consequent, nor transparent, and this has not changed even after the accession of the Czech Republic to the European Union on 1 May 2004. The SAC refused to accept this practice as discriminatory under Union law, insofar as the compensation allowance was paid only to Czech citizens residing in the Czech Republic and not to other Union citizens in the same factual situation. The SAC submitted questions to the ECJ for prelimi-

---

[4] The Treaty between the Czech Republic and Slovak Republic on Social Security of 29 October 1992, Art. 20 (Cz-Sk Treaty).

[5] Art. 3 para 1 Charter of Fundamental Rights and Basic Freedoms, Act no. 2/1993 Coll. (Charter).

[6] Art. 30 para 1 Charter.

nary ruling concerning the compatibility of this interpretation with the Regulation (Article 3 para 1) with basic principles of Union law (Article 12 TEC). The Czech government expressly stated that the CzCC's interpretation of the Cz-Sk Treaty infringes Union law.[7] Although the Court was not a party to the proceeding on the preliminary question before the ECJ, it provided the ECJ with supplementary information and arguments, pointing out that the position of the government violates the Constitution, under which the enforceable decisions of the Court are binding for all bodies (Article 89 para 2). However, this statement was rejected since "(…) members of the ECJ do not correspond with third persons". The Court felt frustrated as a would-be amicus curiae…(CzCC 2012, 13).

According to the ECJ in the case of *Landtová*, the case law of the CzCC on Slovak pensions is in fact not compatible with the prohibition of (direct as well as indirect) discrimination on the grounds of citizenship. However, it may be accepted as long as the rules on payment of the compensation allowance apply not only to Czech citizens, but also to migrating citizens of other EU Member States, who worked in former Czechoslovakia before 1993 and were subject to pension insurance legislation of one or more Member States. The Cz-Sk Treaty, attached since the accession of the Czech and Slovak republics to the Union Regulation, may provide differently coordinated pension scheme from the Regulation's one. But, as the Cz-Sk Treaty has been listed in section A of its Annex III (and not in section B), the benefits that differ from the Regulation scheme may be granted only on a non-discriminatory basis.[8] The ECJ left the decision, compatible with both – the Czech Constitution as well as with Union law, to the Czech authorities: the payment of the allowance could be either extended for all aforementioned persons regardless of their nationality or taken off from those who were eligible under the interpretation by the CzCC up to now.

8.3 The Unprecedented Answer of the Czech Constitutional Court

The immediate reaction of the Czech authorities to the ECJ judgment was motivated by the threat of a flood of Slovak pensioners moving to the Czech Republic with the aim of claiming the compensation allowance. Czech

---

[7] Opinion of A.G. Cruz Villalón in C-399/09, paras 34, 42.

[8] *Landtová* (note 1), paras 31–40; only the international treaties listed in section B of the Annex III may stipulate granting of benefits on a limited group(s) of pensioners.

media largely publicised the information that the costs of such 'pensioners tourism' could burden the social security system with tens of billion Czech crowns. In response to this judgment, the Czech Parliament amended the Act on Pension Insurance and banned any allowances or compensations for periods of pension insurance obtained before 1993, that are considered periods of Slovak pension insurance[9] by the Cz-Sk Treaty. The SAC, at the first occasion, refused the claim on compensation allowance, since – as had just been proven – the CzCC, through its 'broad minded' interpretation of the Cz-Sk Treaty, violated not only Union law, but also – through non-submission of preliminary question to the ECJ – the constitutional right to lawful judgement under Art. 38 Charter. The SAC requested the CzCC to abandon the 'policy of two faces': the Court, if it wants to abide by its case law, should openly declare the ECJ's judgment in *Landtová* case as an unacceptable breach of 'the material core' of the Constitution.[10]

The case of *Slovenské důchody XVII* did not require the CzCC to reflect on the ECJ's critical assessment of its case law', since the petitioner was a Czech citizen, not a Union one (Komárek 2008; Zbirál 2012; Král 2012; Zemánek 2012). On the other hand, the CzCC could have used this occassion to strengthen its position vis-a-vis the general courts (SAC), if it would have demonstrated respect for the binding opinion of the ECJ and accepted the broad, 'European' concept of equal treatment, which was going *praeter constitutionem*, not *contra constitutionem*.

Instead, the Court founded its judicial reasoning concerning the scope of application of 'the right to adequate material security in old age' (Charta, Art. 30 para 1) on unilateral, constitutional grounds, and not on the Union law-based test of equality: (Charta, Art. 3 para 1)

> (…) only citizens of the Czech Republic, and not other persons, can be a differential group when testing for potential differing treatment (…) The tenor of the Constitutional Court's case law (…) is respecting the constitutional principle of equality, i.e. ruling out unjustified inequality, in this case between citizens of the Czech Republic (…) It described as constitutionally impermissible, the discrimination of one versus other groups of citizens of the Czech Republic: an inequality established 'only as a result of a particular circumstance that originates in the dissolution of the then-existing Czechoslovak federation.' (CzCC 2012, 11).

The consequence of this reasoning was directed towards the applicability of the Regulation. The Court found the Cz-Sk Treaty as lex specialis, appli-

[9] Act no. 428/2011 Coll., on the amendment of the act no. 155/1995 Coll.

[10] Decision of 25 August 2011, no. 3 Ads 130/2008-204.

cable with priority over the Regulation[11] and refused to retroactively consider a period of employment, during the former Czechoslovakia in the present-day Slovak Republic, to be a period of employment abroad, in a foreign state. Therefore, entitlements arising from it in this context "do not contain a foreign element, which is a precondition for applying the Regulation". The Court followed:

> Failure to distinguish the legal relationships arising from the dissolution of a state, with a uniform social security system, from the legal relationships arising for social security from the free movement of persons in the European Communities, or the European Union, is a failure to respect European history. It is comparing things that are not comparable (...) based on the principles [stated in *Lisbon I*] we cannot do otherwise than state that (...) in that case [*Landtová*] there were excesses on the part of a European Union body, that a situation occurred in which an act by a European body exceeded the powers that the Czech Republic transferred to the European Union under Art. 10a of the Constitution; this judgment exceeded the scope of the transferred powers, and was *ultra vires* (CzCC 2012, 12).

The CzCC concluded that the case in question was a matter of

> (...) constitutional identity of the Czech Republic, which it draws from the common constitutional tradition with the Slovak Republic, that is from over 70 years of common statehood and the peaceful dissolution thereof, i.e. from a completely idiosyncratic and historically created situation (CzCC 2012, 13).

8.4 Critical Assessment of the CzCC Ruling

One dissenting opinion occurred, arguing, that Article 20 Cz-Sk Treaty (annexed to the Regulation) has been transformed, since the accession of the Czech Republic to the EU, to be a part of Union law, no longer a mere provision of an international treaty.[12] Therefore, its interpretation by the ECJ must also respect the principle of Union law and cannot be regarded as an act *ultra vires*. The specific treatment stipulated by this provision is to be observed in the interpretation and application by the national administrative and judicial authorities, subject to the principles of Union law.

---

[11] In the opinion of the Court, listing of the Cz-Sk Treaty in Annex of the Regulation had only a declaratory, not a constitutive importance.

[12] As a treaty agreed before the accession to the EU between two of its Member States without any special regime in the Treaty of Accession, no exception to the principle of primacy of Union law may be claimed.

The dissenting opinion also referred to a constitutional law argument: the fundamental right to adequate material security in old age (Article 30 Charter) may be enforced only subject to statutory (under-constitutional) provisions that can not guarantee an exactly equal level of pension benefits to all, but must also reflect the economic developments in the respective successor state. The economic developments can take in the future the opposite direction as it was the case until recently. In such a case, Czech citizens, who did not work, during the time of the Czechoslovak federation, for an employer residing in the territory of the present-day Slovak Republic, would become disadvantaged compared to those Czech citizens, who did so and were – thanks to the interpretation of the Article 20 Cz-Sk Treaty by the CzCC – beneficiaries of the compensation allowance. The dissenting opinion disagreed also with the quasi-legislative role of the Court in this matter.

The dissenting opinion is to be taken seriously. No provision of law applicable in a Member State, having a concern (a direct link) with situations governed by Union law, is immunised from judicial review of the background of the principles of Union law. What was at stake in the case of *Slovak pensions XVII*, was the rule based on the judge-made law of the CzCC. If the Court required, that the rule on compensation allowance for Czech citizens was to be followed and could not be questioned by the general courts, the Court's sole responsibility for safeguarding compatibility of this rule with Union law had to move the Court to the submission of a preliminary question to the ECJ under Article 267 TFEU. The ECJ already stated earlier that the Regulation can not govern the pure internal situation without any cross-border element (ECJ 2008, C-212/06).

However, in my opinion, it was not *a priori* clear, whether this is also the case regarding citizens of neighbouring countries (mostly Poles, former GDR-citizens and Hungarians), who had been working during the Czechoslovak federation for an employer residing in the territory of the present-day Slovakia and obtained the status of pensioners in the Czech Republic after its accession in the European Union. The application of the Regulation on their current social status is not the matter of a 'real' retroactivity of law, which is assumed to be contrary to the principle of legitimate expectations and thus *per se* prohibited (with some exceptions), because the Regulation does not govern the initial legal situation of the case (periods of social security insurance before the end of 1992). It governs only the lasting consequences of this initial legal situation (the claim of cross-border recognition of vested rights) within the (new) context of the EU-membership and the obligation to observe Union law; this effect is in law generally not prohibited (with some exceptions). In this respect, the internal situation has been – since the accession – externalized. The application of the Regulation by the ECJ in *Landtová* case cannot be assessed as an act *ultra vires*.

The constitutional law aspect does not justify the behaviour of the CzCC either. The fundamental right of Czech citizens to 'adequate material security in old age', can be attributed to the inviolable 'material core' of the constitutional order. The extension of claiming this welfare standard on some other persons (non-Czech citizens, who worked during the time of the Czechoslovak federation for an employer residing in present-day Slovakia), required by the ECJ, would not result in a violation of the respective constitutional provision (Art. 30 Charter), since the ECJ expressly left the final solution up to the Czech authorities. (On the other hand, the prohibition of any compensations and allowances by the Czech legislature in its immediate reaction on the *Landtová* case[13] was declared by the Court in *obiter dictum* of *Slovak pensions XVII* as making "no sense in and of itself", since "if the reason for the law ceases to exist [the Court declared the ECJ's decision *ultra vires*, i.e. inapplicable in the Czech Republic], the law itself ceases to exist". (CzCC 2012, 16)) The Euro-conform interpretation of the Charter is possible, and not *contra constitutionem*, when the personal scope of application of the Charter's provisions on 'citizens' is – in 'pure internal situations' – limited on 'Czech citizens' (Art. 42 Charter). The 'irradiation' of the principles of Union law into the national legal order (CzCC 2006a, b) requires a broader understanding of the provision in question, i.e. 'Czech citizens and other persons entitled under Union law are to enjoy equal material legal status'. The same is obviously true with some other constitutional rights, such as the right to vote in municipal elections,[14] etc.

8.5 Conclusions

There was neither a constitutional law-based, nor any other justification for the CzCC's rebellion. What can explain its behaviour, indeed? How can the controversy between the CzCC and the ECJ be settled?

First of all, the multi-level judicial dialog of law interpreters[15] did not function adequately. The ECJ in *Landtová* case was not clear enough in its delimitation of persons disadvantaged by the CzCC's practice, being excluded from compensation allowance (CzCC 2012, paras 42–43) by its

[13] See comments above, note 9.

[14] Art. 21 Charter in conjunction with Art. 22 para 1 TFEU.

[15] This notion is well described by Pernice (Pernice 2011).

case law. The Court was, therefore, afraid of a potential influx of Slovak citizens migrating, as pensioners, into the Czech Republic, after the ECJ's ruling, and asking for equal treatment with Czech citizens under the Regulation, applied so far in 'purely internal' situations. If the ECJ would have expressly excluded this group from its ruling, the CzCC should not had to have a reason for rejection the ECJ's ruling. However, the Court was not aware of its duty to remove this uncertainty, forming an obstacle for decision in the case *Slovak pensions XVII*, by submitting a preliminary question to the ECJ. Instead, it decided this question on an autonomous basis, not admitting the limitation of sovereignty of the Czech Republic by European integration.

Second, the rhetoric of both courts was not appropriate to the existing situation and provoked exorbitant reactions. The CzCC, frightened by an envisaged abuse of its generosity, articulated the grant of allowances expressly towards Czech citizens, without being asked to extend this practice to Union (non-Slovak) citizens, who did not complain in this respect. The ECJ did not notice, that the CzCC, when mentioning (only) Czech citizens as beneficiaries, did not exclude other Union citizens as (at least potential) petitioners. The controversy seems to result from a case of mutual misunderstanding.

Third, Czech authorities – CzSSA, the general courts – should have to continue granting compensation allowances to Czech citizens, or they will infringe the binding case law of the CzCC. They should have to extend this practice on Union (non-Slovak) citizens, who had worked during the Czechoslovak federation for an employer residing in Slovakia, since any other approach would infringe Union law (Article 3 para 1 Regulation). It is to be reminded, that the Court excluded the application of the Regulation only on 'pure internal' situations (i.e. on Slovak citizens migrating on a later date in the Czech Republic), not on situations involving other Union citizens. The Czech legislature should annul the amendment to the Act on Pension Insurance and remove the ban imposed on compensation allowances,[16] which the Court in *Slovak pensions XVII* found unconstitutional.

Fourth, the CzCC should have to reconsider its rigid position on implicit changes of the constitutional order by the Euro-conform interpretation, if the autonomous application of its provisions (like Article 30 and 42 Charter in the case in question), disregards principles of Union law, obstructs *l'effet utile* of the latter, and if such interpretation is not *contra constitutionem*

[16] See note 9.

(does not empty the substance of the legal norm). This restoration of routine behaviour would be the most important, positive contribution of the controversy to the Czech doctrine of European law.

Fifth, since the controversy was to be attributed to a lack of the due judicial dialogue, rather than to intolerant and irreconcilable approaches, a peaceful settlement could be expected. On 9 May 2012, the SAC submitted three new preliminary questions to the ECJ. One of these was, whether Union law restrained the SAC from the adoption of the legal view of the CzCC, which – as it seemed – was not in compliance with the Union law?[17] The more precise opinion of the ECJ, concerning the range of persons eligible for the compensation allowance might help the Court to bring the rhetoric of its case law in harmony with Union law, waive its resistance towards the ECJ ruling instead of arguing by national identity and – last but not least – put an end to the hostility between the top Czech judicial authorities.

Later, however, the claim brought by the complainant was satisfied by a social security authority and the Supreme Administrative Court withdrew its questions referred for the preliminary ruling and discontinued the proceedings without entering a judgment. Finally, the Czech Parliament repealed its legislative ban on the provision of compensatory allowance, and, on the contrary, made the provision thereof possible to anyone in need, i.e. also to persons previously 'disadvantaged', regardless of their nationality Act no. 428/2011 Coll. amending Act no. 155/1995 Coll., on Social security). A bitterness from a failed multilevel judicial dialog should have to be overridden at the next occasion.

References

Albi, Anneli. 2007. Supremacy of EC law in the new member states: Bringing parliaments into the equation of 'co-operative constitutionalism'. *EuConst* 3(1): 25–67.

CJEU. 2011. Landtová v. Czech social security administration, C-399/09, 22 June 2011 (Not yet reported).

CzCC. 2006a. Sugar quote regulation, Pl. ÚS 50/04, 8 March 2006.

CzCC. 2006b. European arrest warrant, Pl ÚS 66/04, 3 May 2006.

CzCC. 2008. Lisbon I, Pl. ÚS 18/09, 26 November 2008.

CzCC. 2009. Lisbon II, Pl. ÚS 29/09, 3 November 2009.

[17] Order 6 Ads 18/2012-82 = C-253/12 *JS v. Czech Social Security Administration*, OJ C 273, 8. 9. 2012, 2.

CzCC. 2012. Slovak pensions XVII. Pl. ÚS 5/12, 31 January 2012. See http://nalus.usoud.cz/Search/GetText.aspx?sz=Pl-5-12_1. English translation see: http://www.usoud.cz/en/decisions/20120131-pl-us-512-slovak-pensions/.
Act no. 155/1995 Coll. on Social security
Act no. 428/2011 Coll. amending Act on Social security
ECJ. 2008. Government of Communauté française and Gouvernement wallon v Gouvernement flamand, C-212/06, 1 April 2008.
FCC. 2009. 2 BvE 2/08, 30 June 2009.
FCC. 2010. 2 BvR 2661/06, 6 July 2010.
Komárek, Jan. 2008. Czech constitutional court playing with matches: The Czech constitutional court declares the judgment of the court of justice of the EU *Ultra Vires*; Judgment of 31 January 2012, Pl. ÚS 5/12, *Slovak Pension XVII*, *EuConst* 8(2): 323–337.
Král, Richard. 2012. Otazníky nad posledním nálezem Ústavního soudu ČR, týkajícím se tzv. Slovenských důchodů. *Jurisprudence* 4: 28–33.
Ley, Isabelle. 2010. Brünn betreibt die Parlamentarisierung des Primärrechts. Anmerkung zum zweiten Urteil des tschechischen Verfassungsgerichtshofs zum Vertrag von Lissabon vom 3.11.2009, *JZ*, 4/2010, 165–173.
Pernice, Ingolf. 2011. Die Zukunft der Unionsgerichtsbarkeit. Zu den Bedingungen einer nachhaltigen Sicherung effektiven Rechtsschutzes im Europäischen Verfassungsverbund. *EuR* 2: 151–169.
Thym, Daniel. 2009. In the name of sovereign statehood: A critical introduction to the Lisbon judgment of the German constitutional court. *CMLRev* 46: 1795–1822.
Treaty between the Czech Republic and Slovak Republic on Social Security of 29 October 1992, (Cz-Sk Treaty).
Treaty on the Function of the European Union (TEFU).
Wendel, Matthias. 2011. Lisbon before the courts: Comparative perspectives. *EuConst* 1: 96–137.
Zbirál, Robert. 2012. A legal revolution or negligible episode? Court of justice decision proclaimed *ultra vires*, Czech constitutional court, Pl. ÚS 5/12, 31 January 2012. *CMLRev* 49: 1475–1492.
Zemánek, Jiří. 2007. The emerging Czech constitutional doctrine of European law. *EuConst* 3(3): 418–435.
Zemánek, Jiří. 2011. The two Lisbon judgments of the Czech constoitutional court. In *Europe's constitutional challenges in the light of the recent case law of national constitutional courts*, ed. J.M. Beneyto/I Pernice, 45–64. Baden-Baden: Nomos.
Zemánek, Jiří. 2012. L'arret de la Cour constitutionelle de la République tcheque du 31 janvier 2012 *Les retraites slovaques*: le principe de l'égalité de traitement – un motif de rebellion contre la Cour de justice de l'Union européenne?, *CDE* 9: 709–732.
Zwingmann, Beke. 2012. The continuing myth of Euro-scepticism? The German federal constitutional court two years after Lisbon. *ICLQ* 61(3): 665–695.

Jiří Zemánek JUDr. Ing, CSc., Judge at the Constitutional Court of the Czech Republic; Jean Monnet Chair of European Law at the Law Faculty of Charles University, Prague; former Vice-Dean for External Relations, Managing Director of teaching programs „Czech Legal System in European Context" (Erasmus) and „Introduction to German Law"; former member of the Council for legislation of the Czech Government; member of the academic forum „European Constitutional Law Network" and of the Board of Advisors of European Constitutional Law Review; former president of the Czech Branch of ILA and Czech-ECSA.

Chapter 9
The Infra-Constitutionality of European Law in Romania and the Challenges of the Romanian Constitutional Culture

Manuel Guțan

Abstract This article deals with European Law as a legal transplant facing the Romanian constitutional culture, in the context of constitutionally limiting the Romanian State's sovereignty as a member of the EU. Consequently, the reception of the EU law into the Romanian constitutional system (and culture) is determined by two paradoxically divergent Romanian legal-cultural traits: on the one hand, the necessity (bearing accents of national legal pride) to cherish and fructify the Romanian legal (constitutional) traditions, reified, as I shall denominate, as 'the adapted Romanian law', and stipulated in the 2003 amended Constitution as a 'tradition firewall' / écran de traditionalité. On the other hand, I shall consider the Eurocentric, non-identity-centred and uncritical dimension of the Romanian legal culture. In this context, the reaction of the Romanian Constitutional Court (RCC) can be better understood when it faced the burden of analysing the constitutionality of the 2003 Constitutional project stipulating the limitation of the Romanian state's sovereignty after joining the EU. By analysing the RCC's 2003 decision, this paper highlights the conflict between the two above mentioned legal-cultural traits. RCC acknowledged that EU Law is supra-legal but infra-constitutional. Regarding this, some would deduce that the RCC has assumed what we could name 'the Solange spirit' (i.e. the identity-centred attitude of the German Constitutional Court when coped with the limits of the Community Law back in 1970s) and applied the desired 'tradition firewall'. Instead, someone would be disappointed to find out that the RCC, completely ignoring the Romanian constitutional (democratic) traditions, has accepted the EU Law infra-constitutionality by importing it as a

M. Guțan (✉)
Faculty of Law, Lucian Blaga University of Sibiu,
Calea Dumbrăvii 34, 550324 Sibiu, Romania
e-mail: manuel.gutan@ulbsibiu.ro

R. Arnold (ed.), *Limitations of National Sovereignty through European Integration*, Ius Gentium: Comparative Perspectives on Law and Justice 51,
DOI 10.1007/978-94-017-7471-0_9

positivistic constitutional practice of the European Constitutional Courts, with no preoccupation for the cultural contexts in which those Constitutional Courts dealt with the problem of the primacy of the EU law. All these are conclusive for Romanian constitutional culture, where the identity-centred discourse is only rhetorically manifested, in contrast with the importing mentality which is deepening the weaknesses of Romanian contemporary constitutionalism. This could be a serious problem for Romania's participation in building a European constitutional culture, primarily architectured as a dialog between the national Constitutional Courts and the European Court of Justice.

Abbreviations

EU	European Union
ECJ	European Court of Justice
M. Of.	Monitorul Oficial
RC	Romanian Constitution
RCC	Romanian Constitutional Court

9.1 Introduction

Joining the EU on January 1st, 2007 represented a real *acquis national* for Romania and the Romanian people. This meant entering a political integration process underpinned by a perpetual dynamic and dominated by a strong desire to bring closer the European peoples. This project is inevitably fostered by juridical instruments which are building and legitimising the European political unity through juridical convergence. Having a normative expression, i.e. a *sui generis* juridical order named European Law, the European juridical convergence is a special process which includes peculiar mechanisms of elaborating and applying European Law. At the same time, this process raises delicate problems related not only to the formal juridical interaction between different European national legal systems or between European Law and national legal systems, but also related to the inevitable encounter between European legal cultures.

This final aspect is more evident for someone who would evaluate the meeting between the European Law and national legal systems in terms of legal transplant. Approached from this perspective, the European juridical architecture can clearly reveal its advantages and shortcomings. On the one hand, the European legal transplant seems to be an efficient mechanism to achieve a European legal convergence. On the other hand, by leaving aside the usually addressed problem of the direct application and priority of European Law in the national legal systems of the members states, the legal transplant perspective questions delicate problems regarding the causes and necessity of the European legal transplant, its actors and mechanisms and, last but not least, the chances of successfully transplanting the European Law into the national legal systems. The latter aspect is essential for political and juridical European convergence, as long as its accomplishment depends on the successful adaptation of the European Law to the peculiarities of the national legal systems. But, in order to grasp a full dimension of these peculiarities, they should be understood not only as formal-juridical normativity but also as legal culture or legal tradition. This perspective makes the European legal transplant more than a simple process of formally integrating the European Law into national legal systems: it is a cultural challenge for the receiving legal systems. It is a matter of preserving one's own legal-cultural identity.

By approaching the European legal transplant as a legal-cultural identity's challenger I am turning away from both the idea of European legal transplant as a mechanism of mixing European legal systems and cultures and the idea of European Law as a legal mix. Exploring the legal mixité at the European level is scientifically rewarding but insufficient as regards specific layers of analyses, *i.e.* constitutional law. More than other legal branches, constitutional law seems to be very sensitive to the mechanisms and effects of the European legal transplant in terms of (constitutional) identity. Consequently, more than ever, the problem of the constitution and constitutionalism is addressed in terms of constitutional culture and constitutional tradition at the EU level. Even if the official treaty of the EU[1] is naturally interested in postulating similarities between the member states' legal systems, by speaking of 'the common constitutional traditions of the member states' (article 6, paragraph 3), it implicitly recognises the existence of the national constitutional traditions. But the existence and preservation of the national constitutional identity was not, as the previous decades demonstrated, the only and supreme concern of the EU. The member states themselves and, in particular, their Constitutional Courts, have eagerly protected the national constitutional identity against the EU and European Law. From afar, the problem of European legal transplant is more delicate because, at this level, the encounter between the European Law and the national legal system is not only a problem of cultural irritation but also a problem of

[1] Treaty of Lisbon (2007).

political sovereignty. Consequently, the problem of constitutional identity is currently overlapping the problem of political and national identity. While accepting the Brussels' cultural-juridical engineering at different levels of the national legal system, the majority of the member states were reluctant in accepting a radical change of the classical paradigm of the national state and sovereign state.

The cornerstone of this debate was, and still is, the primacy of European Law over the national constitution and constitutional law. According to the Court of Luxembourg's case law, the European Law should have a direct and priority effect even over the constitutions of the member states. The consequent application of this principle would remarkably enhance the length and the force of the European legal transplant. It would bring consistent cultural irritation and would threaten national constitutional and political identities, even if the European legal convergence would be promoted more intensely than ever. Unfortunately (for the EU), this scenario was not accepted by the national Constitutional Courts in the member states. The majority of them accepted, more or less explicitly, only the infra-constitutionality of the European Law, i.e. that it has primacy over the national legal system apart from the constitution. This principle was actually fed by the need of national (constitutional) identity. The hunt of European legal uniformity was confined, on the one hand, by the national legal and constitutional self-consciousness and, on the other hand, by the ongoing survival of the classical state sovereignty. Thus, 'the fight' for national constitutional identity underpinned 'the fight' for political identity and national sovereignty, with the national Constitutional Court as flag bearer. The success depended on the magnitude of the constitutional tradition, the public discourse about it and, generally, the strength of its sustainment by the (national) epistemological community, the degree of the constitutional tradition's self-consciousness, the weakness of the national legal system, *i.e.* the capacity to produce national legal solutions to different social problems, the importing / exporting legal mentality, the legitimacy of the European legal transplant and of the Court of Luxembourg's activism in the eyes of the national political and juridical elites, the opposition to European Law principles and the political position among the member states.

This well-known intellectual context is relevant for understanding how Romania, as an EU member state, faces the massive European legal transplant and, especially, the principle of the primacy of the European Law developed by the Court of Luxembourg. How important is it for Romania to manage the European legal transplant from the constitutional and political identity perspective? How important is for Romania to preserve its constitutional tradition when facing some alleged European imperialism? How much is it in Romania's interests to promote its national sovereignty by stipulating the infra-constitutionality of the European Law? Finally, what chances really get Romania to successfully assume an identity-centred attitude in constitutional matters? In order to fully answer these questions, a short overview of the legal transplant antecedents in modern Romania is necessary (II). A 3rd part will emphasize the particular balance between the importing appetite and the legal tradition in the context of Romanian EU membership. After setting the scene, the reasons and the way the RCC is understood to assume the principle of infra-constitutionality of the European Law will be considered (IV). At the end I'll try to demonstrate that the RCC, by ignoring completely the Romanian constitutional (democratic) traditions, has accepted the EU Law infra-constitutionality by importing it as a positivistic constitutional practice of the European Constitutional Courts, with no preoccupation for the cultural contexts in which those Constitutional Courts dealt with the problem of the primacy of the EU law. All these are conclusive for Romanian constitutional culture, where the identity-centred discourse is only rhetorically manifested, in contrast with the importing mentality which is deepening the weaknesses of the Romanian contemporary constitutionalism. This attitude really undermines the chances the RCC could have to participate in the process of bottom-up architecting a European constitutional culture through judicial dialog between the national Constitutional Courts and the ECJ. Some final suggestions regarding the possible fructification both of the fight for constitutional identity and the traditional Romanian Europhilia in the European context will be envisaged (V).

9.2 The Phenomenology of the Legal Transplant[2] in Romanian Legal Culture

Legal transplant is not a novelty in the Romanian legal history. Setting aside the old customary Romanian law, the making of the Romanian modern and contemporary law has been done by a constant, sometime abusive, appeal to

[2] Despite the fact that the metaphor 'legal transplant' is, due to its ambiguity, intensely disputed and even contested in comparative law studies, I prefer to use it anyway, being perfectly suited to the Romanian context. On the one hand, it suggests an unconditioned and unaltered import of legal institutions and, on the other hand, its medical flavour suggests the idea of an institutional sampling in the 'donating' society and its transplantation in the 'receiving' society, by expecting them to be compatible and hopping the transplanted institution will develop in the importing society the same function it got in the exporting one. All these aspects were specific to the Romanian legal development.

legal transplant. Being rational or irrational, voluntary or involuntary, this legal transplant has marked all the crossroads that Romanian law has passed through since the middle of the nineteenth century until the post-communist period (Gutan 2005, 156ff.).[3] Paradigmatically balancing between (socio-economic and political) necessity and (juridical) weakness, (Gutan 2004, 66–67)[4] the importing process entered the ideological reflexes and reformist activity of the Romanian political and juridical elite, naturally situated in an ongoing fight for legitimisation. An endemic complex of inferiority coupled with the urgency of the socio-legal change developed a blueprint of modernisation where, somehow magically, the imported legal institutions (the foreign forms) were meant to change the Romanian mentalities and habits (the Romanian substance) overnight. Consequently, socio-economic and cultural engineering through legal transplant, (Gutan 2011) justified by the prestige and authority of the exporting legal systems, become a routine approach of modernisation in Romania, especially at the middle of the nineteenth century. Needless to say this was not a project condemned to be fully successful. Beyond the impossibility to programmatically change mentalities in a short time, legal-cultural engineering through legal transplant is incapable to meet all national projects. Evaluated today by some scholars (Teubner 1998, 11) as a possible irritant of the national legal system / national legal culture, legal transplant became, in the pre-war and inter-war periods, a certain irritant of the Romanian need to construct a national identity, implicitly a juridical one.

Being regularly irrationally undertaken,[5] the legal transplant captured, at the end of the nineteenth century, the attention of the Romanian intellectual elite. Ideologically built either around the idea of Romanian legal tradition or around the idea of legal modernization through legal transplant, this elite

[3] For a detailed account of the Romanian legal transplant's causes.

[4] For the Romanian legal weakness.

[5] I understand by 'irrational legal transplant' the one which has been done without correctly and fully considering the necessity of the legal import, the possible solutions that the national legal culture could provide, the quantity and the type of the legal institutions to be imported, the proper legal model to be accessed and, last but not least, the possible effects on the importing society and its culture. It is important to remember I'm not casting a purely negative connotation on the idea of irrational legal transplant as opposed to a necessary positive rational legal transplant. Both are normal and explainable endeavours in specific socio-economic conditions, with possibly negative and positive consequences. This does not restrain me to manifest a theoretical preference for the rational legal transplant, at least for its interest to consider the compatibility between the imported law and the importing society.

developed a critical analysis of the (legal) modernisation process in the Romanian society named, over the years, the dispute of 'the forms without substance' (Gutan 2010, 53–68). It shaped, for more than a half century, the juridical epistemological perspectives in modern Romania. On one hand the debate implied a vain acknowledgement and sustainment of the Romanian legal tradition, as a normal conservative reaction to the existence of an alternative way of legal change, *i.e.* the legal transplant, which endangered, in their eyes, the national state project of the Romanians. For them, building of a Romanian political, legal and social identity was an act of self-reflection and self-understanding. On the other hand, a relevant part of the Romanian legal-political elite became, in terms of H.P. Glenn, a part of the epistemological community which was sustaining the Western, especially French and Belgian, legal tradition(s). For them, building a Romanian socio-political and legal identity meant self-deconstruction and openness to total change. As long as legal tradition means legal identity, (Glenn 2004, 33–34) to massively assume a new legal tradition would mean a change of legal identity. This is why, because the French and Belgian legal systems have been massively imported in the middle of the nineteenth century, for many Romanian lawyers and scholars to be Romanian meant to be French or Belgian.

Consequently, the Romanian legal-political elite had been epistemologically divided. There had been two interpretive legal communities, each one sustaining two different legal traditions: the Romanian one and the French-Belgian one, each of them offering a different blueprint of legal and political identity. Despite the fact that the strong support for the Romanian legal tradition lost its magnitude over decades, (Carp 2003, 199 ff.) it still survived but it changed its intellectual expression. In the period between the world wars, it finally accepted the necessity of the legal transplant in the nineteenth century, but it assumed the supreme mission was to obsessively demonstrate the original way the Romanian culture (the substance) adapted the imported legal institutions (the forms) to the Romanian society's needs. The quest for legal identity focused less on the necessity and causes of the legal transplant and more on the critical analysis of the legal transplant's effects on the Romanian society and legal culture. The 'original' adaptation of the imported 'forms' to the Romanian 'substance' became a central intellectual element of the Romanian intellectuality and a central benchmark of the communist period legal scholarship. Unfortunately, they missed the problem of success and the failure of the adaptation process and disregarded the fact that adaptation / transposition is a normal central aspect of a successful legal transplant (Örücü 2002, 206–207).

This perspective is important because it has had enough persuasive and creative force to be the proper foundation of a new Romanian legal tradition where the two old interpretive communities finally met. As a consequence, the Romanian modern law was neither understood as old customary law nor as law formally transplanted from the Western Europe. The Romanian modern law was 'the adapted law'. This succeeded to gather together the necessary interpretive community to sustain and perpetuate the new legal tradition. This tradition is referring to all Romanian legal scholarship after 1989, the post-communist Romanian Constitution of 1991 (revised in 2003) and the decisions of the RCC.

The Romanian epistemological community, which identified itself with the French-Belgian tradition, was not very difficult to integrate into 'the tradition of the adapted law'. This reality is explained by this community's impossibility to fully assume the French-Belgian legal tradition(s). Understanding tradition, in terms of H. P. Glenn, as information captured, transmitted and sustained through spoken and written words, it seems easy to speak about adhering to a different legal tradition. But by using, instead of legal tradition, the concept of legal culture, things are changing, even more so if we're accepting a wide meaning of it, i.e. ideas, ideals, attitudes, patters of thinking / mentalities, methodologies, habits, practices (Bell 2009, 247 ff.). If it seems relatively easy to assume and disseminate ideas and ideals, it looks like a real challenge to change patterns of thinking / mentalities, and seems even harder to determine specific practices. Unfortunately, in the case of the Romanian legal-political elite who adhered to the French-Belgian legal tradition, we could notice only the interest in an epistemological identity, especially for a particular discourse about law and not an interest in assuming the ideas with their practical consequences. For a full identification with the French-Belgian legal tradition, the Romanian legal-political elite should have assumed both the information and the typical French-Belgian legal praxis. But this was impossible. The Romanian elite accepted the epistemological dimension of the French-Belgian tradition (as long as this was possible) but fructified it by using the ways of the Romanian (legal) mentality and praxis. This inevitably resulted in 'the adapted Romanian law'.

The above discussed aspects reveal a Romanian legal culture dominated by a considerable appetite for legal transplant, by its indebtedness to the prestige and authority of the Western (legal) traditions, by a decreasing interest for the organic legal tradition and, paradoxically, by a stringent need to postulate a legal identity, even if this one would be detected in the above mentioned 'tradition of the adapted law'.

9.3 The European Law and the Challenges of the Legal Transplant in Contemporary Romania

Undoubtedly, European Law represents the most considerable legal transplant that Romanian law knew since the birth of the Romanian modern state. Unfortunately, it is an irrational legal transplant. Consequently, a debate about the legal imperialism practiced by Brussels would be reasonable, as long as Romania had to accept an 'imposed reception' based on 'take it or leave it' alternatives (Burrows 1996, 311) of the European *acquis*, before the formal accession. The imposed character of the European Law's reception doesn't flow only from the impossibility of the Romanian legal-political elites to fully negotiate the quantity and the type of the European legal norms to be imported, but also from the fact that the European legal model did not necessarily impose itself as compulsory to be followed due to its prestige and authority. This happened because choosing the EU as a model after the fall of communism was rather an economic and political option than a juridical one. Transplanting European Law was not a rational decision made after carefully comparing the legal solutions existing on the international legal market and it didn't envisage, as expected, (Ajani 1995, 115–116) an improvement of the national legal system by discovering better legal solutions abroad. In this case, legal transplant was the subsequent and undesired outcome of a credible and legitimate post-communist Romanian project based on political chance and economic prestige, with clear economic and political finalities and not juridical ones.

In the past, Romanian legal-political elite made irrational legal transplants, determined by the authority of prestigious legal models, but they were envisaged as efficient instruments of social engineering. The Romanian elite was entitled to establish the legal transplant's socio-economic and political goals, as well as its necessary juridical instruments. Even if these instruments have not always been correctly chosen and sometimes malfunctioned, they were at least the result of the Romanian choice. The legal transplant was irrational, although had an aim and was voluntary. When it decided to join the EU, the Romanian legal-political elite detected the political-economic goal and chose the European political-economic model, but was restrained in choosing the legal instruments. As a consequence, the legal transplant from the European Law was not only irrational but also unconscious and involuntary. Irrational because it was not the outcome of a rational balance between the quality of the national legal solutions and the foreign one or between the quality of different foreign legal solutions; unconscious because has been no real evaluation of the legal transplant's impact on the Romanian society and its culture; involuntary because the limits of the legal transplant were not negotiated but imposed. Accordingly, the legal-political Romanian elite was condemned to operate socio-cultural engineering with (juridical) instruments it didn't choose, it didn't know and which it didn't manage. The economic welfare and European peace have been sold free of charge to Romania as a perfectly functional device, under single condition to purchase the necessary accessories but without the functioning manual. Or, to amplify the medical metaphor, we could visualize Romania as an outpatient suffering from brain cancer, which she must operate on herself, but using the procedures and instruments imposed and controlled by another.

In this context, a pretty serious threat for the chances of European Law to be successfully adapted in Romania is the way the Romanian legal-political elite managed the legal transplant in the post-communist period. The appetite for legal transplant seems to be high but not fully unconditional, like in the nineteenth century. Using legal transplant for improving the legislation is a deep mark of the Romanian legal culture but, after 1989, the problem seems to have new coordinates. Unlike the pre-communist period, the post-communist one accepts, in some legal branches at least, legal transplant only as a secondary instrument of legal change. Thus, the need to reintegrate in the West-European interpretive community determined the Romanian elite's use of the constitutional transplant. This happened in the process of making the 1991 Constitution, by more or less rationally using comparative law (Iorgovan 1998) and constantly utilising the Romanian social and political context as a benchmark. The appetite for rational constitutional transplant was not diminished by the inevitable practice of the experimental 'constitutional gardening' (Ludwikowski 2000–2001, 9) and manifested despite the outside perceptions which condemned, for example, the irrationality of preserving institutions like the bicameral parliament (Ludwikowski 2000–2001, 10).

The explanation for the reserved attitude toward constitutional transplant flows from the Romanian elite's need to legitimate itself by appealing to the past's authority, *i.e.* to the Romanian legal tradition. Appealing to this authority is normal in the work of the ruling elite which wants its laws to be observed and to manifest efficacy (Wise 1990, 4). In this case, the need for authority didn't necessarily lead the Romanian ruling elite towards legal transplant, as predicted some scholars, (Watson 1993, 21ff.) but toward domestic legal tradition. The option for the Romanian pre-communist legal tradition, culturally marked by the 'adapted law tradition', was meant both to assume a national legal identity, after 40 years of USSR legal imperialism, and to promote, by valuing continuity, the image of a national juridical strength. This kind of attitude inevitably led to a process of reification of the pre-communist parliamentary democracy and determined the resurrection of the vain discourse about the Romanian adapted law's originality.

Such a cultural-juridical recalibration of the leading Romanian elites remarkably affected the making of a new post-communist constitutional architecture. The 1991 Constitution was the outcome of a premeditated balance between the Romanian society's needs, the possible workable solutions offered by the Romanian constitutional tradition and the analyses of the alternative solutions existing abroad. Paradoxically, despite the fact that the legal transplant was rationally fructified, the final constitutional solution proposed by the Constitution's founding fathers were not always rational. The element of irrationality came this time from the way the Romanian constitutional tradition has been promoted by the Constituent Assembly. Usually, the evaluation of different solutions that the Romanian constitutional tradition should provide was fully equilibrate, by taking into consideration the post-communist reality and socio-political aims of the moment. The fathers of the Constitution had no reserve to give up constitutional tradition when necessary. Notwithstanding, the reification of the pre-communist parliamentary democracy determined the Constituent Assembly to use prestige as a strong argument. Consequently, some parts of the Romanian constitutional tradition had to be recovered even if there were serious comparative law arguments against it.

As a result, regardless if it was recovered for its prestige or for rational reasons, the Romanian constitutional tradition became a central filter of the post-communist constitutional reform. Constitutional values and institutions have been, when necessary, passed through this constitutional identity-centred filter, thus conferring strength to the Romanian legal system and a Romanian constitutional identity to the constitutional reform. This specific legal-cultural treat has been officially stipulated in the revised Constitution of 2003, proving that the appetite for constitutional tradition was not a passing personality crisis of the Romanian legal / constitutional culture. Now, Article 1, paragraph 3 stipulates:

> 'Romania is a democratic and social state, governed by the rule of law, in which human dignity, the citizens' rights and freedoms, the free development of human personality, justice and political pluralism represent supreme values, *in the spirit of the democratic traditions of the Romanian people* (my emphasis) and the ideals of the Revolution of December 1989..'.

As a consequence, the constitutional tradition filter received a constitutional status, as the Romanian constitutional doctrine is crystal clear that this provision

> (...) creates the obligation to interpret all constitutional provisions from the Romanian democratic traditions' perspective, regardless the force of the past normative act in the normative hierarchy and regardless, sometime, the normative character of the act which shape these traditions (Dănişor et al. 2008, 481–482).

For many it would be very interesting to discover what could happen when this *écran de traditionalité* regulated by the Romanian Constitution since 2003 faces the European Law, i.e. a distinct juridical order which needs legal transposition for obtaining relative identical effects in the EU member states, which claim priority over the national law, which expects unitary application by the national legal actors and, last but not least, which undertake juridical-cultural engineering aiming to block the harsh manifestations of the national legal pride. Could this constitutional provision be assimilated with a 'structural safeguard clause' which many of the EU member states' constitutions provide (Grabenwarter 2011, 100–102) in order to set the constitutional limits to the European integration? The question didn't remain unanswered, because, in the same year, 2003, the Romanian Constitutional Court had to present its position as regards the newly introduced constitutional article regulating the relationships with EU and the European Law.

9.4 The Romanian Constitutional Court and the Challenges of the European Legal Transplant

For assessing the fate of the European legal transplant in the Romanian legal system, it is important to address the delicate problem of the meeting between the European Law's principles and the RCC, which, after 2003, has had the competence to interpret the constitutional dispositions through the filter of the Romanian (democratic) constitutional tradition. Apparently, the above mentioned *ecran de traditionalite* represented for the RCC neither 'an apparently utopian and demagogical provision' (Dănişor et al. 2008, 481), nor a constitutional provision to be valued through a purely normative approach. During the period between the making of the Constitution (1991) and its amendment (2003), the RCC made, occasionally, (Dănişor et al. 2008, 479–480) express references to the Romanian democratic traditions. Some would be right to presume this attitude to be a conscious acceptance of the identity-centred policy of the 1991 Constituent Assembly. Considering this context, some would also have expected to observe a firm attitude of the RCC as regards the problem of European Law's application in the Romanian legal system, manifested both before and especially after Romania joined the EU. It would have also been normal that the same *ecran de traditionalite* to induce, at the very least, a Euro-sceptical, if not a Euro-negative, attitude in the work of the RCC. Instead, all RCC decisions since 2003, regarding the European Law, are bewildering us due to their lack of clarity, lack of consistency and timidity in the matter.[6] This would enable a sceptical position to the external observer, who would be entitled to question the seriousness and profundity of the identity-centred cultural attitude of the Romanian constitutionalism and to wonder if the need to cherish the national constitutional tradition was no more than a futile parade of the national legal pride.

Confronted, since April 2003, with the problem of the relationship between European Law and the national legal system, when asked to evaluate the constitutionality of the envisaged constitutional amendments, the RCC only manifested an apparently Euro-sceptical attitude. It formally assumed what I'm proposing to call the *'Solange[7] mentality or spirit'*. Analysing the provisions of Article 148, paragraph 2, of the amended Constitution, which stipulates the priority of European Law over the contrary provisions existing in the Romanian domestic law, the RCC is eager to declare the infra-constitutionality of the European Law:

> The consequence of joining [EU] runs from the fact that the EU member states understood to situate the community *acquis* – the constitutive treaties and the derivate legislation – on an intermediary position between the Constitution and the other laws, when mandatory European legislation is concerned (RCC 2003a no. 148).[8]

Beyond questioning this solution's correctness or lack of opportunity (which do not directly concern the aim of this paper), it is surprising that the RCC did not respond to the European Law pretentions of absolute supremacy

---

[6] In the last decade, the RCC made only two clear references to the 'democratic traditions of the Romanian people', i.e. in the Decision 248/2006 and Decision 919/2009, but without making clear what exactly it understands by 'democratic traditions'.

[7] I'm using the name of the famous decision of the German Constitutional Court in the case Internationale Handelsgesellschaft mbH versus Einfuhr (29th of May 1974), Solange I. In this decision, the German Court is very firm in appreciating that as long as (Germ. Solange) the European Community did not eliminate the possible normative conflict between the Community Law' provisions and the human rights stipulated by the German Basic Law, the latter ones would have priority. Consequently, taking into consideration the almost general diffusion of this type of constitutional safeguard, we could situate in the Solange spirit the attitudes of the European Constitutional Courts which, considering the explicit or implicit provisions of their Constitutions, settled partial or absolute limits to the principle of the European Law's priority. These limits concerned different values pertaining to the legal-political national identity, regulated by the constitutional provisions, provisions which are not accepted to be amended when coming into conflict with the European Law's provisions. On the contrary, it would be rather expected either a European Law's amendment, considering the interests of the member states, or a parallelism between the national-constitutional and European legal orders.

[8] From 16th April 2003 regarding the constitutionality of the legislative proposal regarding the amendment of the Romanian Constitution, M. Of. No. 317 / 12.05.2003.

by adopting its own substantial, explicative position. It preferred to invoke the authority argument, following a specific pattern: if the Constitutional Courts of the EU member states adopted such a solution, they probably have had a strong reason to do that and who are we to establish a different solution? The RCC has adopted this solution by taking it as a formal positivist practice, without questioning its rightness or digging for its cultural roots in the member states, which it only collectively remembers.[9] RCC's judges assumed the Solange-type solution but not the Solange mentality.

After all, the RCC did not understand that the infra-constitutionality of the European Law, the well-known solution adopted by the German Constitutional Court in its famous decision Solange I (1974), reiterated in Solange II (1983) and Maastricht (1993), was not the outcome of a pure process of logical deduction or of a formal scientific application of some constitutional principles, but the result of a cultural-juridical and political identity-centred attitude. [10]

[9] From my point of view, it would have been important to specify the member states that the RCC considered when it accepted the infra-constitutionality of the European Law as the best solution. This demand is justified by the existence of different typologies among the countries which assumed the 'Solange spirit'. On the one side, there is the group (Italy, Germany, Denmark, Belgium, Spain, Sweden, Ireland and Great Britain) which just partially limited the priority of the European Law over the national Constitution, by assuming the right to review, through their Constitutional Courts, the constitutionality of the European Law only as regards some fundamental constitutional values which are crucial for their legal-cultural and political identity. On the other side, there are France and Greece who accepted no kind of priority of the European Law over the national Constitution. See Grabenwarter 2011, 98–104. By making clear its sources of reference, the RCC would have revealed and maybe understood the cultural coordinates of the resistance that Constitutional Courts manifested towards European Law all over Europe.

[10] Considering both the internal constitutional logic and the logic of the classical national sovereignty, the RCC dictum is correct: in order to avoid the violation of the constitutional provisions regulating the limits of the constitutional amendment, especially the one guaranteeing the political independence, there was no other way than to postulate the infra-constitutionality of the European Law. Instead, it is very puzzling the lack of a substantial identity-centred attitude of the RCC. To be very well understood, I must say I do not consider an absolute necessity of an RCC position which would consider the above mentioned *écran de traditionalité* or any other cultural-legal national element (so, a Solange type attitude). From my point of view, RCC could have interpreted the syntagm 'domestic laws', stipulated in the article 148 paragraph 2 RC, as to include the Constitution. Thus, the RCC would have been adopted, by teleological interpretation a supra-constitutionality solution. This one would have perfectly fitted the 'supremacy' of the European Law logic adopted by the ECJ and would have been reached by using the teleological interpretation, considered by ECJ essential for the preservation of the community legal order and its unitary application in the member states. See Fennelly 1996–1997, 656ff.; Snyder 1993, 42–44. My perplexity flows form the fact that, by hav-

The German Constitutional Court 'aggressively' (Mayer 2007, 298) reiterated in its Maastricht decision (1993) its right to review the constitutionality of (this time) all legal acts adopted at EU level, considering the limits of the EU institutions' competences, as they were stipulated in the EU primary law, with the clear effect of declaring inapplicable in the German territory all legal acts which are violating those limits (*ultra vires* acts). Beyond the 'frontal attack on judge-made European Law' and the considerable 'possibility of conflict' between the German Constitutional Court and the ECJ, the attitude adopted in the Maastricht decision could be situated in the larger context of the interest for preserving 'the identity of the German constitutional order' (Zuleeg 1996–1997, 633)[11] Inevitably, the issue of the relationships between European Law and the national (constitutional) law is settled in terms of national constitutional identity and, why not, in terms of national legal pride.

Consequently, the RCC made an apparent comparative analysis and appealed to legal transplant when it was not absolutely necessary. A thorough evaluation of the political and legal context when other Constitutional Courts in Eastern Europe have adopted the Solange mentality would have revealed to the RCC that all this was about cultural-legal attitudes, about an axiological positioning, and not about legal logic or legal transplant. Relevant for our case is the fact that the Constitutional Courts of Hungary, Czech Republic and Poland manifested a Solange type attitude without a necessarily existing explicit conflict between the national Constitutional Courts and the European Law. Moreover, this happened exactly when these Constitutional Courts were formally manifesting deep and sincere respect for the rules of the communitary game. This attitude was rather a strategic positioning, envisaging a possible conflict with the European Law, where the conditions of conflict and 'the weapons' were situated, a clear advertisement that these Courts will not give up their role as guardians of the national Constitutions against the possible threats coming from the European Law (Sadurski 2008, 9, 15, 20). Paradoxically, the legal and political cultural values to be protected from the European 'threat' are the rule of law, fundamental rights and liberties, and democracy, as these Constitutional Courts interpret them.

---

ing a Solange type attitude, the RCC didn't have a substantial, political and legal identity-centred position, despite the fact it would have had a strong reason and a clear benchmark for such an attitude.

[11] Paul Kirchhof, the judge of the 2nd Senate of the German Constitutional Court, as a case reporter, stated that ,... the European States at present do not shield themselves from other States or nationals of other States, but they maintain their originality in a people related by birth and descent, by a territory belonging to themselves, and by a cultural community of language, religion, art and historic experience'.

Therefore, these values are endowed with priority over any kind of legal and political interpretation coming from the EU.

These aspects are relevant for the fact that things are far from being clearly and definitively settled at the EU level as regards the 'supremacy' of the European Law over the national (constitutional) law. The process of establishing a workable equilibrium between the two legal orders, between the competences allocated to the national and European institutions, between the national Constitutional Courts and the ECJ, takes into consideration, for the moment, the legal and political cultural discourse existing in the member states, the cultural values and the mentality of some small epistemological communities, e.g. the Constitutional Courts' judges, the perpetual need to have an identity-centred approach of the democracy in the Eastern member states and, last but not least, the national pride of the old and well-defined constitutional traditions in Western Europe.

In this context, it is intriguing that the RCC's position preferred a simple formal reference to the European 'tradition' of the infra-constitutionality of the European Law by ignoring the constitutionally postulated Romanian democratic tradition, as a determinant element of the national legal culture. Instead of a fairly expected attitude of legal-political pride and of a tradition-centred positioning towards the European Law, the RCC's judges have been tempted to review the conformity of the national (constitutional) law with European Law, thus becoming futile guardians of the European legal order (Tănăsescu 2007, 1–21). Moreover, by publicly assuming the role of 'the warrant of the Constitution's supremacy for assuring a good governance in Romania', (RCC 2008) the RCC has explicitly considered only 'the principles that Romania accepted once adhered to the EU' as the fundamental principles lying at the foundation of the Romanian constitutional order, with no reference to the national democratic traditions. Interestingly, the RCC is positioning itself as a guarantor of the European democratic principles despite or against some implicitly presumed pseudo-democratic national practices. While other Eastern European Constitutional Courts have become protectors of national sovereignty, culturally expressed through a particular national sense of democracy, the RCC seems to become a protector of the European concept of democracy, at the same time kindly explaining, using an elementary legal-political logic,[12] why the national sovereignty must be limited in the context of European integration (RCC 2003b, no. 149).

[12] RCC's logic is correct: if the Romanian desiderate to adhere to EU is legitimated by the country's interests, that national sovereignty cannot become an obstacle on the way to achieve it. See RCC's decision no. 149 / 16th of April 2003 regarding the constitutionality of the constitutional amendment. Somehow, we are told to reconcile ourselves with

It is difficult to explain such an evolution as a cultural attitude and so consequently my perspective is evidently hypothetical. Obvious is only the fact that the RCC missed the chance to manifest a substantial juridical-cultural identity-centred attitude as regards European Law. More could be explained by the weak RCC judge's consciousness of the role that the Court could have in building the Romanian post-communist democracy, in the context of European integration. We could also consider an RCC's judges state of confusion: when confronted with the delicate encounter between the pretentions to supremacy of the European Law and the logic of the classical sovereignty, they preferred the Solange type solution which is, in their perspective, a logical 'consequence' of adhering to the EU, being thus more comfortable and politically correct to hide behind a well-known practice than to assume their own substantial position in the matter. An opportune explanation would be also the revitalisation of the old irrational importing mentality determined by the considerable prestige of the Western democratic models. This type of Romanian cultural attitude was regularly Europhile, uncritical and identity-decentred. In this context I cannot forecast a future conflict between an identity-centred discourse, based on the vain valuation of some uncertain (Gutan 2010, 24–27)[13] Romanian democratic tradition and a (traditional) pro-European discourse. For now, the Romanian constitutional democratic tradition seems to lose the battle with the European Law on the cultural soil of the RCC.

9.5 Conclusions

When the problems of legal transplant and of the latent conflict between the two latitudes of the Romanian legal cultures are discussed in relation with the constitutional culture, specific issues come at stake. Turning the scale in favour of one of the mentioned latitudes is essentially changing the destiny of the European legal transplant in Romania and the role played by the Romanian law in the process of European legal convergence. But this unbalanced situation cannot be accepted. Paradoxically, in keeping a fair balance

the idea of losing political sovereignty, as a necessary consequence of the 'country's interest'.

[13] Despite its constitutional stipulation, the Romanian constitutional scholarship is not interested in debating and clarifying the meaning and the dimensions of the Romanian democratic traditions. Paradoxically, we could speak about a present tradition which lack its pastness.

between the member states and the EU in the matter of European Law supremacy, the preservation of both types of attitude is necessary in Romania.

The logic of the national cultural identity, closely related to the logic of the classical national sovereignty, gives birth to natural tensions between the national legal systems and the European legal order, especially due to the self-awarded right of the member states' Constitutional Courts to review the European Law. These tensions highlight, at the same time, peculiar interpretive perspectives pertaining to some distinct national legal / constitutional cultures as regards a common problem of the sovereign states which is currently solved using the same paradigm: the national state has the monopole of the legitimate political and normative power. The way the abovementioned Constitutional Courts managed the problem illustrated a real need to find an equilibrium capable of satisfying the need of the European legal order to legitimately manifest. This could happily (or unhappily) take place by perpetuating a close relationship between the national legal system and its formal normative sources, hierarchically structured and having the Constitution as a supreme normative expression of the national sovereignty. The fact that a European legal norm cannot be legitimised only by the European legal order, determines the need to be re-legitimised by the national legal system and its supreme law, the Constitution. This is, on the one hand, proof of an eager preoccupation to avoid uncomfortable hierarchies between the European Law and the national law and, on the other hand, the proof of an interest to give a chance to the European Law. In other words, the national Constitutional Courts have avoided the peril of hierarchisation coming from the super-nationality and super-sovereignty of the EU by encapsulating the European Law in the inner normative hierarchy, on a subordinate position vis-à-vis the constitutional norms (McCormick 1998–1999, 31–32; Terré 2003, 243; Grimm 1996–1997, 234ff.; Ward 2003, 105) As a consequence, this results in a fragile equilibrium, quite problematic, ready to be unbalanced in favour of the national legal system by using the Solange mentality. By refusing to amend their constitutional provisions or by exerting political pressure to obtain the amendment of the EU primary law, some member states are not encouraging the idea of a uniform application of European Law and betray the principle of equality before European legislation (Zuleeg 1996–1997, 634). Unfortunately, this is a source for new obstructions. By developing 'parallel interpretations' of the European Law, (Mayer 2007, 303–304) a particular kind of inner equilibrium, some national Constitutional Courts are inevitably adding new prejudices to the community project and undermine the ECJ's vision of a uniformly interpreted and applied European Law. Consequently, a compromise capable of valuing both the legal and political national identity and the logic of European Law is necessary. It doesn't matter that the resulting 'arrangements' will encourage a particular European federalism inside the logic of traditional political sovereignty or the multiplication, in the context of a constitutional pluralism, of the legal-political legitimating centres, beyond the traditional concept of sovereignty (McCormick 1993, 17).[14] A balance must be achieved. The ECJ must understand that a legal-political European convergence is not possible without accepting the constitutional traditions of the member states[15] and the Constitutional Courts must understand that the European legal order is not possible without its pretentions to supremacy. As I. Pernice puts it, the national and European constitutional orders are complementary; they depend on each other, being two elements of the same constitutional system (Duculescu 2006, 283). The ideal solution would reside in the creation of a trusty European constitutional order built concomitantly top-to-bottom and bottom-up by continuous cultural dialog between the political and juridical actors (especially the Constitutional Courts' judges).

In this context, the peculiar traits of the Romanian legal culture would encourage this perspective. Correctly understood and valued, the need to fructify the national democratic traditions and the traditional openness towards Western European legal culture could offer efficient cultural instruments to the RCC's judges, allowing them to participate to the delicate ongoing dialog between the national Constitutional courts and the ECJ. By extension, the continuous exchange of information between the national and European interpretive communities would encourage an epistemological re-configuration at the European level and would strongly underpin the idea of legitimacy and legal validity of the European legal order. It would contribute to the creation of those constitutional principles necessary to give birth to a EU emancipated from the classical national sovereignty obsession (McCormick 1993, 18). Melting these principles into one single European constitutional culture is indispensable for the existence of a common perspective as regards the role of the national sovereignty in the EU, which would be capable of integrating all member states. This could be a very good solution for the national pride's tendency to see the elimination of the European Law's constitutional review as 'a subordination to a foreign power' (Mayer 2007, 309–310).

[14]The idea of a necessary re-evaluation of the traditional concepts of national sovereignty and constitutional supremacy has been developed in the Romanian constitutional doctrine by Vrabie 2006, 321–322.

[15]It is doubtful whether the obsession for uniformity, illustrated by the expression 'common constitutional traditions' of the member states, inscribed in the Lisbon Treaty is the most helpful response to de problem I discuss.

From this perspective, the appeal to the constitutional tradition's filter, stipulated by the amended Romanian Constitution, could have a real utility in the context of the cultural dialog that Romania is compelled to develop in Europe. But the legal-political identity-centred attitude must be really assumed (not just rhetorically), correctly determined (by avoiding futile mythology) and judiciously manifested (by avoiding nationalism). All these are necessary because the cultural identity is not guarded by rhetorical fundamentalism or artificial self-imposition, it is not self-conserved but, instead, it is build and protected by the intensity of the informational exchange (Glenn 2004, 41) inside the interpretive community which is sustaining it. In the same time, it is not necessary to have this Romanian democratic tradition classified and archived as soon as the Romanian elite is following its Europhilic sentiments. On the contrary, it must be firmly affirmed and negotiated through mutual respect and loyalty for the EU. At the same time, to assume a rigid and formal Solange-type attitude, garnished or not with the Romanian democratic traditions, does not represent an aim in itself and, even less, an endeavour to save, by all means, the national sovereignty. It is rather a mechanism of continuous balancing between the national and European Law, between the national identity project and the European one, inside a Europe which is formally respecting both dimensions. Inside this dialog, traditional legal-political values are information which must be sustained and communicate (not imposed), hoping for an adhesion or at least a formal recognition. This is why the Solange spirit is expressing a degree of a continuously increasing level of cultural identity adjustment between the member states and European Law, and not a mental juridical entrenchment for defending the national sovereignty's integrity.

Considering these, the traditional Romanian Europhilia could represent an advantage for a successful political and juridical integration in EU and a cultural preamble for successful dialog. This should allow the RCC's judges to completely assume both the logic of the national cultural identity and the logic of the European Law's supremacy. It seems there is still a long way until successfully setting a dialogical spirit into the Romanian appetite for Western European culture. Europhilia does not mean to revive the usual irrational legal transplant of the past and, on the other hand, to assume the logic of European Law' supremacy is necessary only when the identity-centred cultural 'arrangements' are permitting this.

In the same context, it must be understood that such specific solutions meant to constitutionally regulate the conflict between the national and European constitutional orders, as the RCC interpretive decision for expressly exempting the European Law from constitutional review or a constitutional amendment stipulating the supra-constitutionality of European

Law (Deleanu 2006, 320, 322; Bercea 2007, 282–283) are correct from the classical national sovereignty's point of view, but futile for the logic of European Law supremacy. Being destined to legitimize the European Law supremacy over the national constitutional law by using the national constitutional mechanisms, these solutions could be missing if the full consequences of the European Law autonomy are followed. Apparently, we are in the presence of a paradox: these solutions are meant to promote the logic of European Law supremacy by applying the logic of the classical national sovereignty, instead of appealing directly to the solution proposed by the ECJ. At a legal-cultural level, the Europhilic attitude is promoting the logic of the European Law supremacy through the logic of the classical national sovereignty. This paradox would be easier to understand if we accept that, at the national legal-political identity-centred level, there still exists the need to manifest the European Law supremacy logic only as long as it is perpetually legitimated by the logic of the classical national sovereignty (Kirchhof 2007, 770–772). Therefore, when a conflict between European Law and the national constitutional law occurs, the application of the European Law's logic will be possible only as long as the logic of the classical national sovereignty is willing to accept it, regularly by subsequently appealing to constitutional amendment.

A constitutional amendment stipulating the supra-constitutionality of the European Law would be normal in Romania but it would favour the Europhilic anti-identity-centred legal culture, possibly leading to an unconditional legal transplant as long as the Romanian democratic traditions would be ignored or eliminated. The perpetual disregard by the RCC of the constitutional democratic tradition filter demonstrates that this process is not utterly impossible. From my point of view, this step would endanger Romania's need of legal-political identity-centred determination inside the EU. This kind of determination cannot be acquired without a correct balance between the dimension of the 'Romanian adopted law', which cherished the 'essentials' of the Romanian constitutional culture and the traditional Romanian Europhilia. It is not the moment to give up the logic of the classic national sovereignty, as long as the constructive dialog between the RCC, as the guardian of the Constitution, and the ECJ would not lead to a negotiated equilibrium. In this sense, the presence, beside the usual structural safeguarding clause stipulated in the article 148, paragraph 1 RC, of the special *écran de traditionalité* (article 1, paragraph 3) is important as a prerequisite of a cultural dialog between equals. All that remains to be done is for the RCC to consciously assume in its case law the identity-centred attitude and complete its role in the frame of the political, juridical and cultural dialog with the ECJ.

References

Ajani, Gianmaria. 1995. By chance and prestige: Legal transplants in Russia and Eastern Europe. *The American Journal of Comparative Law* 43: 93–117.

Bell, John. 2009. De la culture. In *Comparer les droits, résolument*, P. Legrand (sous la direction de), 247–278. Paris: PUF.

Bercea, Raluca. 2007. *Drept comunitar. Principii*. Bucharest: C. H. Beck.

Burrows, Noreen. 1996. European community: A mega mix. In *Studies in legal systems: Mixed and mixing*, ed. E. Örücü, E. Attwooll, and S. Coyle, 297–313. Hague/London/Boston: Kluwer Law International.

Carp, Rudu. 2003. *Responsabilitatea ministerială*. Bucharest: All Beck.

Dănişor, Dan Claudiu, Ion Dogaru, and Gheorghe Dănişor. 2008. *Teoria generală a dreptului*. Bucharest: C. H. Beck.

Deleanu, Ion. 2006. *Instituţii şi proceduri constituţionale –în dreptul român şi în dreptul comparat*. Bucharest: C. H. Beck.

Duculescu, Victor. 2006. Dreptul constituţional european – o „sfidare" la adresa dreptului constituţional „clasic" sau un concept nou în dezbaterea juriştilor. In *Liber amicorum Ioan Muraru*, ed. S. Tănăsescu and S. Deaconu, 278–290. Bucharest: Hamangiu.

Fennelly, Nial. 1996–1997. Legal interpretation at the European court of justice. *Fordham International Law Journal* 20: 656–679.

Glenn, Patrick H. 2004. *Legal traditions of the world*. Oxford/New York: Oxford University Press.

Grabenwarter, Christoph. 2011. National constitutional law relating to the European Union. In *Principles of European constitutional law*, ed. A. von Bogdandy and J. Bast, 83–129. Oxford/Portland: Hart Publishing.

Grimm, Dieter. 1996–1997. The European court of justice and national courts: the German constitutional perspective after the Maastricht Decision. *Columbia Journal of European Law* 3: 229–242.

Gutan, Manuel. 2010. Comparative law in Romania: History, present and perspectives. *Romanian Journal of Comparative Law* 1: 9–72.

Gutan, Manuel. 2004. Romanian tradition in foreign law import: Between necessity and weakness. *Imperialism and Chauvinism in the Law. Reports presented to a colloquium on the occasion of the 20th anniversary of the Swiss Institute of Comparative Law*, 65–79. Genevè/Zurich/Bàle: Schulthess.

Gutan, Manuel. 2005. Construind dreptul românesc modern – o cazuistică a importului juridic. *Supllement Acta universitatis Lucian Blaga. Seria Iurisprudentia*, 156–170.

Gutan, Manuel. 2011. *Legal transplant as socio-cultural engineering in modern Romania*. Available at SSRN: http://ssrn.com/abstract=2207718 or http://dx.doi.org/10.2139/ssrn.2207718.

Iorgovan, Antonie. 1998. *Odiseea elaborării constituţiei*. Târgu Mureş: Editura Uniunii Vatra Românească.

Kirchhof, Paul. 2007. The legal structure of the European Union as a Union of States. In *Principles of European constitutional law*, ed. A. von Bogdandy and J. Bast, 765–802. Oxford/Portland: Hart Publishing.

Ludwikowski, Rett. R. 2000–2001. Constitutional culture of the new East-Central European democracies. *Georgia Journal of International and Comparative Law* 1: 1–30.

Mayer, Franz C. 2007. The European constitution and the courts. In *Principles of European constitutional law*, ed. A. von Bogdandy and J. Bast, 281–334. Oxford/ Portland: Hart Publishing.
McCormick, Neil. 1993. Beyond the Sovereign state. *Modern Law Review* 56: 1–18.
McCormick, Neil. 1998–1999. After sovereignity: Understanding constitutional change. *The King's College Law Journal* 22: 20–38.
Örücü, Esin. 2002. Law as transposition. *International and Comparative Law Quarterly* 51: 205–223.
RCC. 2003a. Decision no. 148.
RCC. 2003b. Decision no. 149.
RCC. 2006. Decision no. 248.
RCC. 2008. Comunicat de Presá. http://www.ccr.ro/comunicate/COMUNICAT-DE-PRES-119.
RCC. 2009. Decision no. 919.
Sadurski, Wojciech. 2008. Solange, chapter 3: Constitutional courts in Central Europe –democracy- European Union. *European Law Journal* 14: 1–35.
Snyder, Francis. 1993. The effectiveness of European community law: Institutions, processes, tools and techniques. *Modern Law Review* 56: 19–56.
Tănăsescu, Simina. 2007. Comentariu la Decizia Curții Constitutionale nr. 59 din 17 ianuarie 2007. *Curierul Judiciar* 5: 1–21.
Terré, François. 2003. *Introduction generale au droit*. Paris: Dalloz.
Teubner, Gunther. 1998. Legal irritants: Good faith in british law or how unifying law ends up in new divergences. *The Modern Law Review* 11: 11–32.
Vrabie, Genoveva. 2006. *Implicaţiile Tratatului instituind o Constituţie pentru Europa asupra ierarhiei izvoarelor de drept. Liber amicorum Ioan Muraru*, 315–322. Bucharest: Hamangiu.
Ward, Ian. 2003. *A critical introduction to European law*. London: Lexis Nexis Butterworths.
Watson, Alan. 1993. *Legal transplants. An approach to comparative law*. Athens/ London: The University of Georgia Press.
Wise, Edward M. 1990. The transplant of legal patterns. *The American Journal of Comparative Law* 38: 1–22.
Zuleeg, Manfred. 1996–1997. A community of law: Legal cohesion in the European Union. *Fordham International Law Journal* 20: 623–637.

Manuel Guțan Professor at the Lucian Blaga University of Sibiu, Faculty of Law His main areas of research are history of constitutional law, history of public administration, constitutional transplants, law and culture. Dr. Gutan is currently the Editor-in-Chief of the Romanian Journal of Comparative Law.

Chapter 10
The Europeanization of Albanian Constitutional Law

Arta Vorpsi

Abstract Albania has applied for accession to the EU and it is facing a long process of Europeanization of its economy, its society and its legal system. It has been 2 years since Albania become a candidate country. The term 'Europeanization' has gained currency in political literature over the past decade or so, as scholars attempt to understand the political, economic, and social transformation involved in European integration, especially in the cases of States acceding to the European Union after being governed by non-democratic (fascist or communist) regimes and, in some cases, after violent conflicts.

The Albanian Constitution accepts the primacy of international law over domestic law, but it is not yet explicitly mentioned the Community law. So, on the basis of such national constitutional provisions a dialogue between the European Court of Justice and Albanian Constitutional Court, but also ordinary courts, could be developed, and this dialogue would permit an adaptation of the national legal system to the growing demands from Community law. On the other hand, examples from Germany and Italy show us that their Constitutional Courts maintained certain limits on the transfer of sovereign powers and required that the Community had to respect fundamental rights and that it could not contradict the basic legal structure of the State. Realizing from previous examples in Europe that national courts tend to recognize the supremacy of Community law as being the product of their own domestic legal system, rather than a feature of the unique sui generis nature of Community law, which is the position which the European Court takes, the interpretation of the primacy of Community law could raise problems when Community law conflicts with the national (Albanian) Constitution.

A. Vorpsi (✉)
Law Faculty, University of Tirana, Tirana, Albania
e-mail: arta.vorpsi@yahoo.com

R. Arnold (ed.), *Limitations of National Sovereignty through European Integration*, Ius Gentium: Comparative Perspectives on Law and Justice 51,
DOI 10.1007/978-94-017-7471-0_10

This paper aims to explain how the Albanian legal system is already open to the incorporation of international law and to limit its sovereignty by European integration. There have already been developments in the Constitutional Court's jurisprudence regarding the integration of Albania into the supranational organization or legal system.

10.1 Introduction

The European Union (EU) was initially established as a rather exclusive club; however its present membership of 28 States includes most of the major countries of Europe. Whilst its traditional functions were focused on economic integration, the Union gradually acquired a more universal nature and was also able to exemplify its own catalogue of individual rights and liberties. The EU is a truly supranational organization. Its laws are directly applicable in its Member States and, in case of conflict, prevail over national legislation. The ultimate power to interpret and to enforce EU law belongs to the European Court of Justice (ECJ) in Luxembourg.

In each European country (whether or not it is a member) the domestic and the EU legal systems coexist closely with one another. In other words, domestic legislation is not the only legislation applicable by the national courts. Its sovereignty must be shared with a supranational structure. Some countries still have difficulties in accepting that the traditional understanding of national sovereignty has lost much of its validity. There is always some potential for tension or conflict which goes beyond natural differences in views and opinions. The judiciary remains by no means immune to those dangers.

Albania, as a country which has applied for accession to the EU, faces the long process of Europeanization of its economy, its society and its legal system. Further to this, I will try to present some thoughts on the legal (or constitutional) system of Albania which could prove helpful in understanding the ongoing steps of the Albanian government to fulfill the EU requirements, otherwise known as the *acquis communitaire*.

10.2 Europeanization Defined

The term 'Europeanization' has gained currency in political literature over the past decade or so, as scholars attempt to understand the political, economic, and social transformation involved in European integration, especially in the cases of States acceding to the European Union after being governed by non-democratic (fascist or communist) regimes and, in some cases, after violent conflicts. Europeanization may be seen working through three types of mechanism, which interact synergistically:

> legal obligations in both political and economic spheres flowing from the requirements of accession to the EU, and/or from the Council of Europe membership and accession to its ECHR;
> objective changes in economic structures and the interests of individuals as a result of integration with Europe; and
> subjective changes in the beliefs, expectations and identity of individuals, feeding political will to adopt European norms of business, politics and civil society (Oeter 1999, 902).

European integration and globalization are considered to be the major driving forces of a "transformation process of the State". There is consensus that the power of the EU, mostly derived from the competence that Member States have delegated to it over the years, has been extended from its mainly law making activities into more and more policy fields and also into highly sensitive areas.

Europeanization of law is a consequence of the influence of European integration on the domestic legal systems of countries aspiring to EU membership. The constitution is by no means free from this influence. To put it more simply, Europeanization of the constitution means constitutionalization of matters either related to European Union law ('a sensu stricto' Europeanization) or generally connected with law enacted by European international organizations ('a sensu largo' Europeanization). Constitutional transformation resulting from accession to the EU is mostly reflected in the organizational structure of the State.

In the process of European integration, national constitutional law remains crucial in several respects. The EU Constitution, in its broadest sense, builds on the common constitutional traditions and principles of the Member States, and EU law refers back to national constitutional law in many ways. National constitutional law contributes to legitimizing the EU, in order to ensure that the EU and the Member States as its agents continue to comply with fundamental constitutional requirements, such as the rule of law, democracy and accountability, and the protection of fundamental rights. Also, from a national perspective, national constitutional law remains essential, since it provides the foundation of membership of the EU; it is decisive on the procedures to be followed when powers are transferred at times of accession and Treaty amendment, and it serves to provide the connection between national and EU legal systems.

Participation in the EU requires adaptation of national constitutional arrangements, and national constitutions should not be neglected in the process of the constitutionalization of Europe. Legal Europeanization is often associated with the idea of a "legal transport" (or transplant, transfer, etc.) of EU norms into national laws (Petrov 2008, 330–352). Even if we equate Europeanization with some sort of 'norm transfer', it is still the case that it is an extremely diversified phenomenon, encompassing varying degrees of approximation and always resulting in the creation of something new – more or less similar to, but still different from EU Law. All in all, Europeanization is essentially a process of transformation, involving in its most spectacular forms a "thorough or dramatic change" of domestic legal systems. Legal Europeanization is also a transformation of legal thinking – namely of legal culture and of legal reasoning. This deeper change is a practically unavoidable consequence of the approximation of domestic law to EU law.

I shall first examine the relationship between international law (Community law) and national law in general and then specifically examine the relationship between the Albanian domestic legal system and Community law.

10.3 International Law and the Albanian Legal System

First of all, let me present the constitutional framework regarding the hierarchy of norms. Art.5 of the Constitution of Albania (Constitution of Albania 1998) establishes: "The Republic of Albania applies international law that is binding upon it". Art.116 of the Constitution of Albania foresees that: "Normative acts that are effective in the entire territory of the Republic of Albania are: (a) the Constitution; (b) ratified international agreements; (c) laws; (d) normative acts of the Council of Ministers." As we see, international treaties are legally effective within Albanian territory, making ratified treaties part of the domestic legal system. Therefore, one could say that Art.116 establishes a monistic system uniting international treaties and the domestic legal system.

Art. 122, paragraph 1 asserts: "Any international agreement that has been ratified constitutes part of the internal juridical system after it is published in the Official Journal of the Republic of Albania. It is implemented directly, except for cases when it is not self-executing and its implementation requires issuance of a law. The amendment, supplementing and repeal of laws approved by the majority of all members of the Assembly, for the effect of ratifying an international agreement, is done with the same majority."

Art. 122, paragraph 1 complements Art.116 and clarifies the fact that international agreements become part of the domestic legal system upon ratification and publication in the Official Gazette, furthering the impression that a monistic system prevails and that the doctrine of incorporation applies (Dixon 1996; La Pergola 1993).[1] Consequently, a ratified treaty becomes part of the Albanian domestic legal system without necessitating any further domestic legislative action, except for cases when it is not self-executing and its implementation requires the passing of a law.[2]

Art. 122, paragraph 1 provides some clarity on the subject of the direct applicability and direct effect of international treaties by asserting that ratified treaties which have been published in the Official Gazette are directly applicable, with the result that no Act need be passed to make the treaties applicable; instead, they are directly applicable in the domestic legal system and can be directly employed (Economides 1993). Consequently, all legal and natural persons can explicitly rely on such treaties.

The same could be said regarding the status of the norms posited by international organizations. Art. 122, paragraph 3 of the Albanian Constitution addresses this: "The norms issued by an international organization have superiority, in case of conflict, over domestic laws if the agreement ratified by the Republic of Albania for its participation in the organization expressly contemplates their direct applicability".

Therefore Art. 122, paragraph 3 provides that the norms of international organizations to which Albania is a party have superiority over domestic laws. In this context, the norms of international organizations stand equal to international treaties ratified by an Act of Parliament. Art. 122, paragraph 3 eases the integration of a supranational organization, the communitarian norms of which have prevalence over the laws of the Member State (Albanian Constitutional Court 2006, No. 6).

Art.123 also establishes: "The Republic of Albania, on the basis of international agreements, delegates to international organizations State powers for specific issues. The Assembly may decide that the ratification of such an agreement be done through a referendum." As such, Art.123 authorizes the government to transfer parts of the country's sovereignty to an international organization, an act that must be accomplished through an international treaty. The main way States confer their sovereign powers on an interna-

[1] Most of the world's constitutions incorporate treaties into the domestic legal system.

[2] See the analogous case in Bulgaria: Danov 2002, 36.

tional organization is by concluding a treaty wherein the State undertakes a binding obligation, thereby conferring powers on the organization.[3]

Art.123 of the Constitution contends that the automatically transferred power obligates the Albanian government and/or Parliament to implement the 'transferred power'. There may be different perceptions as to what extent sovereign powers are delegated to an organization (Guerra 2000). The very nature of these powers – executive, legislative and judicial – has led domestic political figures and some amongst the judiciary to question both the constitutionality and the propriety of such broad powers having been passed (Sarooshi 2005, 234). As such the constituent treaty may provide for the conferral of discrete sovereign powers on an organization, but the actual conferral of power only takes place once a State has ratified the treaty.

Nonetheless, based on the Art.11 of the Vienna Convention on the Law of Treaties which was ratified by Albania, the State's consent to be bound by a treaty may be expressed by signature, exchange of instruments constituting a treaty, ratification, acceptance, approval or accession, or by any other means if so agreed. In accordance with these criteria, it is important to emphasize that international agreements are equally binding regardless of the means chosen by the State to express consent to be bound by a treaty. This expression leaves no space for misunderstanding caused by the terminology used in the Albanian Constitution, which uses the term "ratified by law". In this respect, Albania, as a future EU Member already has a legal system which is open to the influence of International/European law. The question that would raise is: how will EU law be implemented by the ordinary courts in everyday cases, especially secondary legislation? It will be a challenge for them as well as for other institutions when it comes to the implementation of EU law in Albania.

10.4 Supra-Nationality of Community Law and Albanian National Law

There is no written supremacy clause in EU law, which leaves a wide margin for interpretation by States (both EU Members and non-Members). The bedrock principle of the supremacy of EC law over national law is the creation

[3] The ICJ has affirmed that the constituent treaty of an organization can act as a mechanism for the State's conferral of express powers on an organization. In the WHOO Advisory Opinion Case the Court observed: "The powers conferred on international organizations are normally the subject of an express statement in their constituent instruments".

of the European Court of Justice, which has already declared European Community law as supreme, directly effective, and autonomous (ECR 1964, Costa Case). A key development in the history of the European Union was the case of Van Gend en Loos (ECR 1963). This was the case which established that provisions of Community law were not just tools of international law, but had direct effect and thus could be relied upon by individual litigants in their national courts.

As European law is founded upon international treaties, the Member States' Supreme Courts tend to argue that treaty law may not be completely autonomous in their internal legal system. Although the supremacy of European Community law is accepted by the national courts of all Member States in reference to the relationship between European Community law and ordinary legislation, the conflict between the ECJ and Member States' Supreme Courts is of great importance when it comes to a conflict between European Community law and national constitutional law.

Today the supremacy of European Community law is indirectly incorporated in the Treaties. The primacy of Community law over ordinary national legislation is also accepted by the Member States' courts to a large extent (De Witte 1999). Yet the idea of an entirely autonomous Community legal system is not shared by the most of the Member States. On the contrary, national Constitutional Courts predominantly take the position that the special legal status of Community law derives from their own national constitutional system. Following the doctrine of the ECJ, national courts are not allowed under any circumstances to review Community law or to curtail the effect of its supremacy. If a national constitutional system apparently limits the transfer of power or the effects of supremacy, it is up to the highest national courts to assess whether such violations have occurred. This raises the question of who has "ultimate authority" (Maduro 2003, 501) and who is the "final arbiter" (Kumm 1999, 351) in the case of a conflict between national and Community law.

The response of constitutional systems of Member States to the needs of supranational provisions in European Community law has been quite different, according to the characteristic of each constitutional system. Although the opening of the domestic legal system is seen as conditional for supremacy by the Member States, from the Community point of view, this doctrine is seen as part of the acquis communautaire.

The Albanian Constitution accepts the primacy of international law over domestic law, (Article 122) but it is not yet explicitly mentioned the Community law. Upon comparison with the French example, the Albanian system seems to have more easily adapted itself to embrace Community law.

The EU Treaty itself shall be ratified by a law enacted by the Albanian Parliament. The primacy of rules enacted by Community institutions over Albanian law could be asserted through jurisprudence, at least in the ordinary courts.[4]

Art.123 of the Albanian Constitution allows the transfer of sovereign powers to international institutions. This provision is similar to Art.24 of the German Grundgesetz and Art.11 of the Italian Constitution. However, partly because the German provision has a more favourable wording which can be more easily adjusted to Community requirements if necessary, unlike the Italian one, and partly because German constitutional law granted the Constitutional Court more pervasive powers than those of the Italian Court[5] – (and also the Albanian Court) – the German system is much more responsive to the requirements stemming from the development of Community powers. It may also briefly be noted that in Germany the idea of the supremacy of Community law over domestic law was asserted more easily than in Italy (Bundesverfassungsgericht 1974, 540 ff; Wunsche Handelsgesellschaft Case 1987, 225 ff.). In spite of the similarity between the Italian and the German Constitutions, the process leading the Italian judges to acknowledge the primacy of Community law was extremely long and arduous.[6]

So, on the basis of such national constitutional provisions (Art.123 of the Albanian Constitution) a dialogue between the European Court of Justice and Albanian Constitutional Court, but also ordinary courts, could be developed, and this dialogue would permit an adaptation of the national legal system to the growing demands from Community law. On the other hand, examples from Germany and Italy show us that their Constitutional Courts maintained certain limits on the transfer of sovereign powers and required that the Community had to respect fundamental rights and that it could not contradict the basic legal structure of the State.[7]

As described above, the pre-eminence of international law is fully accepted by Albania. The particularity of international law is that it is legally binding on States, but leaves to them the task of application within their domestic systems. The provisions of the Community laws addressing

---

[4] For the French Council of State it was maybe a little more difficult, as shown by the 1964 decision in the case of the French oil monopoly. See Conseil d'État (CE 1964).

[5] In Germany, unlike in Italy, even a private citizen can apply to the Constitutional Court.

[6] Art.5 of the Italian Constitution declares that the Republic is "one and indivisible" and this did not help the process in the same way that Art.24 about "transfer of sovereign powers" in the German Constitution did. Besides that, according to the travaux preparatoires of the Italian Constitution, Art.11 was introduced only with a view to membership of the United Nations and to facilitate the entry of Italy into the Organization.

[7] Cases Solange I and II and Maastricht of the German Bundesverfassungsgericht.

domestic law have two characteristics. Some of them only prescribe the behavior that Member States must have; others are more penetrating – and called by many "self executing" – directly establishing subjective rights which are invested in individuals and whose observance can be asserted before courts in Member States. Consequently, I would suggest that it seems to be of some significance that the Albanian legislature should enact a special constitutional provision regarding the adoption of EU law in the Albanian legal system,[8] which would be a separate rule allowing for future accession to the EU. Realizing from previous examples in Europe that national courts tend to recognize the supremacy of Community law as being the product of their own domestic legal system, rather than a feature of the unique sui generis nature of Community law, which is the position which the European Court takes, the interpretation of the primacy of Community law could raise problems when Community law conflicts with the national (Albanian) Constitution.

For example, the accession of Germany to the EEC was based on Art.24/1 of the German Grundgesetz, which allowed the Bund (federal government) to transfer sovereign powers to an interstate organization. This provision – similar to Art.123 of the Albanian Constitution – was interpreted as an expression of 'open statehood' suggesting a break with the concept of the nation State and a possible willingness of the German courts to react positively to the primacy of Community Law. This has not been the case, partly due to the fact that since the Second World War, Germany's Constitution has given particular weight to the protection of fundamental rights, and any provision of Community Law which conflicts with this constitutional protection of basic rights is unlikely to be welcomed.

What would the position of the Albanian Constitutional Court be in these circumstances? Before that question is answered, one must examine the competence of this Court over the international agreements ratified by Albania.

10.5 The Constitutional Court's Review of International Agreements

The review of international agreements is one of the most special competences of the Albanian Constitutional Court, as it is required to assess whether the constitutional principles and norms in the field of foreign relations have been respected and upheld. Foreign relations are not only a

[8] There are many examples from new democracies in Central and Eastern Europe like Bulgaria, Romania, etc.

question of the internal constitutional makeup of a country, but also of international law, to the extent that the State undertakes rights and obligations. In the field of international relations, two separate aspects can be distinguished: the formation of political will and its legal expression.[9] The evaluation of the need or interest in entering into an international agreement is a political act. The question of whether this political act is in conformity with the internal judicial framework (i.e. the Constitution) and with State interests as a whole is of a legal nature. Here the constitutional review executed by the Constitutional Court is particularly focused (Albanian Constitutional Court, decision no.15/2010).

This review is complex in the case of foreign relations, because in some cases foreign relations present difficulties, all the more so given that constitutional review of political acts brings in itself the danger of interference in questions that affect not only internal political interests but also those in relation to other countries or international organizations to which the specific State is a party. Nevertheless, it is now a consolidated practice for the Constitutional Court to also exercise its ability to review to examine other aspects of the decision-making of the executive or the legislature related to foreign relations, taking fundamental constitutional principles as its criteria.

The Albanian Constitutional Court has already emphasized that during the constitutional review of an international agreement, it is important to bear in mind the principle of the rule of law, which prevails over the possibility of conflicting with the general rules of international law, recognized today by the term "international rule of law".[10] When the interpretation of an international agreement is set out for examination before a Constitutional Court, the application of general principles for this purpose is unavoidable. According to those principles, every agreement should be interpreted in an objective manner, such that effect will be given to the parties' intentions

[9] Art. 65, paragraph 1 of Austrian Constitution and Art.59 of German Constitution preempts that every agreement which has to be ratified by Parliament is to be signed by the President of Republic or by an authorized notary (which means the Chancellor, Head of Government or Foreign Minister/Secretary). The agreements regarding integration into the EU are excluded from this regulation because of their nature and special regulation framework, which foresees the expression of the will by the Head of the States or of the Government of the Member States.

[10] Many authors have agreed with the idea that the general rules of international law have supremacy over national constitutions, or at least hold an equal rank. The Albanian Constitution, declared as an "international law friendly" Act, has given the norms of international law priority over its domestic legal system, except for the Constitution. The same regulation can be found in the Constitution of Estonia (Art.123), Bulgaria (Art.85) Ukraine (Art.9, paragraph 2) etc.

lying behind their decision to enter into the agreement. A larger or broader obligation than that to which the parties initially consented should not result from the agreement (Albanian Constitutional Court, decision no.15/2010).

When the Constitutional Court interprets the content of an agreement and reaches a conclusion about its compatibility with the national Constitution, it supports its conclusion only by claiming to uphold fundamental constitutional principles in the text of the agreement. In this case, the Constitutional Court takes account of the fact that the political organs of the State have relied on constitutional principles in order to enter into an agreement and have shown themselves willing to reach a result in compliance with them.[11] That is, constitutionality, good faith, and good will are presumed in the entering into of the agreement, so long as a different conclusion has not been reached by Constitutional Courts (Albanian Constitutional Court, decision no.15/2010).

In respect of this, the Albanian Constitutional Court expressed in an early decision that it considers that the main principles concerning the protection of the fundamental human rights and freedoms sanctioned and even guaranteed by the Constitution of the Republic of Albania, such as: the presumption of innocence; "nullum crimen sine lege" (no crime without law); "nullum poena sine lege" (no punishment without law); the non-retroactive effect of legislation; the right to be legally represented; the independence of the judiciary; the right to be heard by a judge and the right to appeal a decision, have to be also guaranteed by an international agreement in order to be conform with the Constitution and therefore to be applicable in Albania (Albanian Constitutional Court, decision no.168/2002).

In the aforementioned decision, the Albanian Constitutional Court did not raise the question of whether Albania is required to transfer its sovereignty but rather to what extent it should be done. More concretely, the problem presents itself as to how far this transferring of competencies (especially permitted by article 123 of the Constitution) may be extended. Referring to the relation of sovereignty to the acceptance of a supranational jurisdiction (in that particular case the ICC), the Constitutional Court appraises that the problem concerning the quantity of the transferred competencies is of special importance.

Referring to the Albanian Constitutional Court, the answer to this question should be firstly found in the spirit of the Constitution. It can be more concretely noticed in the international constitutional jurisprudence, according to which: "...*the limits of transferring of sovereignty are up to the point*

[11] Decision of the German Federal Constitutional Court regarding the agreement signed between France and Germany concerning the status of the Saar region (FCC 1955).

where the constitutional identity of the State starts to be disputable ..." (FCC 1993) or that: "*the limits of transferring of rights are up to the point where this transferring leads to the violation of the basic conditions for the exercise of national sovereignty*" (Conseil Constitutionnel (CC) 1985).

At the end of the adjudication on the constitutionality of the Statute of Rome, the Albanian Constitutional Court did not consider the transferring of certain (judicial) competencies within a specific field of international interest, – such as that of the prosecution of perpetrators of the crimes of genocide, crimes against humanity, war crimes and aggression – as going beyond these limits. The transfer of State powers to international organizations, according to the Statute of Rome case heard in the Albanian Constitutional Court, cannot damage the country's constitutional identity,[12] meaning that permission to delegate State powers to an international organization is limited to the extent that it does not 'deform' the constitutional and sovereign identity of the Albanian polity. Building upon this provision, the Albanian Constitutional Court has argued that Albania enters into international agreements as a sovereign party, thus supplementing Art. 123.

The Albanian Constitutional Court was and is still aware of the political vision of the government – also expressed in the text of the Constitution – insofar as the integration of Albania into the European Union. For that reason, this jurisprudence was only a step towards taking the correct position regarding the applicability of the EU law, which will be binding as soon as Albanian becomes a member of EU. It is for the Court (not only the Constitutional Court, but also ordinary courts) to find the proper solution or interpretation of the respective constitutional provisions regarding the issue of future integration not only in political aspects but also in terms of (domestic and international) law.

The Albanian Constitutional Court still has a long way to go to implement rules and interpretations which deal with the EU's integration into the country. The latest decision of the Czech Constitutional Court or the earlier decisions of the Bundesverfassungsgericht (Solange I+II) have shown an interesting development of national jurisprudence. We await the practical application of this vein of jurisprudence in Albania with curiosity and eager anticipation.

---

[12] The French Constitutional Council ruled that the Constitution must be amended. See: Pasczolay, Study no. 498/2008 on Constitutional issues raised by the Ratification of the Rome Statute of the International Criminal Court – Supplement to the Report on constitutional issues raised by the ratification of the Statute of Rome by the International Criminal Court (CDL-INF(2001)001;CDL-AD(2008)031) commissioned by the European Commission for Democracy through Law (Venice Commission), Strasbourg, November 2008.

10.6 Europeanization of Constitutional Law and Constitutional Patriotism – Is There Still Any Place for It?

Constitutional patriotism is one of the most attractive yet ill-defined concepts in modern political theory (Müller 2007).[13] The idea has become most closely associated with Jürgen Habermas and his attempt to propose a plausible form of collective identification for a post-national Germany and for the European Union (Habermas 1996). In general, the concept of constitutional patriotism postulates that political attachment ought to center on the norms, the values and, more indirectly, the procedures of a liberal democratic constitution. Constitutional patriotism promises a form of solidarity distinct from both nationalism and cosmopolitanism.

The concept of constitutional patriotism has been frequently proffered as a solution to the difficult issue of political allegiance within increasingly multicultural societies. Moreover, constitutional patriotism has been advanced as a way of conceptualizing political integration at a supranational level – most prominently in the context of the draft Treaty establishing a Constitution for Europe. Finally, constitutional patriotism has also been advocated as the most plausible source of political cohesion in societies emerging from civil wars, pervasive injustice, or theocratic modes of legitimation.[14]

Constitutional patriotism is not in and of itself a theory of justice. Nor is it primarily a theory of the self, although a notion of post-conventional identity plays an important role in Habermas's conception of constitutional patriotism (Müller 2008, 76). Put differently: a theory of constitutional patriotism provides one possible language for an exercise in collective ethical self-clarification. Who and how do we want to be, as far as political rule over ourselves is concerned? The deepest impulse animating a normatively substantive account of constitutional patriotism is the idea of individuals recognizing each other as free and equal and finding fair terms for cohabitation with one another – finding enough common, mutually acceptable ground to answer the question, "How do we want to live together?" Its

[13] The idea was born in postwar West Germany. The political philosopher Dolf Sterberger, a pupil of Hannah Arendts, coined the name in the late 1970s. It was subsequently taken up by Jürgen Habermas and through his work became better known in the English-speaking world.

[14] The leader of Muslims in Bosnia has proposed constitutional patriotism as the best means to hold the State together, whilst Richard Rorty has endorsed constitutional patriotism as an appropriate way to conceptualize solidarity and hope in countries transitioning from theocracy to democracy.

primary focus is on particular, preexisting political structures, not on humanity as a whole.

Nowadays, citizens are asked to attach themselves to, and to maintain, a system of rules for lawmaking that tracks their interests and that they would have no good reason to reject. A country, a city, a nation, a State can all be the objects of constitutional patriotism. The limits are set by the nature of constitutional patriotism itself. Our loyalty to whatever is its object must be a part of the comprehensive battle between efforts to improve the world, based on multiple impartial principles and legitimate ends, and efforts to subject it to the power of the human destructive capacity. A loyalty to any object can be a form of constitutional patriotism only so long as it can be a loyalty to civilization universally. According to this view, a Volkspatriotismus can be a form of constitutional patriotism if it involves a double commitment in favor of principle and against destruction and as long as loyalty to this nation, at this time, and in this form, can be consistent with loyalty to universal civilization. And to take another example, constitutional patriotism directed toward the EU would derive its strength from the EU commitment to universal principles, from its extraordinary success in making war unthinkable, and from its serving as a unique model for a plausible future legal and political foundation of a universal civilization. Whether the EU institutions and especially its courts, have anything they can truly call a constitution does not matter, then, to the strength and confidence of our constitutional patriotism (Soltan 2008, 112).

Constitutional patriotism is thus a strong identity. It does not merely consist of abstract commitments but, rather, it connects an account of the past with a commitment to a concrete set of constitutional arrangements as a framework for the political realization of common aspirations for the future. The future is imagined as creating a more perfect union as defined by a greater realization and deeper understanding of the ideals. In this way, universal values are meaningfully connected to concrete political practices of specific communities.

The preamble of the Lisbon Treaty connects a commitment to universal principles with an account of the past. It connects a commitment to a particularly constituted supranational community in the present to a set of aspirations for the future. Europe, as a political concept, develops specific and distinct contours. It is grounded not just in universal principles but in religious and humanist culture that is its inheritance. It embraces a supranational legal and political form that is neither a European nation State nor a mere intergovernmental organization. It subscribes to a political program, and to an ideal of a liberal civilization that is distinctively European. This is the identity the preamble invites Europeans to make their own by engaging with it, giving substance to it and making it real. This is what the Albanian people are expecting from the integration into the EU family. In that sense it seems difficult to discuss or to implement domestic constitutional provisions without reference to Community values and their effect on the practice of domestic institutions.

10.7 Conclusions

In order to become an EU Member, Albania is obliged to strictly comply with the EU political, economical, and legal requirements (known as the Copenhagen Criteria). Such stipulations have a large impact on this country. This entire process, where European integration has an impact on shortly-to-become-member countries has been dubbed 'Eastern Style' Europeanization. For Albania, Europeanization means adjustment to advanced Western models as well as security and prosperity for the future (Anastasakis 2005, 80). In its current format, we can speak of Albania as being situated in a pre-Europeanization process, since the current transformations have already had effects on the preparation for accession (as entry into the Stabilization and Association Agreement came into force in 2008). Albania has to review much of its legislation, adapt existing institutions or build new ones conforming to EU legislation, policies, and standards. There is a long way to go in this process, which should be characterized not only by a strong political will but also by serious commitments of all organs of State. The executive, judiciary and legislature must become 'behaviorally Europeanized' in order to Europeanize the legal system.

References

Albanian Constitutional Court. 2002. Decision no.186/2002.
Albanian Constitutional Court. 2006. Memishaj Decision no.6.
Albanian Constitutional Court. 2010. Decision no.15/2010.
Anastasakis, Othon. 2005. The Europeanization of the Balkans. *The Brown Journal of World Affairs XII/1*: 80.
Bundesverfassungsgericht. 1974. Internationale Handelsgesellschaft v.EVGF. *Common Market Law Reports*: 540.
Conseil d'État. 19 juin 1964. *Société des pétroles Shell-Berre*. Recueil Lebon 1964, 344.
Conseil Constitutionnel (CC). 1985. Décision n° 85-188 DC du 22 mai 1985. Protocole n° 6 additionnel à la Convention européenne de sauvegarde des Droits de l'homme et des libertés fondamentales concernant l'abolition de la peine de mort.Receuil, 15.
Constitution of Albania. 1998. Constitution of Republic of Albania, aproved by Albanian Parliament in 1998

Danov, Hristo. 2002. *Constitutional courts and European integration*, Science and technique of democracy No. 36, in P. Craig and G. de Burca. Eds. Kosice: European Commission for Democracy through Law, Venice Commission, 27–32.

Danov, Hristo. 2002. Constitutional courts and European integration. *Science and Technique of Democracy*, 36.

De Witte, Bruno. 1999. Direct effect, supremacy and the nature of the legal order. In *In the evolution of the EU law*, eds. P. Craig and G. de Búrca, 177–213. Oxford: OUP.

Dixon. 1996. *Textbook on international law*. London: Blackstone.

Economides, Constantin. 1993. The relationship between international and domestic law, report of the European Commission for democracy through law (Venice Commission). *Science and Technique of Democracy* 6, 85–105, *Venice.*

ECR. 1963. Case 26/62. NV Algemene Transport- en Expeditie Onderneming van Gend & Loos v Netherlands Inland Revenue Administration. Judgment of 5 February 1963. ECR 1963/01.

ECR. 1964. Case 6/64 Flaminio Costa v E.N.E.L. Judgment of 15 July 1964. Rep. 1964/00585.

FCC (Federal Constitutional Court). 1955. Saarstatut. Vol. 4, 157.

FCC. 1993. Maastricht. Vol. 89, 155

Guerra, Luis Lopez. 2000. Conclusions in European Commission for democracy through law (Venice Commission). 'European Integration and Constitutional Law' proceedings of the UniDem seminar. *Science and Technique of Democracy* 30: 16–27.

Habermas, Jürgen. 1996. *Between facts and norms: Contributions to a discourse theory of law and democracy*. Cambridge, Massachusetts: The MIT Press.

Kumm, Matthias. 1999. Who is the final arbiter of constitutionality in Europe? *CML Review* 36(2): 351.

La Pergola, Antonio. 1993. *The relationship between international and domestic law: Traditional problems and new trends*. Speech at the proceedings of UniDem seminar of the European Commission for democracy through law (Venice Commission). Warsaw.

Maduro, Miguel Poiares. 2003. Contrapunctual law: Europe's constitutional pluralism in action. In *Sovereignity in transition,* ed. Neil Walker (ed), 501–513. Oxford: Hart Publishing.

Müller, Jan-Werner. 2007. *Constitutional patriotism.* Princeton/Oxford: Princeton University Press.

Müller, Jan-Werner. 2008. A general theory of constitutional patriotism. *International Journal of Constitutional Law* 6(1): 76–92. New York.

Oeter, Stefan. 1999. Europäische Integration als Konstitutionalisierungsprozess. *ZAÖRV* 59: 902–912. Heildelberg.

Pasczolay, Peter. 2008. Study no. 498/2008 on constitutional issues raised by the ratification of the Rome Statute of the international criminal court – Supplement to the report on constitutional issues raised by the ratification of the Rome Statute of the international criminal court (CDL-INF(2001)001;CDL-AD(2008)031) of European Commission for democracy through law (Venice Commission). Strasbourg.

Petrov, Roman. 2008. Exporting the Acquis Communautaire into the legal systems of third countries. *European Foreign Affairs Review* 13: 330–352. Leiden.

Sarooshi, Dan. 2005. *International organizations and their exercise of sovereign powers*. Oxford: Oxford University Press.
Soltan, Karol Edward. 2008. Constitutional patriotism and militant moderation. *International Journal of Constitutional Law* 6(1): 112.
Wunsche Handelsgesellschaft Case. 1986. *Reports, 1987*: 225.

Arta Vorpsi works as Legal Adviser at the Constitutional Court of Albania and teaches Constitutional Law, Comparative Constitutional Law and Human Rights at Law Faculty, University of Tirana. She serves also as Legal Expert on law drafting and approximation of Albanian legislation with EU law. She has published many articles in various periodicals in Albania and abroad.

Chapter 11
The Supranational Character of the European Union Associations with Third Countries

Viktor Muraviov

Abstract The article elucidates theoretical and practical issues bound up with the conclusion of international agreements between the European Union and the third states. The impact of the acquis on the content of the association agreements as well as the means and consequences of such an impact are analysed. The legal effects of such agreements for the legal orders of the third states are estimated.

This paper is a contribution to the analysis of the topic "Limitation of Sovereignty by European Integration".

11.1 Introduction

One of the main forms of the European Union's (EU) co-operation with third countries and international organizations is treaty-making practice. The Eastern Partnership Policy proclaimed by the European Union in 2008 foresees a substantial upgrading of the level of political engagement with eastern partners, including the prospect of a new generation of Association agreements, far-reaching integration into the EU economy, easier travel to the EU for citizens providing that security requirements are met, enhanced energy security arrangements benefiting all concerned, and increased financial assistance (COM (2008) 823 final) By concluding such agreements, the EU will surround itself with an area of stability and economic, political and

V. Muraviov (✉)
Institute of International Relations, Kyiv Taras Shevchenko National University, Kiev, Ukraine
e-mail: vmour@visti.com

R. Arnold (ed.), *Limitations of National Sovereignty through European Integration*, Ius Gentium: Comparative Perspectives on Law and Justice 51,
DOI 10.1007/978-94-017-7471-0_11

legal cooperation (Ukraine. Country Strategy Paper 2007–2013). Association with the EU will be one of the most powerful legal instruments for the creation of such an area. Such agreements reflect to a large extent the legal policy of the EU, with the supranational nature of the Union being transferred to treaty and institutional mechanisms of associations.

Therefore, research into the effect that EU law has on the character and content of its international agreements, creating legal prerequisites for the expansion of the acquis beyond the EU is a topical problem for the contemporary science of international and European law and its resolution can have practical implications. However, there have been very few publications analysing these issues, a gap that this paper will seek to fill.

11.2 Association Agreements as Legal Instruments for the Incorporation of the EU Acquis into the Legal Orders of the Third Countries

The impact of EU primary and secondary legislation (the founding Treaties and acts of EU institutions) on third countries' legal orders is most often achieved through international agreements whose provisions reproduce the prescriptions laid down in the treaties establishing the EU and in acts adopted by its institutions. However, by no means all international agreements concluded between the European Union and third countries can ensure such penetration by provisions of EU law into the internal legal orders of non-member countries. The most typical kinds of international agreements capable of serving as a basis for provisions of EU law to penetrate into the internal legal orders of third countries are association agreements, partnership agreements, and also agreements on trade and co-operation. These may include acts adopted by organs of the association or co-operation – namely resolutions or conventions constituting part of the institutional mechanism of such agreements.

There are several major routes – through the conclusion of international agreements – for EU primary and secondary law to penetrate into third countries' legal orders: by the incorporation of provisions of EU law into international agreements, by acts of co-operation bodies set up within the framework of such agreements and by references by means of the international agreements or of the co-operation bodies' acts to provisions of EU Treaties and acts of the EU institutions.

In this regard, association agreements may appear to be different from partnership and co-operation agreements in that the former, firstly, appear to reproduce a somewhat greater number of provisions of EU primary and secondary law and, secondly, the association or co-operation bodies created on the basis of their provisions are empowered to adopt binding acts containing the provisions of primary law of the European Union and references to secondary legislation acts of the EU.

This approach is clearly seen from the trade agreements that the EU has concluded with European countries. In particular, Articles 3, 4, 5 and 7 of the Agreement concluded in 1972 between the EEC and Switzerland with regard to the establishment of a free trade area (with the amendments of 2001) (Journal Officiel, 31 Décembre 1972, L 300, 189–280) actually reproduce the provisions of the present Article 30 of the Lisbon Treaty on Functioning of the European Union (EU Treaty) prohibiting the contracting parties from imposing new customs duties on imports and exports and charges having equivalent effect, as well as customs duties of a fiscal nature (Official Journal, 9 May 2008, C 115/01). Furthermore, Article 13 of the same Agreement is in fact a reflection of the provision of Article 34 of the EU Treaty prohibiting the imposition of quantitative restrictions on imports between the Member States and all measures having equivalent effect.

Article 20 of the afore-mentioned Agreement entirely reproduces the provision of Article 36 of the EU Treaty referring to some exceptional grounds allowing Member States to resort to non-fiscal prohibitions or restrictions on imports and exports.

It should be noted that, according to EU law, Articles 30, 34 and 36 have been recognized by the European Court of Justice (ECJ) as having a direct effect (Algemene Transport- en Expeditie Onderneming van Gend & Loos v Netherlands Inland Revenue Administration 1963; Pigs Marketing Board v Raymond Redmond 1978), but, this does not necessarily mean that they may have the same status in the internal legal order of Switzerland.

Article 23 of the Agreement partly reflects the provisions of Article 101, 102 and 107 of the EU Treaty. Article 101 applying to rules of competition (prohibiting, in view of incompatibility with the area of free trade, the agreements between undertakings, decisions by associations of undertakings and concerted practices which have as their object or effect the prevention, restriction or distortion of competition in the sphere of production and trade in goods), Article 102, which prohibits any abuse by one or more undertakings of a dominant position within the internal market or in a substantial part of it, and article 107, which prohibits any aid granted through State resources distorting or threatening to distort competition by favouring certain undertakings or the production of certain goods.

On the other hand, Article 29 of the Agreement empowers a Joint Committee, set up on the basis of this document, to adopt decisions binding upon the parties with the aim of implementing its provisions.

Similar provisions are also reproduced in the 1973 Agreement on a free trade area between the EEC and Norway (Journal Officiel, 27 Juin 1973, L 171/2).

Of special note is the Agreement on the European Economic Area (EEA Agreement) which constitutes a reflection of a great many provisions of EU primary and secondary law. This Agreement was signed in May 1992 (Official Journal, 3 January 1994, L 1/1) between the EU, its Member States, and some of the most developed EFTA Member States as Norway, Iceland, and Lichtenstein.

This Agreement is somewhat unique in the treaty-making practice of the EU, since essentially it entirely reproduces the provisions of the EU Treaty governing the co-operation in the economic sphere. Moreover, annexes and protocols to the Agreement contain references to provisions of various acts of EU institutions and, thus, along with provisions of the EEA Agreement, they fix the vast majority of the norms that make up the EU *acquis* (Muraviov 2007, 2). Such structure is explained by the fact, that when drafters were deciding whether it was necessary to include the relevant provisions of *acquis*, they found that, considering the scale of such work, it would be actually possible to identify and fully incorporate these provisions into the future agreement. For that reason, the drafters decided that it would be better to use the legislative technique of putting references to the respective provisions of the *acquis* into annexes and protocols to the EEA Agreement (O'Keeffe 1992, 6).

Thus, the EEA Agreement can be referred to as a global agreement on association, as it grants associated countries a status which is essentially substitute for their membership in the European Union, not providing therewith any participation in the activities of the EU institutions or their co-operation in matters of foreign and internal policy.

Such a far-reaching character of the EEA Agreement is first of all evidenced by its very structure. The EEA Agreement comprises a preamble and nine parts laying down objectives and principles for the main four freedoms of the common market (free movement of goods, persons, capital, and services), covering the related spheres (rules on competition, social policy, consumer rights protection, environmental protection, statistics, entrepreneurial activity), co-operation outside the scope of the four freedoms, activities of co-operation institutions, etc.

As mentioned in Article 1(1) of this document, "the aim of this Agreement of association is to promote a continuous and balanced strengthening of trade and economic relations between the Contracting parties with equal conditions of competition, and the respect of the same rules, with a view to creating a homogeneous European Economic Area."

In other words, the goal is to create a market encompassing the territory of the European Union and that of the associated countries, with common rules regulating the relations between undertakings of all the parties of the Agreement. The answer to the question of what kind of rules these should be can be found in provisions of the EEA Agreement.

Since the main preconditions for the functioning of a common market are freedom of movement of goods, persons, capital, and services, the EEA Agreement extends to associated countries the applicability, first of all, of those provisions of the EU Treaty which are connected with the maintenance of these freedoms. However, control of boarders remains in force. Freedom of movement of goods is, in particular, ensured by including in the EEA Agreement provisions (Articles 10, 11, 12) essentially identical to those contained in Articles 30, 34, 35 of the EU Treaty – which lay down prohibitions against customs duties, quantitative restrictions on imports and exports, and any other measures having equivalent effect. Article 36 of the EU Treaty is fully reproduced in Article 13 of the EEA Agreement as regards exceptions from such prohibitions. Likewise, a reflection of Articles 110 and 111 of the EU Treaty, which prohibit any discrimination in terms of internal taxation, can be found in Articles 14 and 15 of the EEA Agreement. EEA Agreement provisions on State monopoly of a commercial character (Art. 16) are also similar to EU regulations.

Free movement of workers, freedom of establishment or the right to pursue economic activities are regulated on the basis of Articles 45 and 49 of the EU Treaty which are reproduced in relevant provisions of the EEA Agreement: (Article 28 and Annex 5; Articles 31–35 and Annexes 8 and 11 to the Agreement). The EEA Agreement also envisages measures concerning the mutual recognition of diplomas (formal qualifications) (Art. 30 and Annex 7).

Almost all prescriptions of Articles 56–62 of the EU Treaty in regard to freedom to provide services are reproduced in the EEA Agreement as well (Articles 36–39 and Annexes 9–11 to the Agreement).

Finally, the EEA Agreement excludes any restrictions between parties on the movement of capital, even though these provisions only partly reproduce the respective rules of EU law on this matter (Art. 63–66 of the EU

Treaty), since they keep intact some restrictions on certain direct investments and investments in real estate (Art. 40–45 and Annex 12 to the Agreement).

Other than the rules of the four freedoms, the EEA Agreement also includes EU law relating to transport (Art. 47–52 and Annex 11 to the Agreement), social policy (Art. 66–71 and Annex 18 to the Agreement), consumer protection (Art. 72 and Annex 19 to the Agreement), company law (Art. 77 and Annex 22 to the Agreement), statistics (Art. 76, Annex 21 and Protocol 30 to the Agreement), environmental protection (Art. 73–75 and Annex 22 to the Agreement), protection of intellectual property rights (Art. 65, Annex 17 and Protocol 27 to the Agreement), procurement (Art. 65, Annex 17 and Annex 16 to the Agreement), rules on competition (Arts. 57, 59), etc.

The procedure for examining violations of rules on competition involves the distribution of powers between the EU Commission and the EEA Supervisory Body depending on the category of the case and the trade turnover of those participating in market relations within the free trade area created in accordance with the EEA Agreement (Art. 56).

In addition to the EU Treaty provisions that govern common market relations, the EEA Agreement reproduces other rules of EU law aiming to create preconditions for the normal functioning of the whole legal mechanism of the parties' co-operation. In particular, Article 3 of the Agreement mirrors Article 4.3 of the EU Treaty obliging Member States to ensure the fulfillment of obligations under the Agreement and to abstain from any measure which could jeopardize the attainment of the objectives of this Agreement (the so-called provisions on cooperation).

To ensure that associated countries uniformly apply the EU law provisions making up the *acquis*, Article 6 of the EEA Agreement stipulates that the Agreement provisions reflecting the essentially identical prescriptions of the EU Treaty or acts of EU institutions should be interpreted in accordance with ECJ judgments delivered before the EEA Agreement entered into force, without prejudice to the future practice of the ECJ.

The same purpose is pursued by Article 107 of the EEA Agreement, which refers to the possibility for judicial authorities of associated countries to ask, under a prejudicial procedure, the ECJ to decide on the interpretation of EEA rules corresponding to the rules of EU primary and secondary law. This also suggests that the competence of the ECJ extends to relations arising outside the EU.

As well as EU laws that had been in force before the signing of the EEA Agreement, associated countries may also be subject to provisions of future acts adopted by EU institutions in the form of regulations and directives. This is provided for in Article 7 of the EEA Agreement, which stipulates that EU institutions' acts referred to or contained in Annexes to the Agreement should be made part of the associated countries' internal legal orders. Where the acts are regulations, these have direct effect within the associated countries' legal orders and, where they are directives, they are binding in respect to the result to be achieved, with the manner of their implementation being left with the authorities of these countries.

Thus, the conclusion of the EEA Agreement created legal frameworks for extending – by establishing a free trade area within the EEA – the EU-led European economic integration to the associated countries. This was the first step towards building an internal market comprising the market of the EU and markets of the associated countries. Being included into the EEA Agreement, EU laws regulating economic relations within the internal market have become an integral part of the internal legal order of each associated country. In practice, this suggests that the effect of the rules regulating the main freedoms of the internal market has been extended to the associated countries with the prospect of applying common rules to regulate economic relations within the European Economic Area. Legal frameworks for the functioning of the free trade area within the EEA are created mainly by the direct inclusion of EU laws into the EEA Agreement. The Annexes to the Agreement contain references to the sets of rules applicable to a certain sector of the EU internal market. The Agreement also provides for the incorporation of association bodies' acts into the legal orders of associated countries. Those acts contain provisions of the certain EU regulations or directives or refer to such acts, with the latter keeping those special legal characteristics that they have in EU law. As a result of this process, the *acquis* is deemed to be the basis for the regulation of relations within the framework of cooperation with EU. Such a far-reaching application of EU law rules to regulate relations within the EEA does not give rise to problems for associated countries, since the level of their economic and legal development is sometimes greater than the respective levels of most of the EU Member States.

A similar approach for extending the scope of EU laws to the associated countries has been applied with the EU associations with the Balkan states. The Stabilization and Association Agreement with Macedonia includes provisions (Art. 17, 18, 19, 20) essentially identical to those contained in Articles 30, 34 and 35 of the EU Treaty – which lay down prohibitions against customs duties, quantitative restrictions on imports and exports, and any other measures having equivalent effect. Article 69 of the Agreement also partly reflects the provisions of Article 101 of the EU Treaty, which apply to rules of competition (Official Journal, 20 March 2004, L84/13). However, such agreements do not contain any references to provisions of EU legislation on economic relations in certain sectors of the internal market. Furthermore, acts adopted by the Association organs do not envisage the incorporation of EU institutions' acts into the internal legal orders of the associated countries by way of transposition of or references to EU law rules therein.

Such relatively rare references to EU laws in Stabilization and Association agreements, or acts of association organs may be explained by the fact that European integration was extended to the associated countries of the Balkan region taking into consideration the transitional character of their economies. National economies of these associated countries needed to be gradually adapted to new legal regulation mechanisms of the European Union. Therefore, the body of the EU *acquis* to be accepted by these countries so as to be able to create preconditions for their accession to the EU was considerably less than that for the EEA States.

Association agreements between the EU and Mediterranean countries, which are not candidates for EU membership because of being situated outside Europe, also envisage a gradual formation of the free trade area, and imply that adjacent to the EU will be an area of economic stability, contributing to the development of its integration processes.

A common approach to regulating the relations in associations with Mediterranean countries is to include EU laws or references to provisions of EU secondary legislation in the associated agreements. Detailed examples of this are as follows:

The Agreement on Association between the EU and Tunis, concluded on 30 March 1998 (Official Journal, 30 March 1998, L 97/2), reproduces or contains references to EU Treaty provisions and to certain acts of EU institutions' regulating the conditions for common market competition, State aid measures (Art. 36, paragraph 2), freedom to provide services (Art. 36, paragraph 2), measures relating to the common agricultural policy (Art. 36, paragraph 5), etc.

The Association Agreement between the EU and the Palestinian Liberation Organisation, concluded on 16 July 1997 (Official Journal, 16 July 1997, L187/3), states that the parties are obliged to be guided by provisions of the EU Treaty and EU institutions' acts relating to measures of the common agricultural policy of the EC (Art. 30, paragraph 6).

Article 8 of the Association Agreement between the EU and Israel on 23 June 2006, actually reproduces the provisions of Article 30 of the EU Treaty prohibiting the contracting parties from imposing new customs duties on imports and exports and charges having equivalent effect, as well as customs duties of a fiscal nature. Articles 16 and 17 of the Agreement reflect the provisions of Articles 34 and 35 of the EU Treaty prohibiting the imposition of quantitative restrictions on imports and exports and all measures having equivalent effect between the parties.

Article 36 of the Agreement also partly reflects the provisions of Article 101, which apply to rules of competition (Official Journal, 21 June 2000, L 147/3).

Thus, the creation of legal frameworks for regulating relations within associations between the EU and Mediterranean countries involves the application of EU primary and secondary law for purposes of co-operation only within a limited scope. The association agreements between these countries and the EU only contain certain rules of the EU Treaties. At the same time, they contain a significant number of references to a broad range of rules regulating economic relations in specific sectors of the internal market of the Union. This implies that the EU *acquis* extends its applicability to the associated countries of the Mediterranean region.

11.3 The Supranational Character of the Harmonization of Legislation of the Associated Countries

An important instrument of the EU used to influence the internal legal orders of the third countries is the harmonization of legislation. In relations between the EU and associated countries the compatibility of associated countries' legislation with EU law can be achieved at various levels (level of international obligations, level of EU obligations), and by various means (accession to international treaties, making national laws consistent with legal acts of EU institutions, recognition by the associated countries of national standards of EU Member States, mutual recognition of rules of the other side).

Association agreements usually specify the main spheres in which harmonization is supposed to be achieved by undertaking relevant obligations regarding particular international relations. These mainly include intellectual property, energy, environmental protection, and the prevention of money laundering. The Association agreement between the EU and Ukraine (AA) (Official Journal, 29 May 2014, L 161, p. 1–2) stipulates that pursuant to Articles 40, 46, 158, Ukraine and the EU are to act according to a number of the provisions of the WTO Agreement (art. VIII, XI, XX, XXI) as well as to some WTO agreements including the WTO Agreement on Trade-related Aspects of Intellectual Property Rights, Agreement on Safeguards, Anti-Dumping Agreement, Agreement on Subsidies and Countervailing Duties etc.

However, harmonization by acceding to international legal instruments that set international standards in particular spheres is generally not sufficient. As a rule it requires additional legal measures to be undertaken in the form of national laws adopted with the aim of implementing provisions of the association agreements.

The adoption of national laws and regulations compatible with Community law has become a common harmonization method which Ukraine and the EU rely upon in their relations. The legal bases for such harmonization is established in the AA Ukrainian legislation (Preamble, Articles 1, 20, 56, 58, 59, 64, 67, 84, 114, 124, 133, 138, 140, 148, 149, 153, 151, 152, 256, 262, 264, 278, 337, 338, 342, 343, 353, 355, 358, 363, 368, 375, 379, 385, 394, 397, 405, 410, 417, 424, 428, 474 etc). The spheres of such harmonization include the protection of intellectual property rights, customs, company law, banking, company accounting, taxes, labour protection, financial services, competition rules, public procurement, protection of health and life of humans, animals and plants, the environment, technical rules and standards, nuclear energy, transport, industry, agriculture, social area, sanitary and phito-sanitary rules, European standards on the assessment of conformity of industrial products, small and medium enterprises, statistics etc.

The harmonization of associated countries' legislation with that of the EU bears some traces of supranationality. In the course of harmonization of legislation, associated countries should take into account that this is not a reciprocal process. It does not involve any reciprocal steps of both parties making their legal framework compatible with each other. Associated countries alone are required to change their legislation so as to be in harmony with EU law. The associated countries in fact have no influence on the law-making process within the EU and play the role of a destination for the EU legal precepts.

The AA lays a mechanism that will make it possible to interpret the provisions of EU law with which the Ukrainian legislation is to be harmonized. On the one hand, according to the Agreement the appropriate EU bodies are to advise the Ukraine on amendments in EU law (art. 67). On the other hand, the AA provides that in some areas of cooperation the proper provisions of the EU founding treaties, acts of the EU institutions, EU Court of Justice decisions serve as the legal sources for interpretation (Art. 3, 4, 153, 262, 263). All this may help Ukraine to avoid a situation where national norms may appear inconsistent with EU rules and thus further the efficiency of the implementation of EU law in their national legal order. Therefore, the ultimate goal of the harmonization, which exists as the creation of similar legal conditions for the entities regulated by the basic and harmonized norms, might be achieved.

The AA also provides that the organs of the EU and the organs of cooperation established under the AA will assess the progress of harmonization. First and foremost, the Ukraine is obliged to report to the EU about the harmonization measures. Surveillance on behalf of the EU may then include special missions with the participation of EU institutions and agencies, non-governmental bodies, supervisory authorities, independent experts etc. The results of monitoring missions are then to be discussed in the organs of cooperation established by the AA, which take common recommendations as to the efficiency of the harmonization. These recommendations are submitted to the Association Council, which should decide on further market opening (Art. 475).

In approaching the harmonization process, the Ukraine mainly uses an evolutionary approach, focusing on the meaning and intent of the EU norms with which Ukrainian legislation is to be aligned. Such an approach may be justified by the fact that the national legal system in general has extensive legislation that is codified in the majority of areas relevant to the *acquis*. However, in the areas where there is no extensive national legislation the revolutionary approach is appropriate. That is so-called transposition of the norms of *acquis* into the legal order of the Ukraine (Petrov 2012). Transposition is used when there is an urgent need to precipitate the speed of the process of harmonization and remove pre-existing Ukrainian legal acts by providing for direct incorporation of the EU norms without making any significant amendments to them and avoiding time consuming parliamentary procedures. In such a case more competence is supposed to be given to the executive bodies in adopting normative acts, as it was done in Poland, Hungary, the Baltic states, Bulgaria and some other countries. (Preston 1998, 147–168; Cremona and Meloni 2007, 129–135). The AA provides for transposition of the EU legal acts in such areas as technical rules and standards, cross-border supply of services, public procurement (Art. 56, 96, 153)

So, the transposition of the *acquis* into the legal order of the Ukraine means that legislative bodies of the associated state are excluded from law-making, and EU legal acts in the forms of regulations and directives form the part of the national legal orders of the Ukraine.

11.4 The Supranationality of the Association Institutions

The association agreements lay the bases for the creation of an institutional mechanism with supranational features. The agreements define the powers of the organs of the association and the forms of the legal acts that they adopt. As a rule the institutions of the association are formed on a by-lateral platform, and adopt legal acts on the implementation of the association agreements provisions. Some of these are binding to the association countries and may contribute to the expansion of EU law on the legal orders of the associated countries.

There is quite a complex institutional mechanism created on the basis of the Association Agreement between the EU and the Ukraine with the aim to ensure that the provisions of the agreement and the EU legislative acts are properly implemented by the parties. The functioning of such a mechanism is largely based on the agreement's provisions, and at its top is the Association Council, composed of representatives of the EU Council and the EU Commission and ministerial representatives of the associated country.

One of the Association Council's objectives is to exercise permanent control over the realization and the implementation of AA. The Association Council may consider issues of by-lateral and international relations, and may serve as a forum for the exchange of information concerning the internal legal acts of both parties which are in force, and those which are prepared as well as their implementation measures, their enforcement and their realization.

The Association Council approves by mutual consent the decisions which are binding to the parties and recommendations. What is important is that the Association Council can amend the annexes to the association agreement that contain the lists of the EU legal acts with which the national legislation is to be harmonized, taking into account the standards in force, fixed in international legal instruments.

The Association Council may settle any dispute between the parties concerning interpretation, implementation or execution of the AA, by taking binding decisions.

The Association Committee assists the Association Council and consists of representatives of the members of the EU Council, representatives of the members of the EU Commission, and state civil servant representatives of the associated country.

The Association Council may delegate to the Association Committee any powers including the power to adopt binding decisions. The decisions of the

Association Committee delivered on the bases of the delegated powers are taken by mutual consent and are binding for the parties (Art. 465).

The Parliamentary Committee is composed of the members of the European Parliament and the national parliaments. It has no say in the decision-making. The Parliamentary Committee may only make requests to the Association Council and the Association Committee concerning the implementation of the AA. It also is to be informed about the decisions of the Association Council and may pass recommendations (Art. 468).

Vesting the Association Council and the Association Committee with the powers to pass binding decisions may be justified by the necessity to provide an efficient implementation of the AA. The experience of other EU association agreements confirms this, which is why the Ukrainian side insisted on such provisions' inclusion in the AA in the course of negotiations.

The mere fact that the Association Council and the Association Committee are formed and act on equal bases (Art. 462, 463.1, 465.3) corresponds to the principles fixed in art. 19 of the Ukrainian Constitution. Although some of the decisions are binding they only deal with the subject matter of the AA (Art. 463.3, 465.3); their powers are restricted by the Agreement. This may mean that such decisions do not bear any threat to the sovereignty and independence of Ukraine. They do not undermine the principle of the distribution of powers in Ukraine and do not deprive the Ukrainian Parliament of the authority to pass legislative acts with the aim of implementing the provisions of the AA, in particular, in the directions provided for by art. 92 of the Ukrainian Constitution (the matters that shall be determined exclusively by laws of Ukraine). There are no provisions in the Agreement which could confirm the priority of the decisions taken by the Association Council and the Association Committee over the Ukrainian internal legislation.

Therefore, the supranationality of the institutional mechanism of the Associations with third states reflects to a large extent the supranational character of the institutions of the European Union. The powers of decision-making are vested to the executive authorities of the parties and the representative bodies, like parliaments, exercise consultative functions only. However, such supranationality is used for ensuring the efficiency of the implementation of the Agreement.

11.5 Conclusions

By entering into association agreements with third countries the European Union pursues the same legal policy as in the relations within the Union itself.

The legal regulation of the relations between the Union and the associated countries bears some elements of supranationality, when EU law and the method of subordination become integral parts of the association treaties.

The impact of EU legislation and practice on the legal orders of associated countries is exercised by including in Association agreements provisions analogous in content to those which are fixed in acts of primary and secondary legislation of the EU, or which contain references to EU legislative acts. This impact is also exercised by the incorporation of the EU *acquis* into the legal orders of the third countries by means of the harmonization of legislation of the associated countries with that of the EU. The Association institutions may pass binding decisions for the parties, some of which may extend the list *acquis* for the harmonization.

This, in its turn, sets the stage for the penetration of EU laws into the internal legal orders of the respective third countries. Association agreements of the European Union may provide for direct impact of EU laws both within the legal order of the Union and that of the third countries. The criteria for direct effect of provisions of the EU international agreements have been worked out by the ECJ.

References

COM (2008) 823 final.

Cremona, Marise, and Gabriella Meloni. 2007. The European neighbourhood policy: A framework for mordernisation? EUI Working Paper LAW No. 2007/21.

ECR. 1963. NV Algemene Transport- en Expeditie Onderneming van Gend & Loos v Netherlands Inland Revenue Administration, C-26/62, 5 February 1963.

ECR. 1978. Pigs Marketing Board v Raymond Redmond, C-83/78, 29 November 1978.

European Neighbourhood and Partnership Instrument. Ukraine. Country Strategy Paper 2007–2013.

Journal Officiel, 31 Décembre 1972, L 300, 189–280.

Journal Officiel, 27 Juin 1973, L 171/2.

Muraviov, Viktor. 2007. The Acquis Communautaire as a basis for the community legal order, 4/2007 No. 2. *Miskolc Journal of International Law*: 38–45.

O'Keeffe, David. 1992. The agreement on the European economic area. *Legal Issues of Economic Integration* 19(1): 1–27.

Official Journal, 3 January 1994, L 1/1.

Official Journal, 16 July 1997, L187/3.

Official Journal, 30 March 1998, L 97/2.
Official Journal, 21 June 2000, L 147/3.
Official Journal, 20 March 2004, L84/13.
Official Journal, 9 May 2008, C 115/01.
Official Journal, 29 May 2014, L 161, p. 1–2.
Petrov, Roman. 2012. *Transposition of the European Union acquis into the legal systems of the third countries*. Kyiv: Istina.
Preston, Christopher. 1998. Poland and EU membership: Current issues and future prospects. *Journal of European Integration* 21(2): 147–168.

Viktor Muraviov Academic, Professor, Doctor Hab., Head of the Chair of Comparative and European Law, Institute of International Relations of Kyiv Taras Shevchenko National University, Kyiv, Ukraine. Author of 150 publications including monographs, text-books, articles etc. Visiting Professor University of Minnesota, USA (1989), University of London (1993), Canadian Bureau for International Education, Canada (1994), Osnabrück University, Germany (1994), Central European University, Budapest, Hungary (1996), Turin University, Italy (1997), Nice University, France (1997), Hull University, Great Britain (1998), University Paris II, France (2001), Liverpool University, Great Britain (2005). Participated in international research and education projects within TEMPUS, TACIS, UNESCO, AID etc. Member of the Ukrainian Association of European Law.

MIX
Papier aus verantwortungsvollen Quellen
Paper from responsible sources
FSC® C105338

If you have any concerns about our products,
you can contact us on
ProductSafety@springernature.com

In case Publisher is established outside the EU,
the EU authorized representative is:
Springer Nature Customer Service Center GmbH
Europaplatz 3, 69115 Heidelberg, Germany

Printed by Libri Plureos GmbH
in Hamburg, Germany